PARISIAN SIGHTS

AND

FRENCH PRINCIPLES,

SEEN THROUGH

AMERICAN SPECTACLES.

"Liberté, Egalité, Fraternité."

NEW YORK:
HARPER & BROTHERS, PUBLISHERS,
329 & 331 PEARL STREET,
FRANKLIN SQUARE.
1852.

PREFACE.

"Simul et jucunda et idonea dicere vitæ."

I WISH to take off my hat to my reader. A French bow would be more graceful, but it will take more time, and a greater flourish. I prefer to make his acquaintance with the plain but sincere Yankee nod. In bidding him good morning, I have only to say, that if he read these pages, he will find some truths frankly told, and some opinions frankly expressed. I have admired Paris, the Magnificent, but I have also inquired its cost. I have asked why Republicanism was a curse in France, and a blessing in America. In short, having some leisure hours during the past winter, I employed them in not only examining the outer world of this modern Athens, but in endeavoring to solve its inner life. The result is the following chapters; abruptly various, and full of contrasts like their topic. I commenced my notes for my own amusement. I publish them without being asked for two reasons; firstly, to tell the friendly public what I can make known to them in no other way, and secondly, because I have the curiosity, vanity if you please, to try my hand at making a book. Having brought you, gentle reader, to the threshold of my apartment, your courtesy will not allow you to do less, for my hospitality, than to take off your hat also, and walk in.

PARIS, *June* 1, 1852.

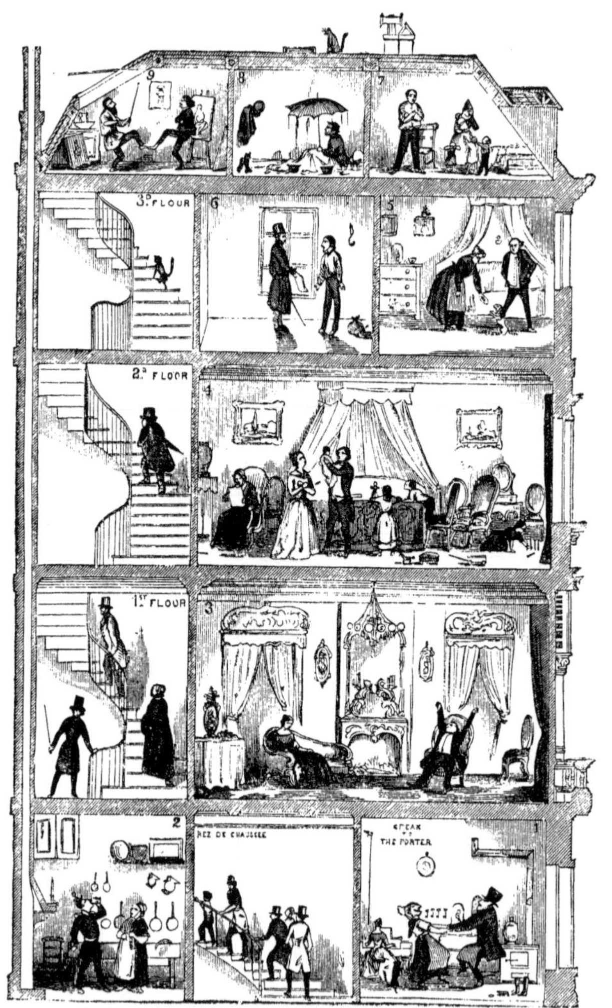

SECTION OF A PARISIAN HOUSE.

PARISIAN SIGHTS

AND

FRENCH PRINCIPLES.

CHAPTER I.

SUNDRIES.

THE different manner in which the Anglo American and the Gaul build their family nests, is pointedly brought home to the former the night of his arrival at Paris. We live in perpendicular strata; they in horizontal. Our houses stand side by side, each like a tub on its own bottom. Theirs, so far as they relate to families, are spread one upon the other, like a pile of gingerbread. With the exception of the principal hotels, and a few recently constructed in the English mode, Parisian houses are arranged after the following fashion. In general, they form a hollow square, allowing a court-yard of sufficient size for a carriage to turn. This shape admits of two ranges of apartments, equivalent in accommodations to houses with us; the one facing the street, the other the court-yard, the kitchen and other conveniences being the two connecting arms. Houses thus constructed accommodate two families on each floor, and are from five to nine stories high. The ground floor is devoted to shops, stables, and the porter's quarters. It is entered by a huge "porte cochère," which is always guarded by the family of the concièrge, who acts as agent for the proprietors in letting their apartments, and watches all the outgoings and incomings of the mansion. Each range has its wide circular staircase for the gentry, leading as high up as what was once considered the only abode of genius; and another—small, dark, and narrow, like the worm of a ram-rod—for the use of domestics.

The porter must be on the "*qui vive*" at all hours of the twenty-four, to slip back the bolt of the outer door, by means of a string connecting with his office, upon the warning ring or cry, "Le cordon, s'il vous plait." Those who enter after midnight, bestow a trifling gratuity upon this Argus, to compensate him for his disturbed slumbers. He replies to all questions relating to his charge, pays postages, receives and distributes all letters and parcels that have owners within his domain, uses your fuel as if it were his own, and is always ready to do the amiable—for a consideration.

The floor above the entrance is called the "entresol," being, as its name indicates, between sun and earth, and it is generally inaccessible to the former, at any season of the year, except in the widest streets or avenues. Being low, it rents low, compared with the floor above, which forms the apartment Number 1, in height, finish, and decoration, and is, consequently, much the dearest. They then progressively decline in price each story, and also in quality, until they terminate under the roof in a series of little chambers, for the servants of the mansion, two or more of these rooms belonging to each apartment.

The apartments themselves are of every variety and size, to meet the wants of the diversified positions of the inhabitants of this metropolis. Some are of sufficient grandeur and sumptuousness to rival the interior of the more pretending hotels, while others dwindle to the means of the most economical bachelor or money-saving grisette.

This mode of building has some prominent advantages over ours. Externally the houses are more uniform, of greater size, and being built of a soft gray sandstone, admit of more architectural ornament. They economize also in ground-room and material, consequently in rent. All the rooms of a family being on one floor, much of that stair-work of which our ladies complain, is saved. In enumerating these advantages, I have enumerated all, unless it may be considered one to be able to bring together the different branches of a family under one roof.

Their disadvantages are more palpable. Each floor having its separate kitchen and drains, contributes its quota to an assemblage of odors, based upon the fragrance of shops or stables beneath, which, in spite of locks and bolts, penetrate with an impartial distribution into every room. This nuisance is not always perceptible, but it is a daily liability; and the plain truth is, that there are few of these gregarious habitations that do not give offense to sensitive nostrils more than once during every twenty-four hours. This fact has doubtless some relation to the enormous consumption of perfumery, which, not unfrequently in the street, overpowers all other smells, as the scented individual goes by.

Again, no amount of cleanliness in one story can always be proof against a want of neatness in the next. If one family cooks onions, the neighbors above and below are brought into unmistakable cognizance of the fact. If there be a frolic overhead, the family beneath participate in the noise, without the fun. There lived in the apartment below me a young lady who, for five months, with scarcely the intermission of a day, practiced on the piano, from four o'clock until midnight, and often until two o'clock in the morning. She played and sang delightfully, or otherwise I should have wished myself deaf. In a city where revolutions have become as periodical and necessary as measles, chicken-pox, and the hooping-cough to childhood, this species of family roosting has inconveniences sometimes of a graver nature. A few shots fired on the 4th of December last, upon the soldiers, from the upper stories of some houses on the Boulevards, caused a return of ball, grape and musket shot, which lasted an hour, broke in their fronts, riddled them in every part; the inmates escaping as they could. One individual has it in his power to compromise a hundred lives.

Although this multiplying of families under one roof may be considered as a species of architectural communism, it is very far from being a social one. No one knows his neighbor. There is no door-plate on the several landings, to satisfy curiosity as to who is to be found within. Somehow or other, the occupants never seem to meet on the common stairway. Of the seven families beside my own that occupied No. — of Rue de ——, foı six months, I knew nothing except that one was English, and another Russian. I could not have distinguished a single member of them all from a casual visitor. It is said that two friends lived for a year in the same house without being aware of the fact, until they accidentally met in the street, and inquired each other's address. An amusing mistake occurred to a friend of mine: He started to call upon a lady with whom he was intimate; after reaching her house, not having taken sufficient notice of the flights of stairs he had ascended, he entered an apartment in the story above, believing himself to be in that of his acquaintance. He found the plate all out, and a display of refreshments, indicating expected company. As his friend did not then receive, he thought this a little strange, but gave it no further consideration, and, with a liberty which his relations with the family warranted, helped himself to bon-bons and fruit. He soon heard a lady's voice, which he supposed was his friend's, calling from her chamber, the door of which was partly open, apologizing for not coming out immediately; to which he replied, "Do not disturb yourself, Madame, I pray you. I will wait."

He had scarcely uttered these words, when she entered the room, and, to his consternation, he found himself in the presence of an utter stranger. She looked equally amazed, as she had supposed it was a gentleman she was expecting. "Madame," said he, "is not this the apartment of Monsieur ——?" "No; that is on the floor below." "Then, Madame, I have to throw myself at your feet for this intrusion; thinking myself in the apartment of Madame ——, I have been eating freely of your refreshments, and can now only offer the humblest of apologies. I am M. de ——." The name was one well known in Parisian society, but he says the lady looked but half convinced, and followed him to the door, keeping one eye on her plate, and the other on him. He afterward met her in the apartment below, and they had a hearty laugh over their mutual surprise. It is unnecessary to add that by this system, duke and laborer, countess and lorette, saint and vagabond; the great, good, bad, and indifferent; wealth and poverty are often brought together under the same roof, alike unknowing and unknown.

The apartments usually taken by strangers, for limited periods, are let furnished with every necessary for housekeeping, except linen and silver, which are hired separately. Inventories are taken on entering and leaving; the lodger being responsible for all damage, other than ordinary wear and tear. These inventories embrace a list of existing damages, including grease and other spots on carpets, table-cloths, cracks or fractures in the glass or porcelain, all minutely detailed, as well as injuries to the furniture, &c. If any are added, they are to be paid for according to the tariff of the landlord, which is not of the most liberal character.

French kitchens are more like a ship's caboose in size, than the domains of an American cook. What room there is, is mainly occupied by numerous little grates, raised upon a brick platform, and adapted in size to the various copper, "*casserolles*," or saucepans, so necessary for the preparation of the indispensable "*entremets*," of French cookery. A Yankee cook would be as much at a loss in one of these kitchens, as she would over a locomotive. One half of the ingenuities of our American furnishing warehouses, would be equally as inexplicable to a French housekeeper. A good broom is not to be found in Paris. Carpets have been introduced into the apartments rented to English and Americans, but the French make but comparatively little use of them, preferring the waxed oak floors, which are cooler and cleaner, but require no little care, at first, for a stranger to preserve his equilibrium. The French use much less fuel than we, warming themselves more by extra clothing and foot-muffs, than by fires.

The search for apartments, which to a novice is a matter of amusement, soon becomes a fatiguing and embarrassing employment. He is ushered without ceremony into any which are taken for a short time, without regard to the convenience of the occupiers; led through disordered bedrooms, unarranged cabinets, and ushered into all the privacy of family matters, lucky for his and their modesty, if among the scattered articles of toilet, he does not pounce upon some fair one in matutinal dishabille. At first, I hesitated upon these domestic thresholds, but the unceremonious "Enter, Sir," soon convinced me that the right of the landlord to exhibit his apartments, was superior to any considerations of delicacy. It was amusing to contrast the coolness and indifference with which French tenants underwent this scrutiny, often saying a word in favor of the lodgings or landlord, and always frankly courteous; whereas, with English or Americans, one was evidently looked upon as an intruder into their temporary castles, from room to room of which the ladies—like quails seeking cover—dodged about, to avoid meeting a man more frightened than they were themselves.

Investigations in the unoccupied apartments are of course

pursued under more favorable auspices. But, to believe the assiduous porters, there was not one that had a single fault, or wanted a single comfort, or even luxury. All of any pretensions had just been vacated by Russian princesses, or English "milords." One proprietor, after a pompous eulogium on the merits of a spacious apartment, whose faded gilt furniture and tawdry splendor, seemed to have descended untouched and almost undusted, from the days of Louis XV., said, as a climax, "The Princess —— has just been to look at them, and was perfectly charmed; she wished to take them at once." "Pray why did you not secure so noble a tenant?" "Because she could not deposit the required security for rent," was the reply. Having just seen in the paper the arrest by the police of a Greek prince, for forgery, I came to the conclusion that the title "prince" was no better security for contracts or morals in Europe, than "colonel," in the United States.

After ascending and descending, in the course of a month, perhaps a thousand pair of slippery stairs, and repeating the same questions, until the thorax is pretty much in the condition of that of Maelzel's automaton baby, whose language was restricted to "Mamma" "Papa," according as the right or left arm was lifted, the lodging hunter growing desperate, affixes his signature to a paper, promising to pay from 100f. to 1200f. per month, in advance. In consideration of this sum, he finds himself, in one case out of two, in the possession of an apartment, in the inventory of which no mention had been made of smoky chimneys, and various facilities for the circulation of cold air, or odors which savor not of Araby the Blest, but which have now become his heritage for the period stipulated in the contract.

In a city like Paris where every domestic want can be supplied almost as it were impromptu, house-keeping is divested of the greater number of inconveniences and vexations attendant upon it in the United States. Labor of any character is at instant command, paid for as soon as completed, and the transaction ended. The sole responsibility of the housekeeper, provided she has made a good selection of domestics, is to give her orders and examine her accounts. Families that intend to make a lengthened stay in Paris, if they would consult comfort and convenience, should proceed at once to housekeeping, but, for a short period, the restaurant-life is preferable, as affording an insight into French manners and cookery to be obtained in no other way. Besides, one meets with, not unfrequently, spicy and agreeable interludes arising from the mistakes and embarassments of novices.

AT VERY'S.

Véry's, Trois Frères Provençaux, and Véfour's have a world-wide reputation, or, at all events, one co-extensive with the love of good eating, and wherever the words gourmand and "gourmet" are still understood in their legitimate signification. These are the places

AT VEFOUR'S.

to test the renown of French culinary art, and the depths of your purse. But one meets mostly strangers at these places. To see the French eat one should visit the restaurants of lesser magnitude and fame, particularly of a Sunday, where the rush to dinner, as no one dines that day under his own roof, is absolutely fearful to a lover of a quiet meal. Infants, dogs, and nurses, all have a seat that day, and the amount consumed would indicate considerable preparatory fasting. Eating and drinking, for the moment, becomes the only business of life. The preparations bespeak the seriousness of the operation. A family enters, consisting of father, mother, maiden sister, two children under five years of age, and a dog. All the tables are filled. They turn to go out. The restaurateur rushes forward, intercepts their retreat, and promises a table "toutsuite." He sees one party have called for their bills, hands them their change, and plumps the new comers into their warm seats, with an array of broken bread, dirty glasses and all the debris of the previous meal before them. Once seated, with bonnets and hats hung up, they are considered as secure as fish fairly hooked. The "garçon," with a dexterity and rapidity peculiarly his own, whisks away the soiled table-cloth and dishes, and in an instant has replaced them with snow-white linen and porcelain. Now commences the "tug of" eating. Each member of the party, except the dog who gravely occupies his chair, too well bred to manifest impatience, plants a napkin under his or her chin, of the dimensions of a moderate sized table-cloth. The females pin the extremities to each shoul-

A FAMILY PARTY.

der, so that in front they have much the appearance of being in their shrouds. The "carte" is studied, orders given, and content and pleasure reign. At these family feasts children are literally crammed, indulged with wines and all the delicacies called for by adult taste, their parents delighted in proportion to the quantity they consume. Eating, under almost any circumstances is to a looker on a vulgar operation. In one of these restaurants it is certainly an amusing one to a veteran traveler, whose sensibilities have long since had their edges blunted. The waiter has a dozen calls at once—the same dish perhaps ordered dressed in a dozen different modes—he is to remember each mode and each table—to supply every change of course, omitting nothing required, and at the end of the meal he has to recall every dish, the quantity and quality—and there may have been twenty different articles called for at one table—that the "addition" may be made out. What wonder then, if in the confusion of orders, he at times mistakes his napkin for his handkerchief, and unconsciously wipes the perspiration from his brow, performing with it the next instant the same service for your plate, or rushes in from the "cuisine" with six dishes piled pyramidically in his hands, a roll of bread under each

GARCON.

GARCON.

arm, and the latest called for "addition" between his teeth. I was exceedingly amused at an incident that occurred at a well known café, in the Passage Delorme. The order "Chef, un bifstake Anglais, toutsuite," was heard, and the article as promptly prepared. The garçon who brought it in vainly sought an owner. Each table supposed its neighbor had ordered it, and the "bifstake" went the rounds unclaimed. The waiter had evidently a mysterious beaf-steak, distinctly ordered but universally repudiated. At last it was discovered that a wag of a shop boy near by, possessing a touch of ventriloquism, had been amusing himself at the expense of "mine host's" kitchen.

COOK.

The French from early habit frequently make themselves very much at home at restaurants and cafés, spending their evenings at the latter, reading the journals, and playing chess or dominoes, paying for the same by calling for a bottle of beer or glass of brandy. I have myself seen a woman who had come in by herself, after finishing her repast coolly throw herself back in her chair and proceed to take a comfortable digestive nap, apparently wholly oblivious to the existence and manifold trials of the race denominated "unprotected females.'

FINALE.

At the same time a Frenchman having completed his meal, washed his hands and face in his goblet, used his napkin for a towel, adjusted his hair over the table, rubbed his hands with lemon and bread, and finally picked up a lump of sugar not required for his coffee, wrapped it in a paper and put it into his pocket. We Americans are not open to the charge of over refinement, but I trust it will be some time yet before we arrive at such free and easy manners.

An Englishman dropped in, and in stentorian tones, called out in his Anglicised French, "Garçon, ōōn beefsteak, avec beaucoup da pōōmmes da terres." "Oui, monsieur," replied the waiter, "avec beaucoup de plasir." "No, no," roared the Englishman, "avec beaucoup da poommes da terres." French politeness was proof even against this trial of risibleness; but I must confess to my own inability to withstand smiling.

At the risk of incurring the charge of mentioning trifling matters, I relate incidents and differences of custom which, after all, are those which come home closest to a traveler, for it is upon such trifles that his comfort mainly depends. To the experienced, they are doubtless flat and unprofitable; but previous to that experience, the knowledge of what to expect would have been decidedly convenient. Besides, it is by comparison of national customs that improvement is evolved. Whatever is better done abroad than at home, should be at once engrafted in our own stock. A traveler may, by *telling* what he sees, find the result in improvements that add vastly to the aggregate of comfort or convenience of his fellow-citizens. Among them are always found some with ears open to friendly hints.

The omnibuses of Paris are superior to all others that I have seen. Each passenger has a cushioned seat, with arms to himself, which of course prevents crowding. As soon as the seats are filled, a sort of weather-cock sign, on top of the omnibus, with the word "*complet*," is elevated, which can be seen a long distance, and announces that no more can be received. Their omnibuses are wider than the American; the central part of the roof elevated so that a passenger can pass to his seat without smashing his hat; and he has also an iron rod to steady himself and keep him from disarranging his fellow-passenger's knees and toes. They have also a system of "correspondence," by which a passenger, without additional charge, is transferred from one line of omnibuses to another, when necessary to reach his destination.

There is as much difference of opinion in regard to the relative merits of the American and French systems of hotel charges, as between their modes of dining. A Frenchman views with disgust the Anglo-American method of mixing meats, vegetables, and sauces upon one plate—mingling flavors that should be kept distinct, and destroying all the delicacy of a repast. He prefers to change his plate as often as he changes his diet; and be it what it may, he never allows but one article on his plate at a time, devouring in the intervals of the changes quantities of bread. For my own part, I have learned to view his fashion as more rational and healthful than our own. So of the system of paying only for what one has at a public place, instead of our plan of lumping charges by the day or meal. A bath with us is a simple 25 cents affair. The reader will be as much struck as I was, with the following list of baths and charges I copied from a French bathing establishment. It illustrates, to a nicety, their system of division of charges:

BATHS, Single......		18 *sous*.	BATHS, Without smell......	3 *f*.	
" Complete....	2 *f*.	10 "	" Chemical.........	3 "	
" Single Barèges	2 "	10 "	Aromatic Baths..........	3 "	
" Complete "	3 "	15 "	Russian "	3 "	

and four others. In all, twelve sorts of baths. The items of charges, at the option of the bather, were as follows. I should mention that he is invariably *locked* in; there being no latch or handle on the inside, he can only obtain an exit by ringing for the "garçon:"

Gelantine	2 *f.*	Towels, hot	2 *sous.*
Bran	1 *f.*	Inside sheet	5 "
½ do.	10 *sous.*	Cake of soap	1 *f.*
Starch	1 *f.*	Boy	4 *sous,*
Cap	2 *sous.*		[or what you please.

What shall I say of servants? I found as good as I could—after having been cheated for the first week to the tune of about fifty per cent. on all supplies, by a Swiss Protestant cook. Upon being confronted with her accounts, and the original bills, which she had accidentally left in her account book, between which the above cash discrepancy was figuratively obvious, with the naïvest innocence, she said they were intended for some other person, though made out in my name, and she would bring the *correct* bills, agreeing with her entries, from the grocer. It is customary here for the cooks to do the marketing, and procure the general supplies, settling accounts with housekeepers periodically. This allows considerable scope for pickings, which the uninitiated, in due season, discover to their cost, if they are unable to speak French, and rely solely upon their servants to purvey. The British Ambassador, but a few days since, in arranging his accounts, previous to his departure for London, discovered that his steward had defrauded him of upward of $15,000. To those who go to housekeeping, I would say, ascertain first the prices of all staple commodities, and then, when orders are given, the correct cost can be known. In all cases require the original bills. Even if it be your good fortune to fall into the hands of "Boutiques de confiance," you must take it for granted that your domestic has a commission for your custom.

The trained politeness of French domestics is worthy of all commendation. It begets good feeling between them and their employers, and inspires a personal interest in their welfare, because, as with coarser natures, there is no fear that kindness will encourage insolence. A French domestic always uses the third person in speaking of or to any member of the family, even the youngest children. "Will Monsieur give himself the trouble to have his coat brushed?" "Will Madame have the goodness to give her orders for dinner?" are invariably the style of questions; and, "I thank you, Madame, very much," the response to directions.

At New Year's they expect, with all the rest of the world, that have ever been paid for services rendered, the gifts of the season; but, unlike the rest of the world, they are generous out of their scanty resources, in making the little ones about them happy, by tasteful presents of their own make or selection. I was greatly amused on this anniversary, after having given the customary contributions of money and good wishes, to teacher, domestics, porter, porter's child, letter-man, newspaper carriers, and I do not know how many others, to see the stately Suisse of the Madeleine, march in with a bun on a silver waiter, by the present of which he modestly hinted, that he was not above the love of filthy lucre, at all events, once a year.

CALLS AT NEW YEARS.

The politeness I have alluded to, is characteristic of all classes whose situations bring them into immediate relations with the higher grades of society. It is no derogation of self-respect, for a seller or an employee to express his thanks in a tone and manner, which makes his patron regret it is not in his power to oblige him or her by still further custom. Courtesy calls for courtesy in return. True, one may be cheated, and know it all the while, but the vexation is more than half neutralized by the politeness of the operator. A Parisian shop-keeper plays with a customer as an angler does a trout. He goes upon the principle of risking nothing, by asking a high price, as he has always on the tip of his tongue a load of reasons why, in your individual case, he should depart from his fixed rule, all of which are most skillfully directed point blank against your amour propre. I was asked two hundred francs for a picture, which, perhaps, was not greatly overvalued, but, being in the mood of testing the abating qualities of my virtuoso, I put on an air of indifference, and offered him much less. "It is impossible, Monsieur, to take less, it is a real gem, all the world comes to my shop to see it. I shall really weep when it is gone." He finished, however, by taking one hundred, "because," said he, "I wish the honor of making Monsieur's acquaintance." Shop-keepers, at times, carry this so far as to send their boys into the streets in pursuit of a customer to accept a price emphatically declined over their counters, on the score of principle. Strangers must make up their minds to pay much dearer than natives, and to *buy* their experience at a larger cost. As a general rule the sum first demanded is very wide from the selling price.

"How many papers have you sold to-night?" said I to an old lady, of whom I bought her last "Patrie," one evening. "Fifty, I thank you infinitely, sir," she replied, as she picked up her little bench, and started for home. In directing strangers, all classes vie with each other in attention. I have had a gentleman run after me out of his own way, some distance, to correct a slight error he feared he had made. On another occasion, a young washerwoman gave me the information sought, and after I had proceeded quite a distance, perceiving that she had made an error, she ran to overtake me, requesting me to wait, while she ascertained exactly where the individual lived, whose residence I sought. She inquired at a neighboring shop, and then came to inform me, with pleasure and courtesy beaming in every feature. I should not forget to add that she left a basket of clothes in the street to perform this kindness, which was done with a manner that effectually forbade any pecuniary recompense. This courtesy extends to preserving a polite gravity of countenance, under the most trying emergencies of ridiculous appearances or mistakes. I once, at a bath, ordered an "*assiette*" (plate), instead of a "*serviette*" (towel), to wipe me with. The waiter, without relaxing a muscle, comprehended my want, and in an instant returned, saying, "Here it is, sir," while I was in a roar myself at the absurdity of my order. I did succeed once, however, in disturbing even the gravity of a veteran garçon, by ordering "un fricandeau à l'oreille," a veal cutlet dressed with *ears*, instead of "un fricandeau à l'oseille," that is to say, with sorrel.

I have often thought it very singular that the French, who are so ingenious in inventing methods of killing time, should manifest such a fondness for clocks. That for looking-glasses is easily explained. As for the talebearers of time, there are more I believe, in France, than in all the world beside. Unfortunately, there is no connection between them and punctuality, for with clocks every where, punctuality is nowhere. This is vastly annoying to the punctilious stranger, but after innumerable disappointments, he reconciles himself to the universal system of promises and postponements. To wait is as natural to a Frenchman, as to "go ahead" is to a Yankee.

The latter must be in motion in order to be at rest. He anticipates every thing; the former waits until he is overtaken. An American business community would be horror-struck at an enactment which should require their day to commence at meridian. A Frenchman breakfasts at noon, and gets to work not much before the time Boston merchants go on "'Change." He dines, while the American sups, and comes home from balls at an hour when his transatlantic friend is becoming restless from over-sleep.

Franklin undertook to convince the Parisians that it was much cheaper to use sun-light than gas-light, but did not succeed. Indeed, were the choice of the two given them, there is but little doubt that gas would receive the universal suffrage. At one o'clock, the Palais Royal, or the Boulevards, displays less activity than Broadway at eight.

At present, there are many experiments making in the use of the electrical light. Should it be economically produced, the sun might as well spare its rays for some other planetary system, for any use the Parisians would have of them. They would be cast aside as decidedly vulgar. A laughable incident lately occurred, arising from an amateur experiment of lighting a fashionable salon, in this manner. There were present some two hundred guests, in full toilets. The ordinary lights were put out, and the more brilliant fluid had just begun to dazzle the eyes of the company, when a terrific explosion was heard, followed immediately by another, and total darkness. Smoke was soon perceived. The curtains were on fire, but were promptly extinguished. There was, however, a universal stampede for the doors, but they opened inward, and the panic-stricken crowd pressed outward. Some one broke the window, and shouted for help. The people in the street called fire, and the *pompiers* and *sapeurs*, with their apparatus, repaired promptly to the spot. Seeing the smoke, they began to pour in a deluge of cold water, and the more the confusion within increased, the greater their exertions to swamp the establishment. It was not until furniture and guests had experienced the effects of a thorough February soaking, that they could be brought to comprehend that they had been giving a gratuitous bath to a select circle of the friends of the "Comtesse de ——."

A "female-rights orator" has asserted, that if women had more of the occupations of men they would be more virtuous. By that rule the women of France ought to far excel in that respect their sisters of America. I will say nothing of their laboring in the field, their driving huge carts through the streets of Paris, and other rude labors which soon rub out of them all feminine softness, but confine myself to the more agreeable duties which they have here usurped from man. Indeed, a man is but a secondary being in the scale of French civilization. The "dames à comptoir" are as essential to the success of a Parisian café as the cook himself. More hats are doffed at their shrines than before the most brilliant belles of the metropolis. My bootmaker, or the head of the establishment, is a woman; my hatter, also; my landlord is a dignified specimen of "fair, fat, and forty;" my porter is of the same sex, older in years and worse in looks; my butcher, milkman, and the old-clothesman, newsboy, and rag-gatherer beneath my window, ditto. They are waiters at the baths, door-keepers at the theatres, ticket-sellers, fiddlers, chair-letters of the churches; they figure in every revolution, and have a tongue and arms in every fight; in short, they are the bottom and top of every thing in France. They have so pushed aside the lords of the creation, that for some time my sympathies were really alive to know what men had left to do, until I finally discovered that they had the resource of becoming chambermaids.

But there is one discovery the reformists of the sex can make in Paris, to which I beg particularly to call their attention, and that is, how to preserve the freedom of their "limbs" and their petticoats also. Bloomerism has no chance of success. A French lady, by a sleight of hand in lifting her dress, can cross the dirtiest streets, promenade through mud and mire, and bring home unsullied the whitest stocking and purest skirt. She does it too, with a natural grace and modesty which is perfectly charming. I have heard American ladies covet her art; and American gentlemen declare that the display of beautifully turned ankles in the finest of hose and fringed with the choicest of lace and linen, to be seen on the Boulevards during a shower, was not the least attractive of the sights of Paris.

Observing a crowd one day gathered around a handsome glass-case exposed at the corner of one of the principal streets, my curiosity was excited to discover the contents. Allowing my reader to be the shrewdest of Yankees, his guessing powers would be at fault to tell what I saw. It was nothing less than a series of corns extracted from the feet of Parisian belles and dandies, of all sizes, from a pea to a scale that would have done credit to the horny hide of a rhinoceros, arranged symmetrically, as an incontestable evidence of the skill of the chiropedist. To have completed the attraction, he should have added under each the name of the original proprietor. The largest were veritable monsters, and would have figured to advantage at the London Exhibition alongside of the great diamond, as the most magnificent specimens of their genus in existence.

The shop windows leave to the inquisitive bachelor little to learn of the mysteries of female toilet. That there may be no mistake as to the use of any article, wax figures with a bountiful supply of artificial charms are exposed, to show off the fit and make. The dentists, however, bear away the palm in practical illustrations of their art. They have elegant gilt frames set with glass, in which are displayed artificial jaws with bright red gums and milky white teeth, others in every variety of loss, decay, and repair, row within row, like the anatomy of a shark's mouth, all opening and shutting in different degrees of velocity and emphasis, by some concealed mechanism, the whole forming the most complete exhibition of gnashing of teeth to be seen this side of "outer darkness." Above are wax heads which revolve every minute on pivots, showing alternately a ghastly, sunken-jawed, toothless face, and the same lineaments freshened and filled out with a new set of grinders spotless from the maker's hands. The effect of this, under the reflection of a powerful gas-light, is easier imagined than described.

It is easy to perceive that the French are a practical people at the bottom of all their gallantry. They make their wants or wares known in the most straight-forward manner. Whatever they do—if there be not a bayonet to stop them—they do openly, and heartily despise the mysterious and abashed way in which their neighbors across the channel seek to arrive at the same results. I read in the "Constitutionnel" recently, that "A female orphan, possessing a good fortune, having *immediate* occasion to marry, desires a husband. Address, &c., &c." All over Paris there are marriage agencies, the objects of which are best illustrated by one of their advertisements, which reads as follows: "48 Rue d'Enghien—26th year—M. de Foy, negotiator of marriages, to mothers of families." "Who would believe in an age of progress like this, that the thousands of marriages made in all classes of society by the mediation of M. Foy, during the past twenty-six years, have not yet wholly sufficed, among certain narrow minds, to demonstrate the striking truth, that it is a precious thing to be able to choose a party according to taste, from a rich list, and to use to advantage the knowledge of an experienced man to marry well? To-day this absurd opinion is vanquished, thanks to the judgments of the legal tribunals, which have at length confirmed and sanctioned the morality, principle, and legality of the profession of M. Foy, as being, for him, invested with a special power. After so brilliant a triumph, an immense increase of his business has accrued to his house in France, and its branches in England, Belgium, Germany, and America. Interpreters for these four languages are attached to his office. Widows and mothers can then continue to address M. Foy in full assurance; he offers them within twenty-four hours honorable situations of all ranks, even among the richest of those nations. The books are kept in a cipher known only by M. Foy. A mystery always envelopes his name in the negotiations and correspondence. The number of his rooms is a guarantee against all awkward meetings; and to conclude, the house of M. Foy is a tomb and a confessional for all secrets. Address post-paid."

At Paris one can order a wife or husband, and have either served up in less time than a new coat. Unfortunately, unlike that, they can not be put off at will whether they fit or not, but must remain until one or the other wears out. While on this topic I should not forget to add, that if France can not boast of a Niagara or the biggest pumpkin, she has at this moment, in the town of Liége, a mother of "une fécondité extraordinaire." She is only thirty-three years old, has been married but nine years, and has presented her husband with *twenty-four daughters*, three at each birth. I had the honor of knowing in California a mother, still fresh and vigorous, of twenty-six children, but at the above annual rate there is no calculating what her French rival may not yet live to do for the State.

A robbery was recently committed under circumstances too good not to be told. The thief entered one of the fashionable ready-made linen shops, and asked to see sundry articles for his wife, for whom he said he was preparing a pleasant surprise. "But," said he to the attending damsel, "I wish to be sure of a correct fit. My wife is about your height; she has, like you, a fine figure—the carriage of a queen. It is necessary to add I have always been the admirer of the group of the Three Graces. Will you be so obliging, since my wife has just your size, or very near it, to try on this chemise over your dress?"

The obliging lass complied. The thief, pretending to draw it down, attached it, by means of a large carpet pin, to all her clothes, including her innermost garment. He then ordered a dozen like it at five dollars each. The shop-girl, well satisfied to have found so attentive a husband, attempted to take off the chemise, but finding that as she raised it, her clothes also came up with it, she ran into an adjoining room to divest herself of the troublesome garment without exposing her person. In the mean while, the thief made off with all he could lay hands upon.

The tribunals witness occasionally scenes no less comical. A man named Grosours was brought before the Correctional Police, for having picked a gentleman's pocket of his handkerchief in the Champs Elysées. Although aged only thirty, the prisoner has passed not fewer than twelve years in jail, and on the day of the robbery he had only been released an hour, when he was arrested. A policeman having declared that he had seen the prisoner pick the pocket, and had immediately seized him, the prisoner cried passionately, "Ask the ass why he seized me by the collar!" "Don't speak in that way," said the president, "or you will be expelled from the court." "I am wrong—I ask your pardon; but I am the victim of that fellow. Remark, I do not call him an ass from want of respect to justice. Why did he arrest me?" "Because he saw you commit a robbery, and he did his duty." "But he was in such a confounded hurry. On my honor, I should have put the pocket-handkerchief back again, as I only took it to blow my nose, because I had a cold. I am above a paltry pocket-handkerchief." "Why," said the policeman, "did you run away so fast, if you did not intend to keep the pocket-handkerchief?" "Oh, it was to get it washed; it wouldn't have been polite to have returned it, after using it, without washing." "That is not very likely," said the officer. "Heaven forgive me, if I do not believe the vile creature of the police suspects my honor!" "Be silent," cried the president, "you insult the witness." "But he attacks my honor." "Silence!" "I have, I suppose, the liberty of defending myself. That brigand—" "Silence, I tell you!" cried the president.

"If I am to be silent," said the prisoner, "the defense is not free, and I will retire." Here he attempted to climb over the dock, but was prevented. "Let me go, will you? I tell you that the defense is not free. If I had an advocate he would retire, and as I am my own advocate, I may retire too." He again attempted to get away, but being stopped, sat down in a rage, and cried, "This is infamous!" The tribunal condemned him to six months' imprisonment. "I protest," cried he with great solemnity, "because the defense was not free."

These Parisians have their attention drawn, every clear night, if not toward heaven, at least toward the heavenly bodies, by ambulatory astronomers, who plant their telescopes in the most favorable sites for observing the planets, chalking on the sidewalks, "Saturn is magnificent to-night—the moon is beautiful, and its mountains and volcanoes exceedingly distinct," &c. The instruments are superior, and the gratification and instruction derived,—for the gazer has the benefit also of a brief astronomical lecture,—well worth the trifling charge of five sous. I have often stopped to get a brief lesson in this science, illustrated by a powerful instrument, such as one in America can only obtain access to with much difficulty. Another, less instructive, but more diverting sight, is to be found among the dog professors, who, by blows and starvation, often force more learning into the heads of their animals, than a pedagogue succeeds in driving into human noddles. There was one hound which invariably played a game of dominoes through, with any opponent that offered from the curious crowd, without making a single mistake. His greatest difficulty was in picking up such small objects from the ground. This he could only do by turning his nose sideways.

The conveniences of life are so multiplied in Paris, that it would be a troublesome task to discover any new occupation arising from human wants in any shape. The great difficulty, for a man supposed to have money, is to find any thing left for him to do. His wants are anticipated on every side with an alacrity and politeness that are really overpowering. He can not shut a carriage door himself. It is of no use making the attempt. A man appears as suddenly as if he dropped from the clouds, closes the door upon him before he can seat himself, and with hat in hand, begs Monsieur not to forget the trouble he has been at.

The bachelor on whose head time begins to show its steps in the changing color of his hair, has but to step into the "Salon épilatoire," and he will find a private entrance to a private room, tastefully furnished, where, in the utmost privacy, for two francs, he can have every gray hair extracted by a pair of tweezers in the pretty hands of a charming grisette, who, if she have not the beauty of Sterne's damsel, may possess equal wit.

ON THE BOULEVARDS

An American is made for in-doors, but a Frenchman's home is the outside half of his house. It is for the street he sacrifices domestic comfort. He eats and drinks in the street; he reads his newspaper and takes his dram in the street. To appear like ladies or gentlemen in public one day in the week, either sex will economize their personal wants the remaining six to a condition bordering almost on penury, to save sufficient money to hire, if they can not purchase, the necessary garments. More can be made of a small capital in Paris than in any other city. There is no occasion to buy any thing. Whatever is needed of clothing, domestic utensils, or any article whatever, even to a newspaper, can be hired at moderate rates for any period of time.

AT HOME.

One of the most striking contrasts between the French and Americans is in their physical appearance. Both sexes of the former look healthy and robust. Their countenances are full and florid, and have an expression of sensual ease and contentment, as if they were on good terms with themselves and the world. They have none of the care-worn, haggard American physiognomy, which gives youth the air of age, and betokens a race in which labor and thought are paramount to all other considerations. On the contrary, the French when old, look young. The pleasures of this life oil the joints of age, so that time slips smoothly by. If any class belie their years it is the children, to whom overdress and physical restraint give an expression of premature gravity or unnatural heaviness. No doubt the outdoor, and "care not for to-morrow," life of the French, combined with their passion for amusements, has much to do in their fine state of preservation. Something must be put down to their superior toilets. For the English, with perhaps a higher condition of health, look beside them, to use a comprehensive term in the female vocabulary, like frights, or in other words, there is about as much difference of exterior between the two races as between a buffalo and a blood horse. This applies more particularly to the women. I verily believe an English lady to be incorrigible in matters of taste; or else it has become a point of honor with her to make herself as unattractive as possible. If both nations would divide equally their respective pride and vanity, the result would be a decided improvement in each. Add to this composition the go-ahead principle of brother Jonathan, and the world would have a specimen of a race that would soon distance all national competition in the essential points of order, beauty, and energy.

For a man whose passions are his slaves, whose sentiments are obedient to his will, whose emotions are made so many sources of epicurean pleasure, who lives only to extract the greatest amount of happiness from the sensual world, regardless of a spiritual life, Paris affords resources which are not to be found elsewhere. It is emphatically the home of the man of the world. All that the head can covet is at his option; but if he has the faintest suspicion of possessing a heart in which dwells the love of the true and natural, he had better withdraw it from the vortex of Parisian life, before it is sucked in too deep to escape.

CHAPTER II.

SITES AND SUICIDES.

In the heart of Paris, in the centre of the Seine, connected to either bank by a series of bridges, which makes it resemble a spider within its web, is a quarter of the city a stranger's foot seldom enters. I mean the "Ile Saint Louis." I had often gazed from a distance upon its antique-looking mansions, all apparently of one character, height, and color, and wondered what sort of a race they sheltered. My curiosity grew until I determined upon its exploration. The suspension-bridge "De la Cité" took me to the Rue St. Louis en l'Ile, which traverses the island lengthwise. The sombre appearance which characterized its exterior became even more apparent in the interior. The houses were high, streets narrow, clean, and quiet; there was no trace of commerce, and the few shops that were to be seen, seemed to be there because they were too poor to move elsewhere. There were no carts or carriages; the few persons in the streets seemed to know each other; to be in reality neighbors. They appeared cheerful and contented. I looked about to detect if there were apartments to let. Although all appeared so quiet, there was scarcely a sign indicating room for newcomers. Had it been at the same hour in a tropical climate, I should have explained the universal calm by the afternoon siesta. But there were 7500 inhabitants on a very small spot of land to be accounted for in some way. I am certain I did not see one hundred. The greatest sign of life was the passage of an omnibus through its narrowest part, on its route to the extremity of the external city. The streets were scrupulously clean—every thing was old and faded, but neat. The quaint, polygonal spire of open stone-work attracted me into the church, the only public edifice on the island. Its interior was deserted except by a stray workman. It had some good pictures. The quiet of this core of Paris contrasted so powerfully with its noisy environs, that "it seemed good to be there." I inquired into its history. I could not learn that it had any. A sure proof of uninterrupted calm and contentment. It was the nearest practical approach to "Egalité" I had yet seen in the Republic. Its manners were unexceptionable. As their fathers lived, so live the present generation. No barricades had ever disturbed the slumber of its streets. No revolutionary hordes had made it a stronghold. Its most treasured souvenirs were, that in the Hotel Lambert, Voltaire planned his Henriade, and Napoleon, in 1815, held his last conference with M. de Montalivet, before he fled from Paris, to return to it no more. But its brightest boast, and one which makes it the white spot of this modern Lutece, is, that it does not contain a single prostitute.

Leaving the "Ile" by another bridge, in five minutes I was again afloat in the mighty current of Parisian life. In the solitude and silence I had left, it seemed that when I had gone I should be missed. It was refreshing to believe that one's presence was necessary, if but to enliven a desert; but here, an atom among a million other atoms, tossed from side to side in efforts to avoid contact with thousands of faces, hands and feet that one has never seen before, and will never meet again, the conviction of individual nothingness grew strong and sad within me. I felt there was nc solitude like that of a stranger in a strange multitude, speaking a strange tongue. Were I to plunge into the rapid waters of the Seine, the crowd would gape a minute, exclaim "Voilà un drôle!" and pass by.

Every step in Paris is a lesson in history. There is scarcely a street but has had its baptism of blood, its barricade, its combats, its slain, and more lamentable still, its martyrs to popular rage, or victims of royal revenge. Who can paint a picture that shall embrace Parisian character in all its shades? To-day, light, buoyant, brilliant, sympathetic, courteous, enthusiastic in art, overflowing with humor, displaying all that makes life attractive and graceful: to-morrow, ragged, disheveled, reek-

PARISIANS AROUSED

ing with the sweat of a hundred barricades, and screaming that dreadful war-cry of crime, "Ca ira!" whose notes carry terror to every throne of Europe, and set millions of armed men in motion from one extremity to the other. Singular race! Equally ready to laugh or fight. Terror-stricken at the idea of death, banishing from memory, as far as possible, its dread reality, yet plunging into crime and slaughter with the levity of buffoons, and the cruelty of Molochs. As I threaded my way through the joyous-hearted crowd, whose faintest jostle called forth a "Pardon, monsieur," with all the interest of tone a mother addresses a child upon a supposed hurt, and from whom the slightest accident or loss drew forth genuine expressions of kindness and commiseration, it was difficult to realize that their fathers, almost on the spot where I stood, had burned by a slow fire, made slower by damp straw, a girl of twenty, stripping her naked, cutting off her breasts, and slashing her fair skin with their sabres heated red hot, while her agonizing screams, borne on the still air of a summer evening, were heard as far as the Louvre. Her crime was wounding a republican soldier. An Iroquois never tortured a woman at the stake. This was reserved for chivalric France. After this deed, it is no matter of astonishment that the heart of an aristocrat became a savory morsel, and the blood of a countryman sweeter than nectar. The cannibalism of Paris put to the blush that of New Zealand. Pity and indignation never grow old at the recollection of the fate of the Princess Lamballe; yet her lot was mercy to that of many of her sex, every way as deserving. In those days of terror so great was the stupefaction, that it was necessary only to say to a victim, "Go to your house, remain there, and to-morrow morning the cart will call to take you to the scaffold," and he went.

The grated archway of the Conciergerie still wears the same look of gloom as it did during the massacres of September, 1792, in an era when even the tribunal of which a Fouquier-Tinville was judge, could not do its work of slaughter with sufficient rapidity to satisfy the desire of the people for blood. Within is still to be seen, deep stained in the very stone, the "damned spot" made by the blood-dripping sabres of the ruffian butchers who, wearied with their work, had rested their weapons against the wall, while they recruited their energies by copious libations of wine. Those days were not the first in which the Conciergerie had seen the people slay the nobles within its walls. In 1418 its vaults for two days resounded to the agony of priests, ladies and lords murdered by an infuriated populace, who thought to avenge in these cruelties the disasters of Crecy, Poitiers, and Agincourt. On the 23d of August, 1572, its bells, answering the ominous signal of St. Germain l'Auxerrois, awoke another generation of murderers to their work of blood. It was the night of St. Barthélemi, and what a night even for Paris! Fanaticism sharpened the weapons of hate. Says an eye-witness: "The continual noise of fire-arms, the piercing cries of the victims, the shouts of the assassins, the headless trunks thrown from the windows or dragged to the river, the sack of more than six hundred houses, made Paris resemble a city taken by assault." The panacea for every ill, has always been blood. Has it ever cured its patient? Let Charles VII. answer for the slaughter of the Armanacs; the edict of Nantes, for St. Barthélemi; and a Bourbon monarch for the blood of September. Monarch, priest, or citizen, imperialist, monarchist, republican or socialist, each in turn adopt the sword and perish by the sword. "Paris," exclaimed Henry III., chief of the kingdom, but a chief too great and too capricious, "thou hast need to be bled to cure thee; also all France, for the frenzy that thou communicatest to it. In but three days, and your walls and your mansions will be seen no more, but only the place where thou hast been." A Dominican, James Clement, bore the reply on the part of her citizens to their angry king on the end of his poniard. His death was received with more exultation than even that of Louis XVI. Fireworks, savage dances, gross caricatures, blood-thirsty songs, and a solemn thanksgiving to Almighty God in the proudest of the temples of the Prince of Peace, announced their joy that another murder was done, while the whole city rushed to bless the miserable peasant mother of the assassin.

The rancor of political strife affords some extenuation for rejoicing in the fall of an enemy, even by the agency of crime But what can we think of that spirit which finds pleasure in the agonies of a fellow-creature? The populace, so sympathetic with the artificial distress which they pay to see in their theatres, weeping at sufferings which have no reality beyond the counterfeit emotions of mercenary actors, crowd with still greater eagerness a place of execution. When Damien was tortured in the Place de la Grève, for stabbing Louis XV., the square, the win dows, the roofs, and every spot whence human eyes could reach the assassin, was occupied, even by ladies. For five hours they glutted their cold curiosity in his agonies. Unmoved, they saw his flesh torn off his limbs with red-hot pincers—molten lead poured into his wounds—those wounds scooped out with knives —disturbing no mortal part, but probing to the quick, the vital. As a coup de grâce, four horses were fastened to his limbs to tear him asunder. They were wearied out in vain efforts—two fresh ones were added, and these failed, until the joints of the misera ble wretch were severed by strokes of a hatchet. The only ex clamations were of pity for the poor horses, flogged to unwonted exertions to perform their part of the tragedy.

The "Conciergerie" can not be the most refreshing sight for the inhabitant of the Tuileries, though it may serve, like the skeleton of the Egyptian banquets, as a moral on the pride and instability of rank. Its walls have imprisoned alike illustrious victims and the greatest of criminals. The confinement and torture of Ravaillac failed to screen Louis XV. from the knife of Damien; and he, in his turn, was no warning to Louvel, who aimed to destroy the Bourbon line in one blow. Fieschi, failing in his attempt upon the Orleans king, here spent the few days that intervened between him and the guillotine. Impartial in its destiny, it receives alike royalty and its assassins. The memory of Marie Antoinette is indelibly affixed to its walls. Within them the Girondins held their last banquet. Louis Napoleon himself has left them too recently to have forgotten that the distance between their towers and the Palace of the Tuileries, has not lengthened since he usurped the throne of Charlemagne.

Simply to enumerate the sites of historical interest, would fill a volume. Yet who can pass unmoved the spot where the great Henry fell a victim to the fanaticism of his adopted faith, after escaping twenty-three previous attempts? The Parisians never forgave the heretic king the siege they had endured. It cost them, from famine alone, thirty thousand men. Though they were reduced to browse upon the grass in the streets, and to make bread of the bones of the dead, they yet found strength enough to fire from their walls upon the Protestants, and to repair to their churches to listen to the exhortations of their monks. Their priests sustained their constancy, under sufferings not exceeded at the destruction of Jerusalem, by promises of paradise, and by themselves guarding the entrenchments, making sorties, and sharing the duties and hardships of the meanest soldier. In their hatred of heresy they stripped their churches of lead to cast into bullets, and were the foremost in every combat, and the last in every retreat.

In the Paris of to-day, one in vain seeks to recall the city of which Henry IV. became master. There were but few houses left entire; the greater number were uninhabited; grass had overgrown the streets; there were no lights; brigands pillaged openly; one heard every where of thefts, ambushes and murders. Strange, indeed, says Lestoile, to say that in a town like Paris, robberies were committed with as much impunity as in a forest. No one dared go out after sunset. All places of amusement were closed at four o'clock. Added to these evils, the civil wars had begotten such a spirit of combat, that the streets were daily stained with the blood of those who fell in duels. In less than fifteen years forty thousand perished in this scandalous manner, and seven thousand pardons were granted.

I never pass the narrow "Rue du Rempart," without recalling to mind the heroic Joan of Arc, who here was wounded by the English, while sounding the depth of the ditch with her lance. Fortunately for posterity, and appropriately for herself, this Maid of Orleans has found in a daughter of Orleans, the Princess Marie, best beloved of Louis Philippe, a genius equal to the perpetuation in marble of her chaste and heroic image. This admirable statue is now at Versailles. It is some consolation to the descendant of an Englishman, to know that the ignominy of the death of this noble girl was shared by a Frenchman, Jean Cauchen, a doctor of the Sorbonne, by whose judgment she was sent to the stake.

Another female, "spirituelle," talented and beautiful, whose life was consecrated to the amusement of the French, and whose melancholy fate is never to be forgotten by those who have once seen it depicted by the present queen of tragedy, lies buried in an unrecorded grave, under the pavement on the banks of the Seine, in front of the Palais Bourbon. The curate of St. Sulpice refused to receive in consecrated ground the corpse of Adrienne le Couvreur, an actress, although she had, in her will, left a legacy to the poor of his parish.

Many of the public edifices have experienced no less strange mutations of fortune than their occupants. St. Lazare, a hospital for lepers, was also the temporary abode of the ancient kings, previous to their solemn entry into their capital, to teach them a lesson of humility and humanity, by a temporary sojourn among the most infirm and disgusting of their subjects. The corpses of the king and queen were also deposited here, previous to interment at St. Denis, to be sprinkled with holy water by these human outcasts. This hospital, of which St. Vincent de

Paule was abbot, and from which André Chenier passed to the scaffold, is now a prison for prostitutes.

The Convent of St. Augustin, for centuries the place of assembly for synods, councils, parliaments, and the Order of the Holy Ghost, has become a poultry market. The cells of Ave Maria, once filled with pious nuns, are now the lodgings of soldiers; the convent of the Jacobins, a prison; that of the Cordeliers, dissecting rooms; the Capuchins of St. Jacques, a venereal hospital; the convent of the Sisters of Visitation, a Protestant church; the Jacobins of St. Germain, the museum of artillery; others are corn magazines, prisons, stamp-offices, city halls, markets; and the abode of the Holy Daughters of St. Thomas has been replaced by the Temple of Mammon, the present "Bourse."

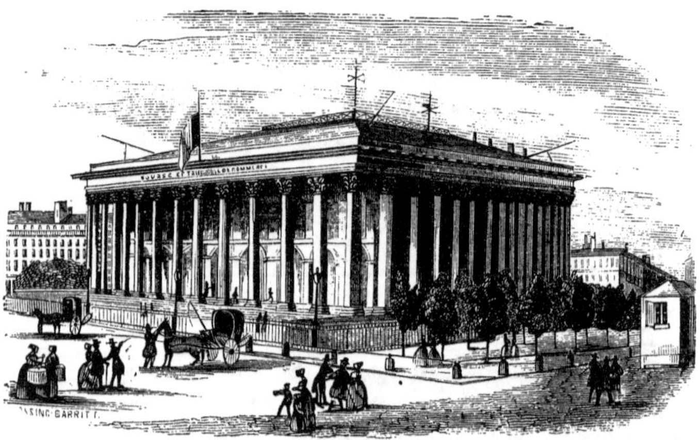

THE BOURSE.

The revolution of 1789 has left so deep an impression upon the minds of the present generation, that, in the vivid recollection of its horrors, we lose sight of the fact that the Parisian populace were but obeying the instincts of a nature transmitted as a legacy from one generation to another; nursed in their mothers' milk, and made venerable by the traditions of their sires. If the noblesse rejoiced in the chivalric and proud Montmorencis, Condés, and the Rohans whose motto was, "Roi je ne suis; Prince ne daigne; Rohan je suis;" the people of Paris were no less proud of their redoubtable butcher chiefs, the Legoix, Saint Yons, and Thiberts, who, for centuries had been the head and front of every insurrection, whose descendants kept up the turbulent glory of their race, in the troubles of the League and the Fronde, and whose names are yet to be found among the butchers of the dreaded Faubourgs. The populace have a hereditary taste for tumult. They have a thousand wrongs to avenge; a thousand examples to move them. Fickle in their attachments, they are true to their natures. In 1227, to a man, they seized their arms, rescued Louis IX. from the hands of his unruly barons, and triumphantly brought him within their walls. Their children, six centuries later, ignominiously expelled from amidst them the last descendants of their saintly monarch. St. Louis grateful for their devotion, took the title of "Bourgeois," and called the citizens to his councils. For the fifty thousand souls that composed its population, he established a police of sixty men; stronger in the love of the people, than the governments of the present day, in the steel of sixty thousand bayonets.

During the reign of Philip IV., the populace undertook, after their usual fashion, to reform the government, by gibbeting the ministers, Labrosse and Marigny, voting the salique law, and driving the king from his palace to the Temple, in which he found a refuge. It was then without the walls of the city. A little later, the king returned the compliment, by hanging twenty-eight of the citizens to the four principal gates. Five hundred years afterward, another Capet, driven by popular fury from his royal abode, was conducted a prisoner to the Temple, from which he only issued, to be led to the scaffold, by the descendants of the very bourgeoisie his ancestor had hung upon a gallows. The successor of Charlemagne was compelled, under the mockery of Royalty, to humiliate himself before the people, from the windows of the Hotel de Ville, with the red and blue cap of liberty on his head, which, with its silver clasp and device, "à bonne fin" (to a good end), had been awaked from its sleep of four centuries, to complete the humiliation of this unhappy king. Little did the republicans of 1364, when they added this motto to their colors of liberty, contemplate to what "end" they were preparing their emblem of authority. Under Etienne Marcel and his friends, they imposed laws upon the Dauphin Charles, regent during the captivity of John in England. Royalty was compelled to abase itself, and sue for favors to the assembled multitude. The regent, and Charles le Mauvais, by turns, harangued the people in the Place de Grève, the place of executions. The populace made themselves merry at these jousts of eloquence, hooting or applauding the princes, as they would comedians whom they paid to amuse them. The Dauphin, having seen his favorites slain before his eyes, in his own chamber, by the partisans of the "Liberté, egalité and fraternité," of that day, was reduced to beg his life on his knees, of Marcel, who replied by giving him his liberty-cap, as a protection, drawing him to the window, and showing him the corpses which had been pitched into the court-yard. "On the part of the people," replied Marcel, "I require you to ratify the death of these traitors, for it is the will of the people that has done this."

The prince fled, assembled an army, and besieged Paris. Marcel was assassinated, and the royalists once more masters, true to their instincts, sought to wash out the humiliation they had endured in the blood of the popular leaders. This game of power has always been "If I win, heads you lose." But, like all depletions, the practice begets the necessity; a truth in political therapeutics, not fully acknowledged, even after so many centuries of accumulated proofs. On the spot where the Danton of the 14th century had met his death, the Dauphin built a triumphal edifice, as a monument of defiance to unruly demagogues, and a prison of state to reform or bury the politics of obnoxious spirits.

This fortified dungeon continued faithful to the interests of its builders, until the day when the popular colors of Paris became again victorious over the royal lilies of France. While royalty battled aristocracy, the Faubourg St. Antoine remained quiet; indifferent whether the cannon of the Bastile won or lost a husband for Mademoiselle de Montpensier. She, with the inexplicable caprice of her sex, intrigued for the hand of Louis XIV., yet fired upon his army, causing Mazarin to exclaim, "Mademoiselle has killed her husband." But after a repose of one hundred and thirty years, its terrible population awoke, and on the 14th of July, 1789, avenged the abasement of their flag, and the wrongs of humanity, by the destruction of that symbol of despotism.

THE BASTILLE

European democracy has learned its trade of barricades from the Bourgeoisie of Paris, who after six hundred years' practice, have well-nigh brought the system to perfection. Whenever the genius of revolutions prompted them to reform the State, Paris found itself transformed in a day into a vast fortress. The entrance of each street was closed by massive iron chains, and, on the appearance of an enemy, these chains were reinforced by stones, barrels, beams, and every obstacle to render them impregnable to the heavy-armed Barons. Alternately victorious and defeated, the democracy and despotism of the 14th century were synonymous with carnage and destruction. In 1382, Paris was full of pride and wealth, with an overflowing, turbulent, swarming population. It had then, according to Froissard, thirty thousand rich and powerful men, armed from head to foot, as well appareled as any Chevaliers, and able to fight for themselves, without the aid of the great lords. "In 1436, Paris," writes Lavallée, its historian, "was ravaged by famine and the plague, ruined by war, deserted by its principal inhabitants; its population reduced one half; wolves infested the streets; it had so many empty houses, that they were destroyed for fire-wood; and it was proposed to remove the capital to a town on the Loire. In 1466, with a view of re-peopling it, criminals of all countries were invited to take up their residence within its walls."—With such precedents in its history, and such a germ in its population, is it astonishing that Paris should in its periodical frenzies, exhibit every form of crime, madness and folly, of which human nature is capable?

Such were my reflections as I passed from one to another of the sites of historical events in which Paris is so prolific. The actors have passed away, but the human nature which gave birth to them remains the same. What does the future hold in store for this city? Emerging from every trial greater, richer, and more powerful, the centre of arts and sciences, if she ever learn wisdom from the lessons of the past, to what may she not aspire? But there is too much living interest in this turbulent, sparkling, ever-changing stream of humanity, for thought to remain long fixed on what lies beneath its waters. I opened my eyes to the world around me and walked on.

Although it was mid February, old women were knitting in the open air on the bridges, patiently awaiting customers for their humble wares. A noisy group was gathered around a large electrical machine, on the ecstasy of being pained by which, a professor in blouse was so eloquent, that he at last succeeded in obtaining a circle of greenhorns, who were willing to test the merits of the harmless looking array of bottles, wheels, and wire before them, even at the sacrifice of a few sous each. The professor touched them up pretty smartly. The shower that followed of "Mon Dieus," and other exclamations of irritation and wonder, in which the French is behind no other tongue, seemed to be peculiarly gratifying to the more cautious, who had kept their hands off the magical wire, while for a moment the carnival dancers themselves might have derived some useful hints from the variety and activity of the hops and gesticulations displayed. However, let a Frenchman make as much noise as he pleases, and he soon grows quiet; so it was here, and curiosity to know how it really did *feel*, soon drew together a fresh set of victims. I had some desire to know how much of an income the owner derived from so striking an appeal to the sensibilities of the public, but the crowd was too great for me to get near enough to question him.

On the Quai du Marché Neuf, I came to one of the sights of Paris, which, like all others, by the policy of the government, is free; but which it would be much more to its credit and to the benefit of public morals, if it charged a large fee for entrance to the merely curious. It was THE MORGUE, a name which, like that of Judas, stands by itself, the sole representative of its genus, species, and kind throughout the world. It is a plain Doric, cold, forbidding-looking building, perfectly in keeping with its uses. I entered, and saw three corpses, behind a glass partition, naked, with the exception of waist cloths, and laid out upon inclined slabs, something like butcher's blocks. Tiny streams of water were directed over

THE MORGUE.

them to keep them fresh. Their clothes were hung above their heads. Two were middle-aged men, the other a young woman, who apparently had come to her death by drowning.

The bodies of unknown persons are deposited here for three days, then, if not recognized and claimed, they are buried at the public expense. In a city like this, such an institution is one of undoubted utility; but to make a public spectacle of the naked bodies of our fellow-beings, whom crime, misfortune, accident, or neglect may have brought to an untimely end, is unquestionably demoralizing in its tendency. Young and old, maiden and mother, the stranger as well as the citizen, one and all of the unknown dead must be brought here, stripped even of the raiment which in most instances would be the best test of recognition, and exhibited to the morbid curiosity of those who, when they were living, passed them heedlessly by. Men, women, and children, even nurses with infants, came, gazed a few seconds on the revolting spectacle, and then left their places to those behind, impatiently awaiting their turn. In making this exhibition so unnecessarily public, I wondered why the government had not, with the system which it displays in every other place, provided a register for names, and a railing with a guard, to prevent crowding, and make the access and egress more facile. Seriously, this is a strange show in the heart of civilization. If it be not classed among the "necessary superfluities," and consequently an institution sacred even from the reforming hand of government, it imperatively calls for a change, by which the modesty, even of the dead, be not outraged, and the sensibilities of the living needlessly blunted.

During 1851, there were exposed three hundred and seventy-one bodies or parts of corpses; of these two hundred and fifty-four were of the male sex, thirty-eight of the female, twenty-six new-born babies, forty-six still-born, and seven fragments of limbs. Among the causes of death, there were one hundred and thirty-nine known suicides, twenty-five supposed, five homicides, seventy-one accidents, and forty-eight natural deaths.

It is stated that the deaths occasioned by carriages had diminished the past year. If so, this can only be attributed to a merciful Providence, for I never was in any city where there is more careless driving and apparent indifference to the safety of the foot passengers. The coachmen make a point to aim at pedestrians, either to see how near they can come to them without hitting them, or to enjoy a malicious satisfaction in seeing them jump in affright at the warning cry of "gare!" as the horses are about to tread upon their heels.

It will be remarked that suicides furnish by far the larger proportion of contributions to the Morgue. The papers teem with notices of, or attempts at, self-destruction. They appear to be more frequent than among any other nation, and for causes often of the most trivial and eccentric character. As illustrating the truth of the latter portion of my remark, I quote a number of cases taken from the newspapers during the winter, and which are well worth the attentive consideration of the student of human nature; or, more specifically speaking, of those who perplex their brains in endeavoring to disentangle the Gordian knot of Gallic character. It may be questioned whether the horrors of the revolution of '89, have not bequeathed even to the mothers of the present generation this unnatural legacy of blood. Succeeding events have not had a tendency to re-establish the peaceful and healthy flow of the vital current.

"Ernest B., of nineteen years of age, being jocularly told by a physician he had not long to live, took the words seriously, and fell into a profound melancholy. In his conversation he made constant allusions to his approaching end. Yesterday he was found hung in the garret of his father's house."

For children of but twelve years of age to seek self-destruction, with the coolness and determination of adults, and for causes as trifling as the pleasures that then amuse, no other country but France can give evidence of, and none others but French mothers can give birth to such offspring. I quote from an evening journal.

"Yesterday, a girl, scarcely twelve years old, climbed upon the parapet of the Quai d'Augustins, and, after making the sign of the cross, threw herself into the Seine. Several boatmen, warned by the cries of those who had seen her jump, detached a boat, and made every effort to save her. But by the time they succeeded in reaching her, she was dead.

"Taken to the Morgue, she was recognized this morning by her parents, living in the quarter of the Palais Royal. It appears that this young girl had felt for one of her cousins a violent passion. He having left for a foreign country, she had conceived a chagrin which prompted her to this fatal act.

"Almost at the same moment, there arrived at the Morgue, the corpse of another young girl, of the same age, who had committed suicide, from a motive more easy to comprehend.

"Toward the end of November last, Hortense R., belonging to a family in easy circumstances, in the Faubourg St. Antoine, left her school, to pass a day with her parents. She carried home an unsatisfactory note. Her mother gravely remonstrated with her, and reproached her, because, although twelve years old, she had not made her first communion. Hortense appeared much affected by these admonitions. At dinner-time, she could not be found. Her absence being prolonged late into the evening, her parents were much alarmed, and made every effort to obtain some tidings of her.

"Since that time, Hortense had not appeared, and no one knew her fate. Yesterday, the body of a young girl was taken from the Canal St. Martin, where it appeared to have been for a long time. It was discovered to be the corpse of Hortense."

The same paper records the suicide of a girl of eighteen, who had been fined twenty cents for some trifling fault.

The "Droit," of February 7, has as follows: "A triple attempt at suicide, accompanied with circumstances of the deepest immorality, has been for several days the only subject of conversation in the town of Batignolles, so seldom disturbed in its peaceful habits, by dramas of this nature. Clementine N., twenty-three years old, had, for a long time, held intimate relations with a young man of nineteen, Mr. P., clerk in a fashionable store, where she was herself a sales-woman.

"By a precocious depravity, which we leave to moralists to analyze, Clementine, without renouncing possession of her lover, made him contract a second liaison with a young girl of fifteen, named Eliza, also employed in the same shop, and who did not yield, except at the end of long and reiterated temptations by her companion.

"Sometime after this, she wished to give to P. a third mistress, and attempted to seduce another young girl, of the same shop; but this one repelled the infamous suggestions of Clementine, and informed her family of the attempt.

"On account of this revelation, the father of Eliza, in his turn, was informed of all these disorders. Indignant at the recital of this shameful prostitution, he threatened to complain to the prosecuting attorney of the Republic, and enjoined upon his daughter, under pain of being sent to a house of correction, to cease all relations with P. and Clementine. When informed by Eliza, that their debaucheries were no longer a secret, and fearing the effects of the anger of the father, they resolved, by common accord, to defeat it by committing suicide. They re-united in the room of P., and having made their adieus to the world, in a joint letter, set fire to the charcoal they had prepared, which soon began to produce the first effects of strangulation.

"Eliza, of a more delicate constitution than the other two,

felt first the mortal symptoms. She then began to be afraid to die, and, recalling her sinking energies, threw herself violently against the window, which she succeeded in opening, notwithstanding the resistance of her companions, and declared she wished to return home.

"Clementine and P., after having made new and useless efforts to induce her to die with them, yielded at last to her tears. They opened the door, and, as it was very late, and Eliza was taken with vomiting of blood, and scarcely able to walk, they led her to her house. Then returning, they relighted their fire, adding a postscript to their farewell letter, stating that Eliza had changed her resolution, and waited for death. Soon their groans attracted the attention of the neighbors, who, having knocked without an answer at the door, proceeded to break it. At the sight of the smoking charcoal, and the two young persons extended on the bed, giving no sign of life, they hastened to purify the atmosphere of the chamber, and to send for a doctor. Owing to the care bestowed, the two miserable beings were recalled to life. A few minutes later, and they would have been dead. Clementine had no sooner recovered her speech, than she overwhelmed with the grossest and most vulgar invectives, the neighbors who had interfered with her "*partie*" sport of suicide. She also declared that it was only adjourned, and that the next time she would take care to prevent any such impertinent interference.

The following case exhibits so powerfully the rationale of a suicide, that it deserves recording. The corpse was found suspended to a tree, near Paris, with the following note in the pocket:

"Those who discover my corpse shaking in the wind, will, without doubt, feel pity or terror, and say, 'another unhappy victim of misery or disappointment.' They will deceive themselves. I have always been perfectly happy. I feel that with age infirmities will arrive, and it is to evade the smallest grief, the minutest trouble, that I have decided to terminate my life. This may appear absurd ; but I find that when one has lived for more than sixty years, one should have had enough of life. I am alone in the world. I do not live in Paris. I believe it will be impossible to discover who I am. Besides, I have taken precautions for that ; and, if there is any respect for the last wish of a dying man, I beg they will make no research on this subject. I have left my resid·nce after having sold every thing, and announcing that I left for a foreign country. My fortune has been realized ; and the bank bills of which it is composed will have arrived yesterday for an honest father of a family, who will be made happy by them. I have so arranged it that he will not know from whom they came. Having nothing more to do in the world, I leave it Adieu."

As I have no desire to make this chapter rival Madame Tussaud's chamber of horrors, I will briefly add two other instances of those before me, showing how powerful a hold this crime has upon those in whom hope and joy usually burn brightest.

The first is that of a girl of fifteen, who destroyed herself from jealousy of the love her mother bore her only sister, an infant of but two years. The other was one of the best pupils of the "Lycée Bonaparte," who, being wrongfully suspected of copying an exercise, disguised his intent, under the appearance of more than ordinary good conduct, until he had provided himself with the means of self-destruction. He then locked himself in his room, set fire to the charcoal, went to bed, and calmly awaited suffocation. Fortunately, he was discovered, just in season to save his life.

The annual number of suicides in France, is about twenty-five hundred. In Paris they vary materially. In 1837, there were two hundred and seventy-seven. In 1840, three hundred and forty-six ; and in 1843, four hundred and twenty-seven.

CHAPTER III.

A SUNDAY'S WALK.

I KNOW no better way to convey a correct idea of a Parisian Sabbath, than simply to relate what one sees in a walk on that day. On the 15th of February, I sallied out at mid-day, and proceeding up the Rue de la Paix, met a troop of cavalry coming down at full trot. Quite a number of the shops were closed, and there were not many citizens in the streets. Indeed, for the dissipated and fashionable, it was about the time to expect them to be rubbing their eyes in bed, aghast at the thought that it was time to get up. The few that were out, were evidently in search, either of breakfast or some means to dissipate the ennui of the day of rest. Around the play-bills were the usual clusters, in meditation deep, whether to listen to Cruvelli at the Italian, to applaud their old favorite Ugulde at the Opera Comique, weep with Rachel at the Française, or laugh at the wit of the Montansier. Among the twenty-six theatres, it is to be hoped that each pleasure-hunter found one to his taste. There was also the usual assortment of concerts and fancy and masked balls. But the extraordinary attraction of the day was a pugilistic exhibition at the Salle Montesquieu, and a general contest with all sorts of arms, the notice closing thus: "The names of the professors who come together will attract, without doubt, all the true Parisian fashion to this solemnity."

Following a crowd into a large hall, I found myself in an-auction-room, filled with rich furuiture, silver-plate, and other articles belonging to some wealthy person lately deceased, whose heirs preferred the ready money. Sunday was selected for exhibiting them, as it was so convenient for the beau-monde to drop in on their way to church. Ladies were fingering specimens of Sèvres porcelain with one hand, while in the other they piously clasped their prayer-books. The bills said the sale was for to-morrow, and the purchasers were to pay five per cent. on the amount sold, to defray the expenses of the sale. I asked a Frenchman why the purchasers were required to pay the commission for selling. "Why should they not?" he replied; "they have the benefit of the articles they purchase." I thought to myself that cash in the seller's pocket was a more convenient commodity than a marble Venus or bronze Antinous in the parlor of the purchaser, and consequently more justly to be paid for. I afterward found, having occasion to dispose of some furniture, that the *seller* was subjected also to a tax of *six* per cent., making eleven per cent. levied on all goods sold at auction. Upon asking the auctioneer why both parties were thus taxed, he informed me that his per centage was less than four per cent., the remaining seven being consumed by government taxes and a public fund. The business, like that of the undertakers, is a sort of semi-municipal monopoly; and, whether well or badly served, the public must employ the few licensed auctioneers. At all sales there are two criers—one repeating from the other—the superior only wielding the deciding hammer. All articles are put up at an auctioneer's bid publicly declared. To an American their system appears very cumbersome and dilatory; and a sale seldom commences within an hour or two of the appointed time. The sales are held in certain fine hotels erected for the purpose.

Leaving the Rue de Jeuneurs, I passed down the Rue Montmartre, finding myself among an entirely different character of population from that of the Boulevards, so far as externals went. Blouses and caps were decidedly in the majority. Mechanics were busy on new buildings, but the shop-keepers looked as if they would much prefer to be any where else than behind their counters. This I attributed to a bright sun, which, having suddenly come out, invited all the world to come out also. The markets were as lively as ant-hills. It was evident there were many good dinners in contemplation.

The stranger who confines his walks to the new parts of Paris can have no idea of how and in what the poor people live. To ascertain this, he must thread the labyrinth of gloomy streets that lie between St. Eustache on one side of the river, and the Panthéon on the other. He will find many in which it is doubtful if the light of the sun ever reaches the pavement; so narrow, that it would be nothing strange should the inhabitants shake hands from their chamber-windows on either side. The houses are all of stone, lofty, and stained with the accumulated grime of centuries. The narrow, dark entrances look as if leading to subterranean galleries. There is dirt within and dirt without; there are no accumulations of filth on the pavements, but there are no sidewalks, and the feet slip about over their greasy surface as if it had been freshly oiled. It is in these retreats that poverty and students make their homes. As I threaded my way through this forbidding quarter, I ceased to wonder that families who live constantly in Paris, in process of time, become extinct. At this hour there was not much stir in this part of the human hive; but to account for this it must be borne in mind, that there are thirty thousand people in Paris who dare not show themselves in the day. Like bats, their safety is solely in the dark. Woe to the stranger who falls into their toils, and no armed guardian of the night nigh. The search for the burial-place of Moses would not be more futile than the attempt to trace his end. I do not mean to say that because a street is narrow, dark and filthy, it is the abode of these land-pirates, but simply that there are streets in this part of the city which no prudent person should enter after night-fall. And in the day-time it is not altogether without risk, owing to a habit in much repute among the dextrous, of coming behind the pedestrian slily, and jamming his hat down over his head. While the victim is disengaging himself, the assailant makes off with his purse or watch.

It was a relief to reach the quays. Near the Morgue were several groups assembled around the usual variety of mountebanks that gather their harvest of coppers on Sunday in every quarter of the metropolis. They reminded me of the truth of a saying of Rabelais—not the demoniacal mocker of the sixteenth century, but a contemporary Protestant doctor of Montpellier: "The Parisians," says Rabelais, "are so silly, so stupid, and so inapt by nature, that a buffoon, a swill-carrier, a mule with bells, or an old fool in a square, will assemble more people than a sound, evangelical preacher."

All the groups were not, however, of this description. The Parisians love fun, but they are as willing to extract it from the sciences as from any other quarter. I was much amused to hear a philosopher in blouse recount the merits of a strange-looking machine before him. He called it a "dynamique physique," recommended by the medical faculty to test the strength of the arms, the blood, the lungs, &c. A fellow-blouse, a young Hercules in looks, paid a "sous" and took hold of the wires attached to a little box, containing, I suppose, the electric fluid, and from which projected a light handle. This the professor began to turn. The blouse resisted with his utmost strength, but the wires contracted and pulled him straight to the box, much to his astonishment and more against his will, as he had evidently calculated upon an easy victory over the slight apparatus before him. He went off, rubbing his arms with ludicrous energy.

Near by was a market of the feathered tribe, guinea-pigs, cats, dogs, and all sorts of birds, and clean and unclean things in cages, which form the usual assortment of pets to both sexes of all ages in Paris. It requires no little dexterity in the crowded thoroughfares, to avoid being tripped up, by the strings by which the puppies—quadrupeds always when so attached—are secured to the belles in their promenades. They are rightly named pets, as no equanimity is proof against that condition of temper, arising from an accident of this nature, especially if, as is not uncommon, there is a *biped* puppy at the other end of the line. After all, what can be more natural than these companionships, if the principle be correct, that " a fellow-feeling makes one wondrous kind ?"

Leaving philosophers and puppies, I followed the Rue St. Jacques, until I found myself in the ancient " *Thébaïde* " of Paris, so called on account of its numerous and extensive religious establishments, the retreats of courtesans disgusted with the world, and high-born ladies who would, like Valliere, expiate by the austerities of conventual life, the follies and errors of their youth. Their sites were judiciously selected, for they are all built over the catacombs, in which now repose a population of the dead, three times as numerous as that of living Paris. The Revolution has left of the past institutions nothing but their names. The Val de Grâce (Vale of Grace) is to-day a military hospital; the Convent of the Visitation of Ste. Marie, made commemorable by the virtues of Mademoiselle de La Fayette, a house of correction for disorderly women; the famous " Abbaye du Port Royal," the abode of celibacy and all the Christian virtues, a lying-in hospital; and, stranger fate than all, the Church of St. Benoit Trinité, a low theatre, where the students and washerwomen of this quarter assemble to applaud the obscene comedies and furious dramas, which resound within the walls that once echoed only the praises of Almighty God. To a far more appropriate use has the Cemetery of Bonne Nouvelle arrived, if the inhabitants of the tomb may be supposed to have the same tastes, as when they dwelt in the flesh. It is now the site of the theatre "Gymnase Dramatique."

The "Thébaïde" of modern times is the abode of a religious, poor, and laborious population. I entered their humble church with far more satisfaction than the Madeleine, for it was built by the gratuitous labor of the working people, devoting, each week, a day to this pious task, their masters giving the materials, and an illustrious penitent in a neighboring convent—the sister of the great Condé, one of the heroines of the Fronde—the Duchess of Longueville, providing the marble and sacred vessels of the altar.

The Chapel of the Vale of Grace, now a military church, is one of the finest monuments of the city. It was founded by Anne of Austria, in fulfillment of a vow to build a church, in case she gave birth to an heir to the throne. She had been married twenty-two years without issue, and her final reconciliation with her husband Louis XIII., of which Louis XIV. was the fruit, is attributed to the noble sentiments with which Mademoiselle de La Fayette had inspired the king, at the sacrifice of her own love. Her life is one of the brightest triumphs of female virtue on record, and stands out in almost solitary relief of perfect purity of thought and action, among the long list of the brilliant and beautiful of her sex, that graced the courts of France, during the reigns of her earlier Bourbon monarchs.

The high altar is a copy of that of St. Peter's at Rome. The dome, painted on stone by Mignard, is called one of the finest frescoes in France. Its colors appear to have a little faded. The confessional used by Mademoiselle de la Valliere, previous to her taking the vail at the Carmelites, is still preserved. As it was not the hour of service, the church was deserted by all, except the curious like myself. Before I left, an attendant commenced lighting the candles for vespers.

Next I sought that of the Sorbonne. On entering the gloomy

court-yard of this celebrated college, I found not a living being to greet me. The silence was as perfect as if the dead languages had literally driven the living from out its halls. The porter was gone, and his lodge was empty. At last I discovered, in one of the cells of the archway, an old woman, who informed me that, by ascending four long flights of stairs in the most remote corner of the quadrangular edifice, I would probably find the sacristan. The tomb and monument of Cardinal Richelieu was worth the trouble, so I commenced the ascent. Midway I met a domestic, who, learning my wants, not only volunteered to find the sacristan, but declined a fee for his trouble. This official soon appeared and let me into the church, which it seems is kept locked up for his special benefit.

The monument is the finest in France. It is of marble, and was executed by Giradon. The Cardinal is in a reclining posture, sustained by Religion, represented by his niece, the Duchess of Guyon. Another, the Duchess of Frousac, personifies Science, weeping at his feet. It was concealed during the Revolution, but the tomb was opened, and the heart of the cardinal placed on a pike, and paraded about the streets. The person into whose hands it fell, bequeathed it to his son, who was finally compelled by law to restore it to its proper resting-place. I asked the the sacristan if the students ever attended church. He shook his head gravely, as he replied "No," correcting himself, however, by adding, "Now and then one."

The Guillotine and entrance to the Catacombs are both in the immediate vicinity, but neither can be seen except by special favor or very considerable expense. For the first I had no curiosity, but I should have been gratified at a view of this immense subterranean Golgotha, which, extending under more than one sixth of the capital, undermines the Pantheon, the Odeon, Observatory, the Palace of the Luxembourg, the streets La Harpe, St. Jacques, and, strange to say, Hell itself. Visitors are interdicted on account of the dangerous state of the roofs, which require constant propping. The entrance to the Catacombs is very appropriately at the "Barrière d'Enfer," (Gate of Hell.)

Making a virtue of necessity, I left the dead below the city in the undisturbed solitude of their abode, and proceeded to visit the Cemetery of Mont Parnasse, outside the barrier of that name. The vacant spaces between the Boulevards and the gate of the city were filled with peddlers, jugglers, and a crowd busy in buying or applauding. The usual array of stone-cutters' shops, embracing every variety of unlettered monuments, awaiting the record of departed virtues, betokened the proximity of the burying-ground. Passing through the gate, I found myself in the centre of a fair of the lowest class. The amusements, gardens, and cafés bore the same relation to the corresponding resorts within the walls, as that receptacle of the débris of the vanities and miseries of Paris, the market of old linen, does to the elegant shops of the Rue Vivienne. Wine was but six cents a bottle, and brandy twenty. The liquor shops abutted upon the very walls of the cemetery. They were filled to overflowing, and the noise that arose from the French tongues, made doubly active by the stimulus of their favorite beverages, can only be conceived by ears that have listened to it. The clatter of fifty cotton mills is silence in comparison. Cake and pie women cried their comestibles at every pace. The clear air of heaven was poisoned by the fumes of the vilest tobacco ascending from the filthiest of pipes. It was too early in the day for intoxication to have made much progress, but the tide of debauch was evidently on the rise. Such was the spectacle allowed by French taste to exist almost over the graves of their parents. And yet the same people uncover their heads to a passing funeral.

In front of the cemetery wall was a line of some forty women, each with a number and her name on a little sign, and having displayed before her an assortment of gifts of all sorts, such as

French affection lavishes upon buried friends. There were statuettes of saints and innocents; crucifixes and Christs; artificial flowers; porcelain vases; natural wreaths; and piles of white and yellow immortelles inscribed on them in black letters, "à mon père," "à ma mère," and so on through the entire degrees of consanguinity and friendship. Some had simply "amour," "souvenir," "regard," &c. Each one of the forty hucksters of tributes of affection assailed the wayfarers with every variety and tone of argument, to induce a sale of her wares in preference to those of her neighbors. The mourner who visits the grave must run this gauntlet of traffic. Habit, doubtless, as in every thing else, renders the nuisance less noticeable; but a custom at the entrance of a cemetery, which reminds an American of the contests of hackney-coachmen at a steamboat landing, strikes him as jarring painfully with the sacredness of the place. I was pleased to see, however, that almost every visitor brought some souvenir to hang up over the graves they came to visit. This was particularly the case with little children, and must inspire them not only with respect for the departed, but divest the grave-yard of that indefinable horror with which it is too apt to be regarded by the young in America.

Mont Parnasse is a pleasing contrast to Père la Chaise. Like all French cemeteries, it is laid out with the mathematical precision of a town, and the graves so crowded, that they literally are in want of elbow-room. Still the greater number were simple and appropriate. All had more or less tokens of the affection of the living about them. There were enough trees to give it a rural aspect, although they were planted in stiff rows. The family tombs had none of the cold and stately magnificence of Père la Chaise. They were true to their intent externally. The interior arrangements were not in keeping with the spiritual world, however much they might correspond with the taste of the living. I counted no less than one hundred and twelve "immortelles" on one grave. These are as touching a memorial for affection to offer as can be devised. But to look into a tomb through a gilt grating, and see upon an altar, in form of a dressing-table, vases of artificial flowers, silver candlesticks, or a gilt lamp, and the usual decorations of a boudoir, recalls too much of the coquetry of life. Yet such is French taste in the decoration of the abodes of death, and the crowd press to see this vain display, with the same light expressions of admiration that they utter around an exhibition of fashionable novelties in a shop-window.

Père la Chaise is the parent of modern rural cemeteries But what a contrast does it afford to the natural beauties of a Mount Auburn, or a Greenwood! Instead of the labyrinthine paths, bordered with flowers and overshadowed by forest trees, nature refined by art, yet leaving undisturbed that solitude which affliction seeks as a repose for its dead, it is literally a necropolis. It has its paved streets and walks, its monuments of every size and fashion, so closely piled together, that nature is entirely banished. It is a wilderness of carved stone, and an album of epitaphs, to read which one would fain believe that naught but virtue and worth ever dwelt in Paris. If these be true, where are the bad buried? What are we to think of the pride of birth, that builds a mausoleum to a

LA FONTAINE. MOLIERE.

"Very high, very excellent,
and very powerful Princess,
aged one day?"

How different the tomb-stone of genuine affection with its simple "Marie." This Mary may have followed Jesus like those who were latest at the cross, and first at the grave. She may have been the infant of a day, or the mother whose eyes were closed by a new-born babe. Whoever she was, modest love retains the secret.

A neighboring epitaph was of a cloth-merchant, terminating his catalogue of virtues with the announcement "His widow continues his business, Rue Saint Denis, 349."

This epitaph, so ultilitarian and business-like, recalls to my mind that of Milton in Westminister Abbey, in which the immortality of the poet is quite engulfed in the egotism of the erector, who, under the pretense of honoring him, to whom neither marble nor consecrated ground can add honor, sought for himself and his titles a distinction which survives only to proclaim his ridiculous and ungrammatical vanity. It is as follows:

A Bust of Milton.

[Underneath.]

"Milton.
In the Year of our Lord Jesus Christ
1707
This Bust of the Author of Paradise
Lost was placed by William
Benson, Esquire, One of the
Two Auditors of the Imprests
to his Majesty, George 2nd.,
formerly Surveyor General
of the Works to his Majesty
King George the First.
Keysbrook was the
Statuary who cut it."

This is about equal in pathos to the famous apostrophe:

"O Sophonisba, Sophonisba O!"

The situation of Père la Chaise, as regards the view of Paris and its environs, is beautiful. Its chief attraction is the monument of Abelard and Heloise, a delicate Gothic structure, more suitable for some sacred edifice, than the open air. From the number of immortelles hung about it, it is evident that the memory of their loves is still green in the hearts of their countrymen.

HELOISE ET ABELARD.

All that wealth and taste can create from stone has been done to honor the distinguished dead that are here interred; yet the most conspicuous monument of all, a light-house in proportions and design, bears the name of an individual known only for its extravagant cost. Napoleon's

MONGE MASSENA. LEFEBVRE. CAMBACERES. DECRES. SUCHET

marshals lie thick here, but the bravest of them all has neither stone nor story to mark the spot where he sleeps. This rivalry of magnificence in the house of death extends so far, that M. Boulard journeyed to the quarries of Carrara to select the spotless marble that now presses upon his remains.

There are already more than sixteen thousand tombs on which have been expended upward of $25,000,000, yet owing to the character of the material of which they are in general constructed, and their delicacy of execution, they will mostly disappear before the end of the present century. I was particularly struck with one monument, composed in part of mutilated sculptures from the resting-place of some subject of Augustus or Alexander, who little thought, in preparing himself a proud sepulchre, he was but furnishing the materials to erect the tomb of a descendant of a barbarous Gaul. I noticed that the government had erased from the gateways the words "Liberté, egalité, fraternité," the only spots where they could with truth have remained.

COUNTESS DEMIDOFF.

While on the subject of monuments I would call the visitor's attention to one of Valentine Balbiano, wife of René Biraque, carved by Pilou. It is on the ground floor of the Louvre, in the Hall of the Sculptures of the Middle Ages and Revival of Arts. Above is a beautiful female, of perfect contour, and richly dressed in the fashion of the era, the whole delicately sculptured in white marble. Below in bas-relief, is the same female lying in her coffin, with her loins only covered, and wasted away to the extremest point of attenuation, leaving her bosom, face, and other portions of the body exposed. The contrast between the lovely figure above and the shrunken remains of loveliness beneath, exhibiting all that is most repulsive in death, is very striking, some would say disgusting. At all events, it is a curious fancy and not without its moral.

To return to my walk. Re-entering the city, I met crowds pushing on to the cheaper wine-shops and amusements outside the barrier. As I passed the stately Temple of St. Sulpice, its congregation was entering for evening worship. Right opposite was a theatre, in which the performers were all "singes savants," learned monkeys. That, too, had its throng. The Faubourg St. Germain wore its usual air of aristocratic quiet, except there were more ladies about than usual, wending their way to the fashionable church of St. Thomas d'Aquin. Most of them were in mourning for the late Duchess d'Angoulême, who was greatly beloved by the Legitimists. It is said, she occasionally visited them incognito from her place of exile, the government considerately turning a blind eye to that quarter on those occasions.

Of the fullness of the Museums it is needless to speak. Next to religious instructions they are the most desirable schools for the people, and it was gratifying to see the interest with which all classes flock to them.

GRAND AVENUE OF THE TUILERIES.

The Garden of the Tuileries swarmed like an ant-hill with children, dressed like show-dolls, and their "*bonnes*" and mammas. It was easy to see how the national taste for display was perpetuated. These little sprouts already manifested an incipient vanity which promised soon to swell into a settled passion. Their personal appearance was their first care. Their toilette preserved, they then frolicked with what spirit and liberty were left them. It required no little dexterity to avoid stepping upon some toddling infant, to prevent being tripped up by a stray

GARDEN OF THE TUILERIES ON SUNDAY.

hoop, or hit by a flying ball. The boys were sailing miniature boats on the ponds, while their sisters fed the swans. There was no quarreling or ill-humor. I returned to my lodgings with their juvenile shouts still ringing in my ears, and had hardly seated myself, before a strolling musician, with a dancing monkey let off a whole volley of polkas and mazourkas from his hand-organ, right under my window; but as I gave him no copper he removed his quarters to some more propitious neighborhood. He was succeeded by another of his species, who played, and admirably too, what seemed to me the strangest of all the strange things I had seen and heard that day, the good old familiar psalm tunes of Old Hundred and Granville. These last were indeed a treat in Paris.

I do wrong to say the strangest of all the strange things I had seen that day, for I think my readers will agree with me, that the following notice, which I copied verbatim from the shutters of a shop on the Boulevard Madeleine, merits for Paris that description: "Pour obvier un désagrément qui par le temps qui court, arrive trop souvent de venir quelque fois de fort loin les dimanches et fêtes chomées frapper nos portes avec persévérance pour se procurer de nos denrées. Commc la trève qui fesons aux affaires les jours fériés nous est dictée par nos croyances, il est bien qu'on sache que les ventes du Bazar Provençal n'ont bien que les six jours ouvrables de la semaine, le septième etait consacré au repos comme l'on fait nos pères sans interruption par la tradition jusqu'a la promulgation du décalogue dicté par le tout puissant à Moise sur le Mont Sinai. Héritiers des croyances et practiques religieuses de nos aïeux, nous suivons ponctuellement la ligne qu'ils nous ont tracée sans en devier un iota." In free English as follows: "To obviate the inconvenience which, as the times run, happens too often, that persons come from a distance sometimes, on Sundays and holy-days, to knock perseveringly at our doors to purchase our merchandise, this is to give notice, that we open our shop only on the six working-days of the week, the seventh being consecrated to repose, as was done by our fathers without interruption, ordered by tradition and the decalogue dictated by the Almighty to Moses on Mount Sinai. Inheriting the religious faith and practices of our ancestors, we follow strictly the line that they have traced for us without deviating an iota."

The restaurateur of Paris who closes his doors from religious principle on Sunday, is deserving of respect for his abnegation of his pecuniary interest. But to add to this a sermon in an indelible inscription on his window-shutters, on the observance of the Sabbath, is an evidence of moral courage one little expects to find in this gay and pleasure-loving capital. I must add, however, that our sermonizing shopkeeper notified the public that he would send purchases home on Sunday morning, when required.

CHAPTER IV.

PRODIGALITY OF THE ROMAN CHURCH.

To the lovers of vocal music the Church of Saint Elizabeth in the Rue du Temple affords a rare treat in the voice of one of the choir, a boy of thirteen, the son of a shoemaker. His celebrity is such that opera singers and the amateurs of Paris flock to hear him. Large offers have been made him to sing at the Madeleine, but he has refused to leave his parish church. A friend in describing to me his voice, compared it to that of an angel. Although no musician, and never having had the satisfaction to hear a celestial songster, yet I must confess, that my enraptured ears were ravished with the melody of his rich notes, now filling every portion of the church with their sonorous harmony, then subsiding into a strain scarcely audible, yet thrilling every nerve with pleasure. His organ is wonderful, and if its power is preserved will lead him to eminence.

The Catholic ritual is undoubtedly an impressive form of worship. But, like the stage, it requires to be seen from a certain distance to preserve the sacred illusion. Where there is so much machinery and ceremony, there can not fail to be a proportion of tinsel and heartlessness, which ill accords with a Protestant's idea of the simplicity and sincerity to be exhibited in divine worship. It is true, education shapes our ideas, but it is equally true that common sense does not always yield herself blindly to habit, and reason will protest at the violence done her judgment. A Catholic is armed at all points on questions of faith, but it would puzzle the most zealous proselyte of Rome to defend on any grounds of consistency with the doctrines of the meek and lowly Jesus, many of the practices introduced by his church into their rites. In the United States a clergyman who requires a sexton to open and close for him the pulpit-door is viewed as trespassing somewhat on the humility he preaches to his congregation. The conscientious sensitiveness of such critics would be alarmingly agitated in attending worship in this city.

I was at Saint Elizabeth's during vesper service, and took my station in the rear of the altar, by the choir door which leads to the sacristy. The position was well chosen to observe the ceremony. Of what Sydney Smith calls "man millinery" there was the usual variety; each of the different orders that take part in the service having its peculiar costume. With the various genuflexions, lighting of candles, ringing of bells, elevation of the host, every reader who has attended this service is familiar. To those whose faith they quicken, they are well. But the going to and fro between the choir and sacristy of the various assistants, often smiling and winking as they passed, the dodging about of the little boys with red skull-caps, the obsequious holding up of the skirts of the priests by their juniors bespoke a service cumbered with much serving. The most striking figure, and, if there is any reliance to be placed in Lavater, the most important in his own opinion, in the scene was the "Suisse." Every church has one or more, caricaturing in costume the uniform of a field-marshal. Those of San Roch, glitter in gold lace, rich embroidery, chapeau de bras, white tights, gloves, side-arms, halbert in one hand, and an immense cane with an enormous gilt

LE SUISSE.

head in the other. My friend at Saint Elizabeth was the most modestly arrayed that I had seen of his class. He was of the orthodox height, six feet and upward, shoulders in proportion (for this size is a "sine qua non" to the office), wore a black uniform with crimson facings, and silver embroidery, chapeau, rapier, silver epaulet on one shoulder, and a ribbon knot with three ends silver-worked on the other, buttons and stripe to pants of same, gilt. He appeared so ill at ease, that I judged him a novice in this harness. I noticed that he alone was privileged to stand before the altar uncovered, and indeed his sole avocation seemed to be at certain intervals to bring the metal ends of his spear and cane down upon the pavement with an emphasis that made my toes involuntarily shrink within my boots. Whenever the curé or vicars passed to another part of the church he preceded them, causing the stone pavements to ring to the pounding of his two weapons. On meeting his superiors, he gave a half-military salute. The Suisse leads the way for the priests who take up the collections during the service, crying out in an imposing voice—"Alms, if you please, for the church, the poor, the worship of the Virgin," or whatever may be the occasion. Indeed when the church is full, without the aid of their colossal proportions and the salutary terror inspired by their manner of handling their insignia of office, it would be difficult for the priests to make their way from the high altar to other spots where their functions call them. Before the service concluded, there were several infant baptisms. The "Suisse" ushered the parties into the baptismal chapel, and I followed him to witness the ceremony. The first infant had only a mother present, and the priest ordered the Suisse to stand sponsor. To my surprise, he told him to take off his chapeau, which appeared to surprise him too. As on every other occasion that I have seen this sacrament performed, it was done with such a rapidity as to render it utterly unintelligible; the only word distinctly uttered, being at intervals by the Suisse, who responded "amen" in the sharp, ringing tone that Jack gives when he replies "Ay, ay, Sir," to an unexpected hail. In the mean while he was occupied with adjusting his shoulder-knot, and glancing about him evidently to count the number of admiring eyes. As the Catholic rite requires not only to wet the hair but the skin, this was so liberally done that the infant uttered a most vigorous protest, in accents any thing but in concert with the musical prodigy, who at that moment was pouring forth his notes at the other end of the church. The ceremony concluded with a lighted candle, and the usual signing and kissing the cross, turning of robes, and holding the end with the embroidered cross over the child's head.

In this church there is a Mater Dolorosa by Bézard. It is a dead Christ of the size of life sitting bolt upright, with nothing on but a waist-cloth, in the arms of his mother, who looks

CHURCH OF ST. ROCH

younger than he, and is holding him with much the expression and attitude any woman would assume with a corpse in her lap. I have never seen a sacred subject more incongruously treated, unless it is in a painting in the long gallery at the Louvre, by one of the old masters, representing the three Marys assisting in the descent from the cross. The mother of Jesus, who is supporting her son's legs, is dressed in the fashionable costume of a grand lady of the fourteenth century, with rich bracelets on her bare arms, kid gloves deeply edged with fine lace on her hands, and a profusion of pearls and diamonds on her neck and bosom. St. Roch not long since boasted a painting of a black Christ, the work of a Creole artist, but it has been removed.

In the Louvre there is also a ludicrous bas-relief, representing Joseph at work at his carpenter's bench, while about him is a squad of little angels piously picking up all his chips, and quarreling as to who should get the most. The Virgin is watching the Infant Jesus asleep in a sort of Pilgrim Father's cradle, buried up in heavy bed-clothes. Other infantile angels are rocking the cradle and holding the thread for Mary's distaff, which she is nimbly plying. The Almighty seated on a cloud, with the Pope's tiara on his head, is watching the group with a very parental air. Sad liberties are often taken by Catholic artists with sacred subjects under the most devotional impulses.

The clergy are adroit in taking collections, if there is faith to be placed in the power of beauty to draw the purse-strings. The following is a sample of the usual notices given through the newspapers. "An Assembly of Charity will be held at the Church of St. Eustache, Sunday, 25th of January, on behalf of the poor, assisted by Monsieur the Curé, the Sisters of St. Vincent de Paule, and the work for the visitation of the sick. At half past two, vespers and sermon by Monsieur the Abbé Duquesnay, Chanoine of Paris, the raising of the host by My Lord Margueirie, Bishop of St. Fleur, named to the See of Autrens.

The collection will be taken by Mesdames the Duchess of Grammont, 38 Rue de la Ville l'Evèque, the Marquise de Vesins, 23 Rue d'Anjou St. Honoré," and so on, naming the title and residence of each lady.

The office they undertake is no sinecure. I was present at the fête of St. Cecile in the same church, when a collection was taken. The ladies in rich toilets were conspicuously placed in the stall of the trustees. At the termination of the discourse, they sallied out on their errands of benevolence, each with a beautifully wrought crimson velvet bag, with gold tassels and strings in her hand, to receive the offerings of the charitable. The church was densely crowded, and they were obliged to push their way from chair to chair, as only a French lady knows how, through the numberless knees that intercepted their progress. There were moments when I thought that even they considered their philanthropy sorely tested. They persevered, however, each taking a section, leaving no person unvisited. They then stationed themselves at the gates of the nave, and the doors of the church, kneeling on "Prie-dieu," so that every one was compelled to run the gauntlet of their charitable pleadings, and the still more irresistible language of their lovely eyes, for the third time. These successive depletions, joined to the original one of a franc for a seat, upon entrance, lightened most purses very considerably. Besides the pleasure of bestowing charity through so fair a medium, three hundred and fifty of the best musicians of Paris, executed a musical mass of Haydn's in a manner worthy of the author.

Near the doors of most of the churches there are placed a kind of sentry-box with seats, closed in front by a sort of desk. In them sit the day long, with a patience that reminded me of the hermit crab, while they themselves looked like venerable rats peering from their holes, the smallest, grayest, wrinkledest specimens of the human species now extant. Indeed to the man of the street they bear about the same resemblance that dried and pressed plants do to the fresh and verdant. The oldest of our revolutionary fathers would appear like a stripling beside them. If Barnum wants a male "Joice Heath," I recommend to him to select from these antediluvians. Their sole duty is to hold out to the faithful the "toupet" or brush, which is dipped into holy water. A little American girl in asking me its name and use graphically described it "as a thing with hairs sticking out in the end of it, which every body felt of as they went by."

TOUPET HOLDER.

There are in Paris forty-eight churches, all belonging to the government. A church like the Madeleine has about sixty individuals attached to its service. They consist of a curé, vicars, deacons, sub-deacons, chanters, wardens, sacristan, beadles, Suisse, children of the altar, and choristers. The Archbishop appoints the curés to the several churches. They are selected from the oldest vicars, and have control of all matters in their parish.

The Roman hierarchy has as many ranks and as rigid a system of discipline as the army. The total of Catholic clergy in France is about forty-two thousand, beside eight thousand five hundred theological students in the different colleges. There are fifteen archbishops, sixty-five bishops, one hundred and seventy-six vicars-general, six hundred and sixty-one canons, three thousand three hundred and one curates, and twenty-eight thousand eight hundred and one priests. These last, who belong to the "églises succursales" (chapels of ease), are poorly paid. Indeed, compared with the Protestant clergy of England and

America, the incomes of their French brethren are very small. The Archbishop of Paris has $8000 per annum; the other archbishops, little less than $3000; the bishops, $2000; curés, from $250 to $1000; the vicars, $200; and subordinates in proportion. These incomes are augmented by the fees arising from occasional ceremonies. In Paris for a grand marriage the curé receives $5; each vicar, $1·50; the beadle, $1; and the other assistants according to their ranks. Louis Napoleon has increased the stipends of the superior clergy about one third, by which the budget for 1853 gives 3,000,000 francs more for Public Worship than that of 1852, which amounted to 41,000,000.

The churches enjoy also a prolific source of revenue, from the ceremonies which their creed makes incumbent on all believers who would shorten their stay in purgatory, or be considered as zealous for the faith. The price of a grand mass varies from $10 to $60, according to its splendor; a low mass, which consists solely of *silent* worship before the altar, can be had as cheap as 15 cents; funeral services, from $4 to $40; marriages, $3 to $40; a grand marriage made at the high altar, with carpets, gilt arm-chairs, choir, &c., costs from $40 to $60. What remains of these receipts after the apportioned division among the clergy and assistants, is deposited in the church treasury, to defray the expenses of robes, ornaments, and candles. For the last, the rich ladies of the parish contribute liberally. The burning of candles must be considered as particularly efficacious in cleansing from sin, if a judgment can be formed from the numbers offered and consumed before the different altars by the devout women, for it is rarely that a man expends a "sous" for this purpose. In each church there is a "magasin" of these commodities under the charge of a woman, who has before her a sort of triangular iron frame with points, on which the lighted candles are placed. The shrine of the patron saint of Paris, St. Geneviève, in the Church of St. Etienne du Mont, is kept constantly illuminated, and generally there are to be seen persons of both sexes praying before her tomb.

Collections are taken every Sunday for the poor, and to support the church. Baptisms, absolutions, and extreme unction are administered gratis. The finances and books are in the charge of "fabriciens" or trustees: generally six of the oldest and wealthiest members of the parish, chosen by the parishioners at large. They have a seat of honor fronting the pulpit, inclosed like one of our pews, richly cushioned and slightly elevated above the other worshipers. There are two ranges of seats in this stall, on the lower of which the clergy sit during sermon time. The total cost of the Catholic clergy of France is estimated at $7,260,000 per annum. Before the revolution of 1789 it was $28,000,000. The government gives in aid of their worship proportionally to the Protestants and Jews; to the former about $260,000, and to the latter $22,000. There are six hundred and forty one Calvinist and Lutheran ministers, forty of the Church of England, eighty-six of other denominations, and eight Grand Rabbins.

Architecture and the decorative arts are largely indebted to the Catholic church. Henry VII.'s Chapel at Westminster is justly considered a fine specimen of florid Gothic architecture, but the gem of this style is the Sainte Chapelle, erected by St. Louis in 1245–8. To visit this chapel a written permission from the Minister of Public Works is required; but on two occasions I found a "douceur" equally as efficacious to the gentlemanly officer who had it in charge, and who informs visitors of its history. I should not have known this fact, however, if it had not been for a man in a blouse, who, as I was gazing at the exterior with a look of raw admiration that told the stranger, inquired if Monsieur would like to go in. Upon my informing him I was minus the indispensable billet, he gave me some mysterious directions as to what course to pursue, to elevate the "complaisance" of the door-keeper to the point necessary to allow me to speak a few words to Monsieur his superior within. Once within, a franc is as good as the signature of the Minister, and when out, a few sous sent my informant on his way rejoicing, to waylay another greenhorn. There seems to be an unaccountable itching in our nature to see what, in nine cases out of ten, is not worth seeing, if it be forbidden. I have seen five francs open the doors of the Chapel of the Invalides, where the only recompense is a mass of stone and masonry in process of being wrought into the most magnificent tomb in Europe, but which at present scarcely proclaims what it will be. The Sainte Chapelle, like all gems of art, to be described must be seen. Neither dimensions, technical terms, nor the cost added, give any adequate idea of beautiful structures. A landscape may be described, because the general beauties of nature are familiar to all ; but a description in which to be exact, crocheted gables, tripartite archings, and perforated spandrels must figure, would be like the attempt to convey the idea of the beauty of the loveliest flowers by a repetition of their scientific nomenclature.

Near the altar is a side chapel with a small window, accessible only from below. In this chapel that amiable sovereign Louis XI. said his prayers in fear and trembling, lest even the defense of stone and mortar should not prevent an assassin from getting in his rear and destroying him in sight of the very relics, among which was a piece of the true cross and the crown of thorns, which this chapel was built to hold. These relics cost St. Louis enough to be authentic. They are now deposited at Notre Dame. I inquired of the faithful guardian of the Chapelle if they were visible. He sagely replied, he really did not know, but added with a smile that savored of five franc pieces, if the proper means were pursued, he really had no doubt that that pleasure could be had.

Externally, Notre Dame is the most beautiful ecclesiastical

structure in Paris. Internally, it is gloomy and simple to a fault. The reverse is true of St. Eustache, where the exterior is an odd medley of various styles of Gothic and Grecian architecture, incrusted in part on two sides with old buildings, giving it the appearance of a beautiful shell disfigured with barnacles. The northern doorway of the transept is magnificent, but to my mind the pro-

NOTRE DAME.

portions and character of its interior harmonize far better with the spirit of Christian worship, than the gorgeous splendor which characterizes the churches of Madeleine and Notre Dame de Lorette. A French writer says of the latter, that it is worthy of the incredulous and sensual age that constructed it, where the worst taste is shown equally in the *tout ensemble* as in the details, where one finds pictures of Saints in the postures of prostitutes, and where are heaped together the furniture of a coffee-house, the seductions of a theatre, and the blandishments of haunts of dissipation; it is a sort of appendage to the opera, of which it is the parish: a boudoir worthy of the quarter, and which has had the honor to give its name to the grisettes of its neighborhood. This may be too severe, but it needs but a glance at the meretricious character of its decorations to make the visitor fear that he has mistaken an opera-house for a church. In keeping with the character in this respect, it is said to be, by excellence, the church where the vain and beautiful most do congregate to exhibit themselves and their newest fashions.

THE MADELEINE AND THE BOULEVARDS

St. Vincent de Paule partakes somewhat of this glitter of gold, but in better taste. The roof is very beautiful. The most curious church in Paris is St. Etienne du Mont, in which are beautifully blended the Gothic style, and that of the revival of the arts. Its stained glass and magnificent rood-loft, a chef-d'œuvre of lightness and delicacy, attract crowds of visitors. But the church on which modern art has exhausted its genius, is the Madeleine. Situated on one of the most commanding positions of Paris, the stranger of but a day is sure to see it. Externally it is the Parthenon, but to rival that edifice, it requires the purer material and clearer sky, as well as the matchless sculpture of its Athenian prototype. It is strictly a temple, but neither in plan nor finish adapted to the simplicity of Christianity. It should have been, as Napoleon contemplated, dedicated to the military glories of France. Then, the luxuriance and perfection of its decorations, harmonizing with its design, it would have been viewed as a specimen of the wealth and resources of art of the first military nation of modern times, appropriately devoted to perpetuating the memory of the achievements of those who have won fame for themselves and their country. As it exists, it is an incongruous Museum of sculpture and painting, so combined that all sense of the sacredness of the objects is merged into admiration of the skill that executed them, while the display of gilding and velvet, recalls rather the attractions of an opera and the luxury of a palace, than the mysteries of faith. The greatest admirer of Napoleon would scarcely have claimed for him the most conspicuous position in the decorations of a Christian church, putting into shade, by the splendor of his imperial robes, the gilded glories of the second person in the Godhead and the Virgin Mother.

Six beautiful paintings on the tympans of the lateral arches above the chapels illustrate events in the life of Mary Magdalen. The southern end of the church is surmounted by the largest sculptural pediment in existence. In the centre is the figure of Christ, eighteen feet in height, and at his feet, in an attitude of suppliant penitence, is the Magdalen. Other figures, representing the virtues and vices, fill the remaining space. The bronze doors in front are thirty-three feet high by sixteen and a half wide, barely inferior in size to those of St. Peter's at Rome. They are divided into ten compartments, illustrating subjects from the Old Testament. The most beautiful object, and worthy of a place in any Christian temple, is the delicately sculptured high altar, containing the feast of Cana in bas-relief. It is surrounded by a group of the size of life in spotless marble, of Magdalen borne to heaven by attendant angels. On either side is an archangel in the attitude of prayer. These figures, so exquisitely wrought, so pure in conception, and so appropriate in design, atone, in some degree, for the incongruity displayed in the other decorations of the edifice.

But neither by association nor shape is a Grecian temple adapted for a Christian house of worship. Christianity, new to the world in spirit and doctrine, required to model for itself its sacred edifices. The middle ages have given us the specimens best suited to its grave yet hopeful character. Architects, having since traveled through a cycle of unsatisfactory novelties, are now rapidly returning for their models to that genius which produced those matchless samples of Gothic architecture, that still remain the pride and delight of Europe. For myself, the simple steeple of a New England meeting-house, or the antique belfry of one of the village churches of France, gives rise to emotions far more consonant with the spiritual wants of the soul than the Madeleine and its sister edifices, with their untold wealth lavished in displaying rather the pride of man than the glory of God.

To those who love to witness the different forms in which bereavement seeks consolation, it is worth their while to visit the Chapel of St. Ferdinand, erected on the spot of the death of the Duke of Orleans, July 13th, 1842. It is on the road to Neuilly, and but a short walk from the Arch of Triumph. The building is small, fifty feet long by twenty in height, in the form of a mausoleum. It contains touching memorials of the sad scene, placed there by the bereaved family. On the altar, dedicated to St. Ferdinand, is a marble group representing the Prince on his death-bed, with an angel kneeling at his head, imploring the divine compassion on the sufferer. The angel of this beautiful group was the work of his sister, the Princess Marie, who, when she wrought it, little thought her hands were carving the monument of a brother. There is also a painting of the death scene. The unconscious prince painfully gasping away his life, is watched in mute grief by his father and mother, near whom are the Princess Clementine, his brothers Aumale and Montpensier, Marshals Soult and Gerard, and the Curé of Mery. Low oaken presses, a confessional, a chair and prayer desk, all covered with black, and an ivory crucifix, give a painful reality to this hour of mourning. A clock in an adjoining room perpetually marks ten minutes past four, the time of the duke's death. Another represents in bronze, France grief-stricken, leaning over a broken column, while the hand stands arrested at ten minutes before noon, the moment of the accident. In the court-yard is a cedar tree brought from Lebanon by the Duke of Orleans, and planted by his son, the Count of Paris. Now that the fortune of politics forbids, except the dead alone, of this family to remain in their native land, this monument possesses an increased interest.

In the Rue d'Anjou St. Honoré, we find the Chapelle Expiatoire, a beautiful and appropriate memento of the more miserable fate of the elder Bourbons. It is erected upon the site of the graves of Louis XVI. and Marie Antoinette, who were here obscurely buried immediately after their execution. If it had not been for the faithful care of M. Descloseaux, their remains would have been mingled and lost among the crowd of other victims of the Revolution who were here interred, including the Swiss guards, and by a just retribution, little foreseen, many of their enemies also. Danton, Hebert and Robespierre, were here obscurely and unceremoniously buried. Strange mingling of dust! Swept away in the vortex of the storm they knew how to raise but not to direct, they found only in death that "égalité" which was the mockery of their lives. I know no more touching comment upon the misfortunes of the mistress of Versailles, than the simple cash entry made by the sexton, yet to be seen in the parish records of the Madeleine, "Paid seven francs for a coffin for the widow Capet." Her remains and those of the king were transported to St. Denis in 1815, by Louis XVIII. The exact spots whence they were taken are shown. Mass, for the repose of their souls, is performed here daily.

If the arts have gained by the lavish expenditures of the Catholics in their places of worship, it may be questioned whether the true interests of religion have not proportionally suffered. Magnificent temples proclaim the genius of man, but do they fulfill the true intents and purposes of that religion which was to exhibit itself in visiting and consoling the widows and fatherless in their affliction? Far be it from me to condemn the desire to glorify God by the dedication to him of the proudest works of man. But it becomes a question, whether the means are adapted to the end. While immense sums are expended on the building, we find not only the spiritual but the temporal wants of the worshipers and clergy neglected. The salaries of the latter are notoriously low, and no one will suppose that forty-eight Catholic churches are adequate to the wants of a city like Paris. Their congregations are larger since the cholera, but having attended various churches punctually for several months, both at morning and evening services, I am satisfied that although they are comparatively as well filled as Protestant churches in the United States, yet five hundred to each would be a fair average of worshipers who remain during the entire service. I do not include the crowd that is to be seen continually entering and leaving, after carelessly crossing themselves and bowing before the altar. Allowing these five hundred to be changed entirely at morning and evening services, we have less than fifty thousand worshipers each Sunday, out of a population of upward of a million. It must be considered, however, that the Catholic churches are open daily, and that the entire population have the opportunity to hear mass during the week if they see fit But for the regular service of the Sabbath, with a sermon, certainly not more than one twentieth of the Catholic population of Paris are provided. This results from concentrating magnificence on a few churches instead of building more and plainer for the actual accommodation of the people. The Madeleine cost $2,615,800, and can accommodate not over one thousand persons within hearing distance of the pulpit, though more can witness the ceremonies. $5,000,000 have been expended on the Pantheon, and the result is an architectural monument which one knows not whether most to condemn or admire. Useless as a church, it serves to mark the spot where repose the ashes of Voltaire and Rousseau, either of whom, deists though they were, lies with more consistency within the walls of a Christian edifice than does the infamous Cardinal Dubois, a man who pursued his career on principles of avowed villainy, mocking alike at virtue and religion in every form, when hypocrisy would not serve him better. The holy Catholic Church found place for his remains in the same edifice that contains the ashes of the father of the deaf and dumb, the Abbé de l'Epée—the church of St. Roch—and that too in an age when it refused a Christian burial to Adrienne Le Couvreur, on the ground that she was an actress. But, as the lapse of a century leaves but little to be desired on the score of religious liberty in France, I will return to my comparison between the results of the economy of the Protestants and the prodigality of the Catholics in their sacred edifices. Boston, with its one hundred thousand inhabitants, has more churches than Paris with its one million, and all of its churches combined have not cost more than one half the sum spent on the Pantheon alone. Consider the different results! The Pantheon exists as a proud monument of national architecture; lifeless as its own naked vaults; useful only thus far in demonstrating from its dome, by means of the pendulum, the rotary motion of the earth. Yet not useless as a warning souvenir through all time, of the folly of reason placing itself above revealed religion. It was here that took place the apotheosis of Marat, under the auspices of the painter David. The heart of this monster was inclosed in an agate vase, and placed upon a civic altar. The high priest of reason, dressed in red, recited the following apostrophe:—"Oh heart of Marat! sacred heart and adorable bowel! hast thou not as much right to the religious homage of the affranchised French, as the heart of Jesus had formerly to the adoration of the fanatical Nazarenes? The labors and philanthropy of the son of Mary, can they be compared to those of the friend of the people and his apostles, to the Jacobins of our holy Montagne—the pharisees to the aristocrats, and the publicans to the bankers? Their Jesus was only a prophet, and Marat is a God. Live the heart of Marat—but what say I? It has become cold dust—O Marat!" Such was the substitute reason offered for "Glory to God in the highest, and on earth peace and good-will to mankind."

Who can correctly estimate the extent of the religious influences of the Christian churches of Boston! Destroy them and substitute a Pantheon, and the void would be felt in the moral reaction, not only throughout New England, but from one end of the Union to the other. The religious education of the Americans is at the bottom of their republicanism. Pantheons, Madeleines, and a ceremonial heirarchy may gratify the taste of a people for magnificence, but they are a poor substitute for the Bread of Life.

CHAPTER V.

RELIGIOUS EDUCATION.

THERE are no Roman Catholic Sunday Schools. The nearest approach to them is that, during four months of the year, children of twelve or thirteen, are expected to pass an hour each Sunday in the church to be instructed in their catechism, which teaches them there is no salvation out of the pale of their creed.

I have before me the "Alphabet Chrétien, oû Règlement pour les Enfans à l'Usage des Ecoles Chrétiennes," a little book from which the children of France are taught the first principles of religion. The following extracts, turned into English, will show to Protestant parents the points of difference between this and the catechisms they place in the hands of their children. The confession of sins reads thus: "I confess to God all powerful, the very happy Mary, always virgin, to St. Michael Archangel, to St. John Baptist, to the Apostles St. Peter and St. Paul, to all the saints, and to you, my Father, that I have greatly sinned, by thoughts, words, actions, and by omissions; it is my fault; it is my fault; it is my very great fault. It is why I pray the very happy Mary, always virgin, St. Michael Archangel, St. John Baptist, the Apostles St. Peter, St. Paul, all the saints, and you, my Father, to pray for me, to the Lord, our God." Confession and communion are enjoined at least once a year. Two years' study at the catechism is required, previous to the first communion. The young girls dress all in white at this sacrament. The reason given for the invocation of the saints, is, "because they can greatly aid us by their intercession." Children are advised, whenever they drink, "to pronounce inwardly the holy name of Jesus;" "every time you name or hear named Jesus or Mary, you should make a respectful inclination;" "when you pass before any cross or any image of the Lord, or of the very Holy Virgin, or of the Saints, make a respectful bow." The Act of Faith, reads, "My God, I believe firmly all that the holy Catholic, Apostolic, and Roman Church orders me to believe." "Outside of the church there is no safety. Thus all those who do not belong to the church or do not obey it, will be damned. The church is composed of the Saints who are in heaven, the souls which are in purgatory, and the Faithful who are on earth; we participate in the merits of the Saints and the Faithful, and we can solace the souls in purgatory by our prayers and by our good works." "All these truths are included in the Creed of the Apostles. I believe them firmly not only upon the word of the men who announce them, but because they are revealed of God himself and taught by the church, which is infallible. The church is the Catholic, Apostolic and Roman. It is necessary to obey those who have the government by the authority of Jesus Christ; these are the Bishops, and especially our Holy Father, the Pope, who, as chief successor of St. Peter and Vicar of Jesus Christ, has authority over all the Faithful."

"The Eucharist is the most august of all the Sacraments, because it contains Jesus Christ all entire, true God and true man, his body and his blood, his soul, his divinity; at the Mass, by the words of the consecration that the Priest pronounces, the substance of the bread and the wine is changed to the body of Jesus Christ, and there remains only of it the appearances. Thus, when the Holy Sacrament is exposed upon the Altar, or when it is in the Tabernacle, it is Jesus Christ really present that is adored; and when we commune, it is Jesus Christ that we receive to be the spiritual nourishment of the soul. It is not his image nor his form, as upon a cross; but it is Jesus Christ himself—that is to say, the Son of God, the same Jesus Christ who is born of the very Holy Virgin Mary, who is dead for us upon the cross, who is raised, ascended to heaven—who is as really in the Holy Host, as in heaven."

Here in a nutshell are the contested points of faith between the Catholics and Protestants. I quote them because prejudice too often throws the controversialist wide from truth, especially where, as in the Roman Catholic Church, ceremonies and splendor are apt to vail the simple truths which lie at the bottom. With these exceptions, there is nothing perhaps which any Trinitarian would not subscribe to, in the "Alphabet Chrétien," which contains all "it is necessary to know, believe and practice to be saved." In passing judgment upon the religion of a nation, it is of the first importance to know what it believes. Outward observances have their origin in other causes beside faith. They often spring from, or are modified by necessity, expediency, or the prejudices or the genius of a people.

In its infancy, Christianity, true to the principles of its Founder struggled with paganism, until, by the blood of martyrs, its eternal truths found their way to the throne of the Roman Empire. Then, assuming the form of Papacy, it welcomed to its arms Pagan Europe. Instead of a pure and rigid faith, it became an inflexible creed and mighty ceremonial. Paganism, but half weaned from its errors, was received into its bosom. The unnatural embrace has left its traces even upon this age, in ceremonies and fêtes which have their origin far into remote heathenism, and in a deference to usages which, if the church refuses to sanction, its policy permits. Catholicism, corrupted by its victories, but relentless in its animosities, has been obliged to renew its strength at different epochs of its history, by a partial plunge in the pure spring whence it arose, rewarding those who would wash it clean, with ignominy and death. At the present time, the Catholic Church of France is the most enlightened and sincere of Europe. In its day of strength it dealt exile and death to reformers. Battening on its spoils, it experienced the fate of all powers that permit inglorious ease to succeed the virtues that were their earliest nurture, and became sensual and corrupt. Then, indignant humanity gave birth to a philosophy which, while in its cradle, well-nigh strangled the Church of Rome. This philosophy, flashing its uncertain light for a moment over France, drove Catholicism in affright from its territory. But born of man and owning no divinity except reason, it lacked soil to sustain its growth. The Roman Church, strong in the contests and victories of fifteen centuries, stronger yet in having its foundations in the most sacred principles of the human heart, principles coeval with Adam, has returned to its post strengthened and improved. How much more powerful for good it would be if its reforms were not always begotten of necessities! Until the work of its own purification is accomplished, the ritual reduced to its primitive simplicity, and the creed to the standard of its origin, the church will continue to be false to itself and to its mission.

France is nominally Catholic, but indifference or deism are the prevailing sentiments. This, or ignorance, must ever be the case, while the wealth of a church is chiefly expended in fostering the arts, and the labors of the clergy wasted in a ceremonial worship.

I do not desire by these remarks to give offense to any conscience. But that I am correct in the opinion that the efforts of the Catholic clergy are more directed to gratify the senses, than to purify the heart, those who examine their churches and witness their festivals will not deny. The people, educated to this show, estimate a church in proportion to its wealth and ornaments. The greater the attraction for the eye, the larger the congregation. St. Roch, during the recent fête of the Very Holy Sacrament, has been crowded with spectators to witness the elaborate decorations of the high altar. With its countless candles, rich velvet hangings, and profusion of flowers, it was indeed a beautiful sight. The maidens clothed and vailed in white, bowing in adoration before the sacred symbols, added greatly to the effect. But that nothing be wanting to perfect the spectacle, music, that is renowned even in Paris, lends its strains. The leader of the choir, Alexis Dupont, has a salary of 10,000 francs. Some came to pray; many because it is the rule of the church; but the mass, as spectators. For my own part, setting aside the respect due to all houses of worship, I should be perplexed to decide whether High Mass at the Madeleine or an Opera gives me the most pleasure. In either case, the eye and ear are ravished by the combinations of external beauty with the harmony of sound and the grace of action. Where early training has made this an indispensable accompaniment of religion, the heart, perhaps, is enabled through all this sensual crust to reach Him who is to be worshiped in spirit and in truth. But that the clergy here find it politic to add to even these attractions, is evident from a notice I read in the Madeleine on the occasion of the fête above mentioned, promising plenary indulgence to all who would join in the solemn procession, and stating, as the exhibition of the Very Holy Sacrament required a more brilliant light, the members of the parish were requested to contribute to its expense.

The Bible is a rare book in France, and works on religion and moral education, so common in the United States, comparatively unknown. The writings, however, of Voltaire, Rousseau, and Volney, are to be met every where and in every variety of editions. I speak from a careful inspection of the bookstores and stalls of Paris. French literature is prolific in works of science, wit, and amusement; in journalism and memoirs it is unexcelled; but the Abbotts for youth and Taylors for adults are yet to arise.

Chateaubriand, Lamartine, and other writers of their stamp, who have treated of religious topics, have attempted rather to poetize and refine upon the spiritual sentiments than to place before their readers religious truth practically applied to the actual character and condition of man. The cause of this lies undoubtedly in one of the elements of French character. They aim to decorate what they touch. They possess a keen sense of the beautiful in art, and the nicest relish for what the English tongue has no synonym, the "spirituelle," whether in conversation or literature. The term "spirituelle," can only be defined as the fragrance of the mind—an incorporeal essence felt, but not to be grasped; a flashing of an idea like the glimpse of an angel's wings, or the perpetually recurring brilliancy of the fire-fly, sparkling a new beauty before the last has dimmed on the sight, or it can be told whence it was or whither it has gone.

There is another element, in which wit and irreligion are equally blended. It justifies the common saying, that a Frenchman fears neither God, man, nor the devil. At all events, he had rather fail in his respect for the first than to lose his point. What other nation would have dramatized the Fall of Man? It is not two years and a half since there was brought out at the Vaudeville a piece called "La Propriété c'est un Vol."—(Property is a Robbery.) The scene is laid in the Garden of Eden. Satan is tempting Eve to pluck and eat from the prohibited trees, on which is the "affiche" or notice "it is forbidden to take this fruit." Eve says to Satan, "Do you not see that I am commanded to let it alone?" "Eat," he replies, "and you will possess and know every thing." Eve, at these words, rushes up to the tree, and plucks the fruit, exclaiming, "Je m'en fiche de l'affiche"—equivalent to, I do not care a fig, or something more profane, for the notice. The wit lies in the pun, which is not to be turned into our tongue. Soon after a celestial voice is heard, ordering Adam and Eve to leave the garden. They run off, snatching more of the apples as they go. The new and magnificent Opera of the "Wandering Jew" represents the Day of Judgment, raising of the dead from their graves, and heaven and hell, with the fiends tormenting the damned; all got up on a most effective scale.

A French engraving depicts the Devil poking over the earth with a stick, stirring up all manner of trouble, while the Almighty, in the shape of an old man with a white cotton cap on his head, is watching him through a spy-glass.

When the government shut up the cemetery of Saint Medard, on account of the pretended miracles of the Jansenists at the tomb of the Deacon Paris, a wag placed upon the door this verse·

"De par le roi, defénse a Dieu
De faire miracle en ce lieu."

In plain English, The king forbids God to work any miracle in this place.

In the Rue St. Jacques there formerly existed a chapel of Saint Yves, the patron saint of lawyers, though on what grounds he attained this honor, has not been discovered. Our authority says, that the lawyers, without pretending to imitate his disinterestedness, and without being ambitious of the honors of the kingdom of heaven, contented themselves very humbly with the goods of this world. He contrives maliciously to add, that when Saint Yves presented himself at the gates of Paradise, St. Peter repulsed him, confounding him with the rest of his profession. The Saint hid himself in the crowd, and managed to slip in. Being recognized, St. Peter wished to drive him out, but he resisted and said he would not leave until he had been notified so to do by an "huissier" (door-keeper in French courts of law). St. Peter was embarrassed, and searched every where for one, but as one had never entered Paradise his search was in vain, and St. Yves remained among the elect, to the great confusion of St. Peter.

The Egyptian Saint Mary had a chapel in the Rue Montmartre, the stained glass windows of which represented the events of her life. One of these was not of the most exemplary character. Beneath, it bore this inscription, " Comment la Sainte offrit son corps au batelier pour son passage" (how the Saint offered her body to the boatman for her passage). By what process canonization was derived from this event, history fails to inform us. By a chance sufficiently bizarre, Madame Dubarry, after the death of Louis XV., lived for several years close by this chapel.

Among the fancy names given the shops, there is one in the Rue St. Honoré, called "The Infant Jesus," and another in the Rue St. Jacques, named "The Sacrifice of Abraham," and in the Rue de l'Echelle a dram shop very appropriately termed "Fountain of the Devil."

The irreverence of Frenchmen is not a plant of modern growth. When Cardinal Dubois announced to Louis XIV. the death of his brother, the Duke of Orleans, the monarch piously exclaimed, "I hope my poor brother is in paradise." "Sire," replied Bontemps, "Dieu regarde à deux fois pour condamner des princes," "God looks twice before he damns a prince."

Camille Desmoulins, when asked his age by the revolutionary tribunal, answered, "Of the same age as that "sans culotte" Jesus Christ when he died."

Visiting one evening a friend in the Faubourg St. Germain, the Count De ——, in describing the crowd at the Madeleine to hear the Father Lacordaire's Christmas sermon, said he was obliged to stand over the "Grille" (furnace bars) where he was roasted, and he had directly in front a chandelier that put his eyes out. "Ah!" exclaimed Baron, "your legs were roasting in hell while your eyes were being dazzled by the brightness of heaven."

These gentlemen were of the old noblesse, distinguished at the court of Charles X., and stanch Catholics. I quote the jeu d'esprit, which it is impossible to do justice to in English, to show that the temptation to this spirit of wit is as irresistible to the higher classes as the lower. A successful bon mot on any subject establishes a reputation. Earthly powers fare no better than heavenly. A bystander lately remarked in witnessing the erasure by order of the President of the words, "Liberté, Egalité, Fraternité," from the national buildings, that he supposed they were to be replaced by "Cavalerie, Infanterie, Artillerie."

The churches themselves have witnessed so many incongruous spectacles before their shrines within the last three-quarters of a century, that the prestige of their sanctity must be greatly weakened in the hearts of the present generation. Witness the Pantheon, from the worship of the true God changed to a monument of the deification of man; polluted by being made the sepulchre of Marat, whose remains, soon after, *depantheonized* by the same authority that glorified them, found a more appropriate receptacle in a common-sewer in the Rue Montmartre. This church, the last survivor of the Temples of Reason, has been lately restored, by order of the President, to the Catholic clergy. During the first revolution the beautiful edifice of St. Sulpice became the Temple of Victory and the place of assembly for the theophilanthropists. In 1799, its sacred walls looked down upon a banquet given to Bonaparte. In 1831, Notre Dame and St. Germain l'Auxerrois were sacked by one of the tornado mobs, in which Paris has been so fruitful. In consequence, the latter remained closed for seven years. Were I a Frenchman, I should have wished that every vestige of it had been swept from the earth; for while it remains, its sinister-looking walls must remind every stranger of the darkest crime with which history is stained. Its belfry gave the signal on the eve of the fête of St. Barthélemi for the appalling massacre that deluged France in blood, and its bells continued to toll during the whole of that awful night. I never pass it without an involuntary shudder. In the vicinity, until within a few weeks, could be seen the hotel in which Admiral

Coligny was murdered. It has been taken down to enlarge the street.

The Marquis de la Grange, in his "Mémoires de la Force," gives the relation of the miraculous escape on that night of the youngest of that family as told by himself. "The father walked first, the eldest son next, and the youngest in the rear. Having arrived at the end of the Rue des Petits Champs, near the rampart, the soldiers cried, Kill! kill! They first stabbed the eldest boy, who in falling, cried, Ah! my God. I am dead! The father, turning toward his son, was also stabbed; the youngest covered with blood, but who, by a miracle, had not been wounded, as if inspired by Heaven, cried out I am dead! at the same time falling between his father and brother, who prostrate received several more stabs, while he had not even his skin grazed. God protected him so visibly, that when the murderers stripped them all to their skin, they did not perceive that he had not even a single wound. As they believed their work finished, they went off, saying, they had done for the three. The young Caumont remained naked as he was until toward four o'clock, when the neighbors, attracted by curiosity, or to plunder what the butchers might have left, examined the corpses. A tennis-marker, of the Rue Verdelet, wishing to take a linen stocking which still remained on one leg, turned him over, as his face was toward the earth, and seeing him so young, said to himself, Alas! it is only a poor child. Is not this a great wrong? What evil can he have done? Caumont hearing this, gently raised his head and said in a whisper, 'I am not dead, I beg you to save my life.' The marker immediately put his hand on his head and said, Do not move—they are still about here. He then walked about for a little time and returned and told him to rise, for they were gone. He threw over his shoulders a filthy cloak and feigning to strike him, he made him walk before him. Who have you there? asked his neighbors. It is my nephew who is drunk, and I shall whip him soundly, replied the marker. In this way he got him safely to his house."

A gentleman who resides in the quarter referred to, related to me the following incident, as showing the relative effects upon the value of property in Paris, by the erection of theatres or churches.

The government some years since, wishing to improve the vacant land now comprising one of the finest and most populous quarters of the city, proposed erecting churches thereon, to attract to it other enterprises. It was represented to them that to build churches would defeat their project, but if theatres were substituted, there would be no doubt of a favorable result. Several were soon built, and it has in consequence grown into the present magnificent Boulevard du Temple. The friend who told me this is so sensitive a Catholic, that he declined reading a history of the Popes, for fear he should learn something to lessen his good opinion of the heads of his church, "For," said he, "it is better not to know than to hate."

The Catholics condemn servile labor on Sunday, but admit that which appertains to the mind and amusements. The result in Paris, is, that about a third of the shops are closed on that day, and the Parisian world devotes itself to pleasure. Of late the Minister of the Interior has discountenanced labor on the public works on Sunday; but it is common for workmen to be employed on private enterprises.

On this day Paris disgorges its population upon the Boulevards, the Champs Elysées, Bois du Boulogne, public gardens, and museums. The throng is interminable, but a more orderly, happier looking and better dressed crowd is nowhere to be seen. The working faubourgs send their population outside the barrier. In fine weather the Champs Elysées present the appearance of a fair. Every species of jugglery, Punch and Judy, concerts and dog shows, booths, games, and mountebank tricks are in full

CHAMPS ELYSEES.—FETE SUNDAY

blast, and each becomes the centre of a curious circle. The roll of carriages and pleasure vehicles is incessant. Paris dines "en ville," or in other words, as pleasure is a part of a Frenchman's creed and he is fond of good eating, he dines on that day with his family or friends at a restaurant, takes his coffee and brandy in the open air or on the sidewalk in front, and passes the evening at some theatre or ball. However remiss he may be at mass, this part of his religion is never neglected.

The government encourage this mode of its observance by selecting it for grand reviews, races, launches, and whatever can add to the already seemingly superabundant sources of amusement. The grand waters at St. Cloud and Versailles play on Sunday, and the throng of people on the excursion trains of the railways is immense. Sunday is taken literally in the sense of a day of rest from ordinary work; consequently a day of liberty for what otherwise the necessary labors of the remaining six might derange. The elections are then held, but, what appears most questionable, Sunday, the 16th of November last, was selected for the great lottery of "l'ingot d'or." The question of the moral effect of lotteries has of late been agitated here, but it did not prevent, in this, the sale of seven million tickets at one franc each, indeed most of them at a premium, though the chances were but one prize to thirty one thousand two hundred and fifty blanks. The government by this operation pocketed about five million francs, destined, as it was said, to send emigrants to California. The attraction was the grand prize of four hundred thousand francs. A chamber-maid, I was told, held fifteen hundred tickets, being her entire savings. They all proved blanks.

A Frenchman is as conscientious in defending his manner of keeping the Sabbath as an American would be in condemning it, though there are some, even Catholics, who agree with the latter. Education makes the difference. As the highest authority has declared Sunday was made for man, the surest way to test the relative merits of the two systems is by the effects on national character. The balance of physical happiness, and the enjoyment of the senses in works of art, would seem to be in favor of France; but in the acquisition of religious instruction and the strengthening of moral principles, the graver course of the United States stands out in strong relief. The former renders the individual more joyous because less thoughtful—the latter more thoughtful and less joyous. The first, like their own champagne, sparkles, exhilarates and is gone; the last, a solid aliment for the soul, nourishes strength for the hour of trial. A happy combination of the two would temper the one and adorn the other.

The Protestants of the United States can learn two useful lessons from the Catholics of France, in the arrangement of seats in the churches, and the manner of preaching. Pews are unknown. In lieu of the luxuriously cushioned stalls of the United States, with their elbow-rests and every convenience for an easy posture, which, by the way, causes more than one half the somnolency to be witnessed in our churches, they use the simplest kind of chairs. The privilege of supplying these chairs is let out annually by the church, generally to women, who charge each service one sous apiece for those outside of the nave and two for those within.

MASS AT EIGHT O'CLOCK.

The moral advantages of these chairs are more than at first glance would be supposed. They preserve that equality before God *within* the church which is as active a principle of the Catholic faith as it is dead in the Protestant. Prince and peasant, Caucasian and African, side by side offer their orisons to their common Father. Never by glance or gesture have I seen aught to disturb this idea of human brotherhood, and I have repeatedly beheld the blouse kneeling by the noble, the femme de chambre with her snow-white cap and apron brushing the satin of a duchess, and the coal-black negro beside the exquisite of

MASS AT ONE O'CLOCK

the Boulevard. All is republicanism and harmony within the church. Picture the sensation in any of our Trinity's, St. George's or Grace's, should any of the humbler members of society find their way into the pews of these churches. No American would construe wrongly the remarks and looks which would be directed by the proprietors of these pharisaical partitions toward those who came thus between the wind and their nobility. Pews beget exclusiveness, strengthen artificial distinctions, deprive many of a place of worship, from their expensiveness, and make religion with a popular preacher a dear bought luxury. Abolish them, and the equality in law becomes equality in the house of God. Those who object to the mixture as it is termed, have the example of the highest and most refined of Europe. Whoever saw a maid go to church with her mistress in the United States? In France it is a constant practice. A preacher who expects humility to effect an entrance into a church divided into sumptuous and exclusive compartments, the doors of which none can enter but those who count their incomes by thousands, shows himself deficient in knowledge of human nature. Such churches are moral Japans, into which Christians at large can not enter. Replace pews by chairs, and each church can accommodate twice as many hearers as at present. There would be no sleepers. I have never seen a slumberer in a French church.

The average of attention and external devotion is in favor of the French congregations, whether Catholic or Protestant. Both use chairs, and in both the preachers deliver their discourses without notes. They *preach* and do not *read* to their hearers. This of itself is widely in favor of arresting and fixing the attention. Is it inferiority of talent or education, that prevents our pastors from imitating the example of the apostles in this respect? Clergymen or laymen would blush to acknowledge this fact. French sermons are rarely less than an hour long, and are delivered extempore with more ease than is usual with American clergymen who read their essays. Those that I have heard, have been in general on the practical duties or common elements of the Christian faith, delivered with an earnestness that bespoke self-conviction of divine truth.

The "Confessional" is a tender point with the Catholics of France. The most devotional classes are the highest and lowest —the well-bred and highly educated legitimists and the ignorant but honest peasantry. Both these extremes of society may be said to be attentive to the requirements of the church. The great mass of irreligion lies rather between them. Husbands frequently forbid their wives to confess. Those who do, go but seldom, perhaps but twice a year. I was greatly amused at the naïveté with which a young lady related to me her experience. She had selected for her confessor a pious but somewhat indulgent curé, whose humor was often more apparent than his severity. "My daughter," said he to her, after she had disburdened her conscience of a load of trifling omissions and commissions "have you no other sins—little sins—reflect and answer." "Yes," said she, "I have overlooked one—pardon me—I will confess the whole. I was walking with my maid along the quay and I heard a noise in the water. I looked and saw a number of young men swimming." "What did you do?" "I put my hand over my eyes," but, said she to me, I did not tell him I could see through my fingers. "Ah! beware of idle curiosity, my daughter, it will lead you to evil." "But I could not help seeing them." "What where your thoughts?" "Nothing bad, my father, I assure you." "Be sure now, have you no other secret sins; you come very seldom to confession—I am fearful your memory is treacherous." "No, father, nothing more than looking at these boys in the water, which you know I could not help. I was so curious to see what was making such a splash." "Well my child you must repeat three Pater-

Nosters and Ave Marias upon leaving the church, and go and sin no more."

The Calvinists possess four churches and chapels, at which seven pastors preach in rotation. The celebrated M. Coquerel, and his scarcely less eloquent son, are among them. Their largest church is the ancient Oratoire, Rue St. Honoré, ceded to their confession in 1802. It has been adapted as far as possible to the simplicity of worship of the present occupants, but the side-chapels converted into semi-galleries, give it a very awkward appearance. M. Coquerel was a member of the late Legislative Assembly, elected jointly by Catholics and Protestants—the former having confidence in his politics, though detesting his religious principles as a seceder from their ranks. It is a striking proof of the perfect equality in the eye of the law of all sects in France, that in 1848, M. Crémieux, a Jew, was appointed Minister of Justice under the Provisional Government. There is no charge for chairs at the Lutheran and Calvinist churches, but free will offerings for the poor are made at the doors. At the Chapel of the English embassy the price is twenty cents a seat.

Among the Catholics, the most celebrated preacher is the Jesuit, Le Père Ventura, who makes an annual visit from Rome to preach during lent at Paris. On certain occasions, I am told, he officiates only for men, and on others for women. The crowd is so great, that even for the gigantic dimensions of Nôtre Dame it is necessary to issue tickets of admission, and to have a military guard to prevent accidents from the immense influx of hearers. Once, preaching in this church to men alone, he chose for his subject the difference between divine and human love. Such was the power of his eloquence over his excitable auditors, that they burst out repeatedly into lively applause. At last, he stopped, and remarked, if an action so unbecoming the house of God was repeated he should descend from the pulpit. Unable to restrain themselves, his hearers again interrupted him. He was as good as his word, and it was with the greatest difficulty he could be prevailed to re-enter the pulpit and finish his discourse. In preaching a charity sermon to ladies only, he is said to have so excited their sympathies, that they not only emptied their purses, but stripped themselves of their jewels, and even added their watches to the pile of offerings.

During the reign of Louis Philippe, another celebrated divine commenced a series of discourses upon the vanity and luxury of the sex. He made such an impression, that the ladies "en masse" began to abandon their ornaments, to study simplicity and economy in their dresses, forsake their dissipations, and devote themselves to charitable works. To use a theatrical phrase, his success was complete, and to be pious became a furore. Such was the effect upon the traffic in luxuries on which the merchants of Paris subsist, that they represented to the Minister of the Interior that they were being ruined, and that the commerce of the country was actually suffering, while thousands of workmen were starving from want of employment. He quietly sent for the reverend father and informed him, that although he entertained the highest respect for his talents and labors, and believed that vanity and luxury were in themselves sins, yet they were the means of livelihood to a large portion of his countrymen. Paris was also the dictatress of fashion to the civilized world; if the ladies of the "ton" here simplified their tastes and studied economy, ladies elsewhere would imitate them. By this economy the most productive branches of French industry would be ruined, for there would be no markets for the silks, velvets, ribbons, and bijoux. He concluded by advising the orator to travel, until time restored to the ladies their accustomed tastes.

At present Le Père Lacordaire, a Dominican of fifty years of age, carries away the palm of clerical oratory. In 1822, he practiced law with success, and was a Voltarian and Deist. Two years later he renounced his opinions, entered the Church of St. Sulpice, and in 1837 went to Rome, where he took the white habit of the order he now wears. His eloquence is original, brilliant, vigorous, yet melting. His illustrations are striking, and he speaks straightforward to his point. I will give a few examples, weakened necessarily by being rendered into English, and unaccompanied by his impressive tone and gesture:—"The role of an apostle," says he, "is in effect to convert the infidels, the skeptics, of which in the nineteenth century we are all more or less. The old serpent of error changes his colors in the sun of each century. Thus, while in the preaching of proper conduct to those of our own church, we do but aim at diversity of style to impress the matter more fully on their hearts and imaginations, it is necessary that instructive and controversial preaching, pliant as the ignorance it would elevate, subtle as the error it would pierce, should imitate their powerful versatility, and combat them with never-yielding weapons constantly renewed in the Armory of Truth."

In a funeral oration pronounced upon General Drouot, he gave utterance to the following patriotic apostrophe: "All at once, even from the heart of the country, there arose a prodigious cry; the descendant of Cyrus and of Cæsar, the master of the world, had fled before his enemies; the eagles of the empire returned in full flight from the bloody banks of the Dnieper and the Vistula, and folded their wings upon their native soil to defend it from its foes, astonished to clutch in their powerful talons victories which won for them only death. God, but God alone, had vanquished France, commanded even to the last by genius, and triumphant still to the moment that witnessed her fall. I shall say nothing upon the causes of this catastrophe. Not only do they not belong to my subject, but it is repugnant to a true son to probe so deeply his country's wounds ; and he willingly leaves to time alone the care of demonstrating the lessons hidden by God in the depths of misfortunes."

The following, from the same oration, is a picture of domestic life, which goes directly to the heart. Speaking of the General, he says : "Issue of the people by Christian parents, he early saw in the paternal mansion a spectacle which left him neither envy of another lot, nor regret for a higher birth ; he witnessed order, peace, contentment ; a benevolence which knew how to share its resources with the poor ; a faith which, in acknowledging every thing as from God, elevated almost to him its simplicity, generosity and nobleness of soul ; and he learned from the joy he tasted himself in the bosom of a position by the world judged so humble, that every thing becomes good for the man who devotes his life to the work and grandeur of religion. Never was the recollection of those cherished days of his youth effaced from the memory of General Drouot ; in the glorious smoke of battles, at the side even of the man who held all Europe's attention, his heart yearned toward the humble mansion that had sheltered him, and the virtues of a father and mother which were the happiness of his own infancy. Just before his death, in comparing the several phases of his career, he wrote, 'I have known true happiness only in the obscurity, innocence, and the poverty of my early years.' "

After describing the youth of Drouot, the orator concludes thus : " Such was the childhood of which the memory pursued the General, even amid the splendors of the Tuileries. You are astonished, perhaps, at it ; you ask what charm was there in all that ? He has told you himself ; it was the charm of obscurity, innocence, and poverty. He grew under the triple guard of these strong virtues ; he grew as a child of Sparta and of Rome, or better and truer yet to say, he grew as a Christian child, in whom the beauty of the natural, and the effusion of the divine grace formed a mysterious feast, which the heart, that has once known it, can never forget."

The preaching of Lacordaire being too democratic for the taste of Louis Napoleon, he has been politely exiled, or in other words, it has been notified to him that he had better employ the coming twelve months in visiting the convents of his order throughout Europe.

CHAPTER VI.

SUPERIOR EDUCATION.

Whatever may be the deficiency of means for primary education in France, in all that appertains to the superior branches of knowledge, the government displays the most laudable zeal. To individual talent every facility is provided, gratuitously when necessary, to attain knowledge and skill in its particular branch. Judging from the disproportion of the resources to the wants of the population in primary instruction, and those afforded for the successful prosecution of all studies connected with the arts and sciences, one may be allowed the conclusion, that the government, in education as well as in civil administration fosters the principle of centralization. It prefers the more gratifying task of educating eminent men, who may add to the literary and scientific fame of the nation, to the humbler duty of bringing elementary knowledge within the reach of every fireside. It concentrates learning as it does power, making Paris the centre of each; the great heart through whose arteries runs the stream of knowledge destined to enrich the mind of the world. This system is in accordance with the natural love of distinction, which cherishes the individual, that he may add to the glories of France. The country is the idol to be gilded, and personal vanity or ambition find their sweetest triumph in increasing that lustre so dear to the hearts of all Frenchmen.

France has worthily earned her high position in the perfection of arts and sciences, by the encouragement and facilities which she furnishes to students of all nations. Her liberality is of no selfish character. She aspires to be the Minerva of nations, and reaps her reward in the tacit acknowledgment of her claim, by the multitudes that flock to her shrines of learning, or light their lamps at her altars. Toward genius France is thoroughly democratic. No where is intellectual worth more ardently welcomed and more richly rewarded. Its source is not questioned; merit is the sole criterion. The consequence is, that, in every department of knowledge, she has an accumulation of experienced and cultivated intellect, ready to serve her in those points which render a nation illustrious in the eyes of mankind.

Kingdom, empire, or republic, France has cherished learning. In her legacies from Louis XIV., she has not much cause of congratulation, but the encouragement he bestowed upon men of letters, placed talent in its true position. Francis I. paid a homage to learned industry, worthy of its appropriate position in the scale of humanity, when, in visiting the printing-office of Robert Estienne, he refused to disturb him, but waited quietly, leaning upon an arm of the press, until Estienne had finished correcting the proof upon which he was employed. This was at an epoch, when his rival, Charles V., picked up for Titian the pencil he had accidentally dropped.

In France the assistance or encouragement of merit proceeds directly from the government. The Council General of the Seine, in one of its late sittings, voted twelve hundred francs to a young man named Desforges, to enable him to cultivate his extraordinary mathematical talent. He is a stone-mason, and although *he does not know the common ciphers of arithmetic*, he is able to perform intricate mental calculations. He first attracted attention by some observations he made on the power of a steam-engine employed in the repairs of the Pont Neuf, which astonished the engineers, who called the attention of several members of the Institute to the phenomenon. They were equally astonished, and brought him at once to the notice of the city government.

The President has lately sent ten thousand francs to the professor engaged in experimenting by means of the pendulum upon the movement of the earth, as an encouragement to prosecute his researches. He has also offered a reward of fifty thousand francs to the individual of any nation, who discovers the method to make electricity available with economy to the various practical arts. The Institute of France, which is divided into five academies, offers annually the following encouragements for the various objects within its sphere of action. A prize of two thousand francs for poetry or eloquence; a prize for the best treatise on public morals, and one for the most distinguished act of virtue performed by a poor native of France; ten thousand francs for the best work on French history, and fifteen hundred francs every second year to some deserving but indigent man of letters. There are prizes varying from five hundred to three thousand francs for the best treatises on medals, antiquities, statistics, mechanics, experimental philosophy, discoveries in medicine or surgery, and all matters of public utility, and for the best works in the fine arts. The successful artists are sent at the expense of the State to prosecute their education at Athens and Rome.

In the various scientific, literary, and superior schools of Paris, there are between four and five thousand students. In 1851 there were thirteen hundred medical students, and two thousand seven hundred and sixty nine students of law. The numbers of the two latter vary materially from year to year. In 1844 there were two thousand four hundred students of medicine, and three thousand one hundred and forty-three of law. The professors of these schools are paid by government.

Education is regulated by a "Supreme Council of Public Instruction," composed of four dignitaries of the Catholic church, two of the Protestant, one of the Jewish, three Counselors of

State, three members of the Court of Cassation, and three of the Institute. These are all elected from their several colleagues. Eight members are appointed by the President of the Republic, from counselors, inspectors-general, or professors of faculties; and three from the heads of private establishments of instruction. This Council is presided over by the Minister of Public Instruction.*

It would be tedious to the reader to go through all the details of a system, which, emanating from one supreme head, extends its care to every department of public instruction. I will confine myself to brief notices of a few only of the institutions and collections which are placed by the government at the service alike of all nations, for the advancement of art and knowledge, not exclusively professional or scientific, merely observing that the requirements at the examination of all regular students, are of the most comprehensive and rigid character.

The National College of France has twenty-eight professors, who give gratuitous lectures on the following topics: astronomy, mathematics, philosophy, medicine, chemistry, natural history, political economy, archæology, the Oriental tongues, natural, comparative, and national law—history, classic literature, and philosophy, French, the languages, and history of Europe generally.

The "Conservatoire des Arts et Métiers" is a National Museum of machines, models, drawings, &c., connected with all branches of industrial art, somewhat upon the plan of the Patent

* The President of the Republic, on the 9th of March, issued a decree, doing away the elective principle in the Supreme Council, making all officers and professors connected with public instruction, dependent upon himself for their situations, and removable at his pleasure. This is a step beyond the Emperor, who, if he appointed them, allowed them to remain during life. The decree calls this a provisional arrangement, until the new law relating to public instruction can be perfected.

Office at Washington. It is an extensive institution, and supports fourteen professorships for the gratuitous education of workmen in mechanics, manufactures, and agriculture, by annual courses of lectures.

The "Ecole des Mines" gives gratuitous lectures on geology and mineralogy; the school of modern Oriental languages has nine professors, who gratuitously lecture on all matters connected with Asiatic philology. The School of Fine Arts disseminates knowledge on all topics within its sphere, by twenty professors, besides yearly prizes, and an exceedingly interesting museum of architecture, containing, among other objects, models in cork or plaster, in the proportion of one to one hundred, of the Parthenon, Coliseum, Propyleine, Leaning Tower of Pisa, Hanging Gardens of Semiramis, Baths of Augustus, the Amphitheatres of Arles and Nimes, and the wonders of Egyptian art. The western side of the Amphitheatre for the distribution of prizes, is beautifully painted in oil by Delaroche, representing the most celebrated artists of all nations, ancient and modern, assembled for the bestowal of prizes, and presided over by Zeuxis, Phidias and Apelles. It contains seventy-five figures of the size of life, one of which, a lovely blonde on the left of the judges, is a portrait of Madame Delaroche.

Besides the institutions mentioned, there are free schools for the instruction of artisans in drawing and building; of young women, in design—I mean the mechanical branch only—and for music, declamation, and the education of civil engineers, directors of manufactories, and application of the sciences generally

In July, 1850, the government created a Central Agronomical Institute, or School of Agriculture, with nine chairs. Pupils of all nations are received gratuitously; and those of French origin, if their circumstances require it, obtain pensions. The most successful scholars are sent to travel abroad at the expense of the State for three years.

The National Museum of Natural History, better known as the "Jardin des Plantes," has a world-wide celebrity. Attached to it are fifteen professors, who lecture gratuitously on every portion and object of the wide domain of Nature, illustrating their subjects by living specimens or collections in all departments of the science, unrivaled in extent and methodization.

In the botanical department alone of this garden, there are cultivated upward of twelve thousand species of plants; in the Cabinet of Comparative Anatomy there are fifteen thousand prepared specimens, from the skeleton of the whale, to that of the assassin of General Kleber, and every variety of the human species, from giant to dwarf, down to the minutest vertebrated frame This collection was prepared by Cuvier, and is the most complete in existence.

The number of mineralogical and geological specimens exceeds sixty thousand; and of dried plants, woods, fruits, and grains, three hundred and sixty thousand. In the library there are ninety portfolios of original designs, embracing more than six thousand drawings, magnificently colored, and valued at four hundred thousand dollars. The gallery of zoology contains more than two hundred thousand specimens, arranged in progressive order, from the apparently inanimate zoophite, through every link in the animal kingdom, until it reaches its climax in man.

The menagerie forms a varied and extensive colony of animals, birds, and reptiles, from the four quarters of the globe, arranged with the nicest regard to their habits and comfort, and so disposed as to make them feel as completely at home as any creatures can be in confinement. Indeed, with the exception of the more ferocious animals, which have a dejected and pining look, they appear to be very happy. They would be ungrateful if they were not; for they are better housed and fed than one hundred thousand human beings living within sound of the roar of the forest king.

The military man and the partisan of peace visit the Museum of Artillery with very contradictory emotions; the former looks with interest and pleasure, upon more than four thousand specimens of armor and weapons used in war, from the earliest ages, down to the Vincennes carabine and Colt's revolver; while the latter shudders at the thought of the bloody work they have done, and the unnecessary additions they have made to human suffering, during their career of alternate victory and defeat. They have not all been in actual use. The greater part are only samples of the various instruments man has invented to slay his fellow-man. They are sufficiently numerous and ingenious to leave the impression, that all are here except one—the club used by the first murderer.

The firearms intended as a present by Napoleon for the Emperor of Morocco, are most richly set with diamonds and precious stones, of very considerable value; but looking as sadly out of place as would Valenciennes lace around a mailed hand. Imprisoned in their glass cases, reflecting their brightness on cold steel or rusty iron, they give rise to many a fervent wish for their release from their unnatural imprisonment, from the fair, to whom alone, by right of kindred beauty, they belong.

The suits of armor are exceedingly interesting in point of history or tradition. Thus we have a helmet that claims Attila for its original owner; another belonged to Abderama, whom Charles Martel prevented from giving a succession of Moorish sovereigns to France in 730, by slaying him, together with a hundred and fifty thousand of his countrymen. The gallant Francis I. is to be seen on horseback as he rode on the fatal field of Pavia. The miserable assassin of his subjects, Charles IX., with his scarcely more worthy successor, appear as they appeared in life,—in armor. The helmet, sword, and breast-plate of Henry IV. are as battered and bruised as were at one time his fortunes; and the Duke of Mayenne looks more peaceable than he ever did alive. The greatest wonder of all, is how the knights who survived a field of battle, were able to survive the weight of their armor, which cased horse and rider in a solid wall of steel from head to foot, with holes for eyesight through which a mole could scarce see and much less breathe. Gunpowder was a blessing to the fighting trade in releasing them from the stiffest and most unwearoutable costume ever invented. I have always considered that the inventor of hats deserved impalement; but he was a humane wretch, compared with the diabolical fabricator of a suit of mail, which, if it were any protection against being stuck through, created a much more imminent danger of suffocation Indeed, history insinuates that in every rout there were more of these doughty champions smothered than slain in fight. Once down, they were unable to rise without help, and the unencumbered foot soldiers had nothing to do but to cut their throats as they lay; a deed which the fields of Crecy and Agincourt attest they were nothing loath to perform.

If the contemplation of the iron garments of our warlike ancestors, left me no cause of regret in modern broadcloth, I found no more cause to sigh after the "good old times," upon an examination into the domestic comforts of these said lords. In the Hotel de Cluny, we have a fine specimen of one of the mansions of the fifteenth century, restored by the government in furniture and architecture to the standard of that period, and made a museum of interesting objects of the Middle Ages. Here the visitor has an opportunity of drawing a practical comparison between the kitchen and boudoir of a lady of the chivalrous court of Francis, and the "*cuisine*" and "*cabinet de toilette*" of the modern dame. The fire-places of the former have undergone a wonderful contraction. Then there was no difficulty in roasting an ox entire; now they will scarcely accommodate a turkey. My attention was attracted among the arms to what appeared to be and really was an eight-chambered revolving pistol, constructed precisely upon the principle of Colt's. The handle and date showed that it had anticipated his two centuries. There was another near it, of much more clumsy make, but intended for the same amiable service.

Here is to be seen the famous but equivocal safe-guard, or rather, lock-up of chastity, made for, if not worn by, Diana of Poitiers, by order of Henry II. It is a curious relic of the curious habits of a curious age. As even the most modest visitors look at it, at least sideways, I trust there will be no indecorum in my mentioning it. Human nature is unfortunately so innoculated with curiosity, that there would be disappointment to hear of this "exposition of manners" after having left the Museum without obtaining a view of it.

If the glum guardians of this old mansion would permit it, one could lie down in the very bed on which Francis I. as Duke of Valois, had slept. It is profusely carved, and looks stiff and uninviting. Elaborate carving was the fashion of that day in all furniture. The interior of articles had not much to boast of in way of finish, the expense and skill being lavished on the exterior. There are several splendid specimens of carved ebony buffets or wardrobes, that no work of like character now excels. We have also Flemish tapestry, beautifully wrought, with the history of David and Bathsheba; these personages and the whole court of the royal harpist being in grand toilette of the time of Louis XII. This is carrying the prophet's knowledge of coming events into a province of which there is nothing in Scripture to warrant that he was better informed than any of his contemporaries. However, this is less ridiculous than the vanity of a certain French noble, who in a painting had his ancestors represented as among those who came to make offerings to the infant Jesus. The Virgin Mary, suddenly recollecting their exalted rank, says to them "Pray be covered."

On other tapestry, Henry IV. figures as Apollo, and his pious mother, one of the few good as well as great names that her sex has given to France, is metamorphosed into a nude Venus. There is a great variety of the nameless and curious nicknacks that constitute woman's delight in all ages, and without which her " étagères" would have no more value than firewood. The Hotel de Cluny is a sort of semi-modern Pompeii—a connecting link between the expiring luxury of Rome and the dawn of the still more refined magnificence of France.

Under its foundations, and projecting beyond them toward the Rue de la Harpe, we come upon the oldest monument of Paris—the remains of the palace of her Cæsar kings. In it, Julian was proclaimed emperor in 360. There is nothing remarkable in what time has spared except its gloomy hall, which was formerly the *frigidarium*, or chamber of cold baths, and the still more gloomy subterranean vaults beneath, which formed the apartments for warm baths. This relic is preserved with the utmost care and veneration. Why is it that nations are so exceedingly anxious to be reminded of their age, while individuals wish to keep it as far from their thoughts as possible?

Paris is no less prolific in libraries than museums. In nineteen, open to the public, it numbers two millions three hundred and eighty-two thousand books, and one hundred and thirty-four thousand three hundred manuscripts. The library of Ste. Geneviève, recently erected near the Pantheon, has its external walls covered with the names of celebrated writers of all centuries, from the earliest ages down. Among them I noticed that of Washington; honored, probably, more as great and good, than for literary fame.

The leviathan of libraries is the " Bibliothèque Nationale," now deposited in the vast and prison-like hotel in the Rue Richelieu, formerly occupied by Cardinal Mazarin. The census of this library, like that of the world, is only taken by computation. They *guess*, therefore, the number of books and pamphlets to be one million four hundred thousand, and of manuscripts one hundred and twenty-five thousand. The catalogue alone of these last fills twenty-five volumes. The arrangement of the whole is bad for facility of reference; the most valuable or curious works being lost in the common mass, so that, to find them, it is as much a matter of chance as to meet an acquaintance among the million souls that crowd the streets of Paris. There is also danger from fire in their present locality. It has been under consideration for a long time to erect an appropriate edifice elsewhere, from the proceeds of the sale of the land now occupied, which is valued at 2,400,000 francs.

I never wander through its cold and gloomy halls, cased from floor to ceiling with long files of books, whose titles are almost obliterated in the wear of ages, and whose bindings once gay are now gray with time, without feeling that I am in an intellectual catacomb—a veritable place of skulls, that, having done their duty while living, are now quietly laid on the shelf, without even the hope which attends mortal remains, to rise again. This then is the immortality of thought! Millions of brains have delved for fame, wearied their aching sense over midnight oil, starved their bodies to feed their minds, laboring as no laborer can, distracted with doubt, burning with hope, ambitious of a name—and have found at last, in this cemetery of learning, a few inches of shelf-room so elevated from living eyes, that, unlike the epitaphs over their graves which stare at every passer, they can neither be read nor seen. The ideas to which they gave birth may exist, however, like coin in the outer world, passing from hand to hand, recognising no master, but blessing alike him who gives and him who receives. Ambition is a useful stimulus, but he who seeks other reward than the self-consciousness of rectitude, will find that he bites the apple of Sodom.

This library is replete with interest to the bibliomaniac and antiquarian. Here are preserved the earliest specimen of print-

F

ing, which, in less than half a century, attained a beauty and perfection that modern art scarcely rivals. The luxury and extent to which various governments have carried the editions of works undertaken at their order, and limited to a few presentation copies, are surprising. In this respect France is wisely munificent. Works of general utility or scientific and historic value, which would not remunerate private enterprise, are printed at the national printing-office at the expense of the government. This establishment is on so liberal a scale, that when Pope Pius VII. visited it, the Lord's Prayer was printed in one hundred and fifty languages, bound and presented to him before he returned to his carriage.

In the engraving department there are more than one million three hundred thousand plates, including ninety thousand portraits and three hundred thousand maps and charts; furnishing a complete history of the art from its rude commencement to its present perfection.

The cabinet of medals and coins numbers one hundred and fifty thousand, many of which are exceedingly rare, and some unique. The series of Roman and Greek medals is very complete, and exhibits beautifully finished portraits of the most eminent rulers of antiquity, including Alexander, the Cæsars, and earlier illustrious men of the Roman republic. Here is preserved also, perhaps, the oldest relic extant; the remarkable oval black marble carved with rude figures, underneath which is the inexplicable cuneiform writing to which learning has as yet failed to find the key. It was brought from the site of the Tower of Babel.

The collection of ancient and modern gems and cameos is very full and valuable. The autographs are neither so numerous nor interesting as those of the British Museum. Among them, however, we find Fenelon's original manuscript of Telemachus; writings of Galileo, letters of Racine, Molière, Corneille, and Voltaire; the last wrote a remarkably good hand, fine and distinct; Henry IV., the fair Gabrielle, the repentant Vallière and devout Maintenon; and lastly, what will most attract American curiosity, the famous note of Franklin to Madame Helvetius, in which the impassable philosopher of more than threescore and ten distanced French gallantry with its own weapons. It is too good to be turned into English; I copy it verbatim.

"M. Franklin n'oublie jamais aucune Partie oû Me Helvetius doit être. Il croit même que s'il engagé d'aller a Paradis ce matin, il ferait supplication d'être permis de rester sur terre jusqu'à une heure et demie, pour recevoir l'Embrassade qu'elle a bienvolu lui promettre en la reunion chez M. Turgot."

Franklin was no favorite with the old noblesse. Louis XVI. detested him, and, to express his dislike, sent one of his lady admirers a certain nameless domestic utensil of the purest Sèvres, in the bottom of which was his portrait and the well-known motto, "Eripuit Cælo fulmen, sceptrumque tyrannis."

Madame de Créquey, whose hand was kissed by Louis XIV. and who lived to receive the same homage from the Emperor Napoleon, relates, that she was one day invited to meet the celebrated American at dinner, the post of honor next to him being reserved for her. In her aristocratic eyes he was only a low and disgusting republican. She says she revenged herself by not speaking a word to him during the meal, but amused herself in observing his manners. He had a brown coat, brown vest, brown breeches, and "brown" hands. She was horrified in observing him break several eggs into a glass, mix them up with butter, pepper and salt, and eat the unsightly mess with a spoon.

The sepulchre of Thoutmes III., after reposing in quiet at Karnac for some thirty-five hundred years, has been removed to the court-yard of the Bibliothèque Nationale, on the walls of which the world of to-day may read the hieroglyphical tale of the deeds of the ancestors of this Egyptian Pharaoh. Another room contains the famous zodiac of Dendarah, with which at one period French philosophy frightened the Christian world by its astronomical interpretations. If they had proved correct, they would have given the lie to the Mosaic chronology. Happily for believers, the stone of four thousand centuries was soon shown to have the very juvenile age of but twenty.

PERSPECTIVE OF THE LOUVRE.

There yet remains the greatest Cæsar of them all,—the Louvre; a gem of architectural beauty, worthy of the treasures it holds. It ranks with St. Peter's, the Vatican, the Palazzo Uffizi, the Museo Borbonico and the British Museum, as one of the established wonders of the world. The simple catalogue of its contents would form a respectable library. It needs, however, some cleverly arranged guide-book that the visitor may not only know what is most worthy of his attention, but where to find what he seeks. There are so many halls and entrances, that much time is often lost in fruitless research. Indeed, a stranger not unfrequently leaves with the impression that he has seen all the collections of the Louvre, when he has, perhaps, not entered more than half the number of museums. The mere list is formidable.

The Museum of Antiques is a series of apartments on the ground-floor, containing statues, bas-reliefs, vases, candelabra, &c. It is here we find the most beautiful discovery of modern times ; the mutilated but still incomparable statue known as the Venus de Milo. On the same floor we find the Assyrian, Egyptian, American and Algerine Galleries ; the Museum of Casts, of the Middle Ages and Revival of Arts ; of Engraving on Brass and of Modern Sculpture, the last occupying five halls.

Ascending by a magnificent marble staircase, we enter the Salle Ronde, remarkable for its fine mosaic pavement. On its right is the splendid gallery of Apollo. Passing through this, a carved ebony passage-way conducts the visitor into the Salon Carré, which is of itself elaborately beautiful, and contains the gems of the paintings of the Louvre, so disposed as to be advantageously viewed from luxurious velvet divans, in which I am sorry to say I have seen, at least, one visitor sound asleep.

The gem of the Soult gallery, The Conception, by Murillo, by some claimed to be his master-piece—has been placed here since its purchase for 123,060 francs by the French government. Great as was the price paid for it, fifteen minutes after it was struck off, a telegraphic dispatch arrived from Spain to buy it at *any price.* A close examination discloses only a mass of confused coloring, more or less damaged. Let the visitor withdraw a few steps and the full beauty bursts upon him. The angelic children are literally floating in the air, while the Virgin is radiant with heavenly beauty. There appear to be places where some less skillful hand has retouched the canvas. The faces of the children are of a vulgar cast ; too physically healthful. The expression of the Virgin struck me as tinged with an expression of sorrow, a Magdalen sadness, instead of wearing that celestial joy which should belong to the mother of the Saviour in the announcement of the glad tidings to mankind. Soult's pictures brought 1,500,000 francs. In 1829 he offered them for sale for 90,000 francs, the purchaser to get possession of them at a time when there was some risk of confiscation.

On the right is the Hall of Jewels, containing, in elegant presses, vases of precious stones, and silver and gold church utensils, some of which date back to Charlemagne. Here are also the jeweled looking-glass, and other articles of toilet, the gift of the republic of Venice to Marie de Medicis, and many other curious and valuable objects. That which interested me most, was a little statue of our Saviour, of about ten inches in height, of a greenish stone as compact as porphyry. It is of most exquisite workmanship, with an expression of mingled humility and compassion on a face of divine beauty.

The long gallery, in which are the paintings of the older Italian, Flemish, Spanish, and French schools, is nearly a quarter of a mile in length. On entering it for the first time I was disappointed. Repeated visits, however, taught me that taste expanded and improved in the contemplation of its master-pieces. The paintings which, on the first glance, gave me the same impression as does a confused crowd of strange faces, soon appeared in all the pleasing variety of individual acquaintances. Each had its peculiar talent and its definable attraction. Each struck a different mental chord, and the whole gave birth to that quiet harmony of the mind, which is to the intellect what an approving conscience is to the soul. It is the realization of artistic beauty; the joy of seeing actually defined what only existed as a flitting shadow in the brain. Almost all possess the power to appreciate beauty, but few the talent to give it form and expression. This gallery possesses fourteen hundred and eight paintings. Napoleon made it the finest in existence, but in the capture of Paris, the allied powers compelled the restitution of the *chefs-d'œuvres* of the world to their respective owners.

The Hall of Bronzes is full of valuable relics of ancient art. Next is that of the Sept Cheminées, in which are found the master-pieces of the modern French school. This leads into the Galerie Française, also appropriated to the works of eminent French artists. This gallery is sub-divided into nine halls. Then we enter upon a series of apartments, in which are displayed the arts of ancient Egypt, Greece, and Rome. These collections are exceedingly choice and comprehensive, and present a vivid picture of the domestic life of those defunct nations. The Middle Ages and ecclesiastical history are equally well exhibited in halls devoted to their arts. There are others which I do not enumerate. Merely to name them would convey no more adequate idea of their intrinsic interest and value than would a brick, shown as a specimen of a house. In addition to the present attractions, Louis Napoleon has ordered the formation of a museum of articles belonging to the sovereigns of France, in which the souvenirs of his uncle will occupy a conspicuous place.

In the "Salle des Séances," among a crowd of paintings of gigantic dimensions and comparatively little interest, there is to be seen one about two feet and a half long by two in height, in a dingy, time-worn frame, without a name or even a number, yet there is none in all the Louvre I have more admired for its perfect finish and lifelike tone. It is of the Dutch school, and is a skating scene, with a multitude of figures, dwindling in the perspective into almost imperceptible dimensions. No miniature of Petitot is more perfect in the minutest details. This is the more remarkable as it embraces a great variety of objects, and all equally well drawn and colored. All the other treasures of the Louvre I was contented to admire or study as they were, but this I coveted. An idea may be formed of the labor expended on it from the price asked by the artists of the Louvre for a copy. Good copies of the most admired paintings can, in general, be had for from two to four hundred francs. For those of this, two thousand francs are demanded.

I have been able to give but an imperfect idea of the extent of the treasures of art and science which the government of France places at the disposal of the entire world. The palaces and museums of the Luxembourg, Versailles, Fontainebleau, St. Cloud, Meudon, and other places of interest, are equally at the disposal of strangers, without charge. The government undoubtedly reaps a reward in the immense sum of money expended by foreigners in Paris, drawn thither by this liberality, and to gratify their tastes in the enjoyment of these refined and elegant superfluities of life, in the production of which French genius excels that of any other nation. It was computed that 200,000 strangers arrived at Paris to witness the distribution of the eagles to the army on the 10th of May, and that they left in the city 40,000,000 of francs. The number of troops under arms at the review has been greatly exaggerated, even by the official journals, some of which quoted them at 80,000 and none under 60,000 men, which numbers will doubtless go down in history as the true statement. The actual number was 36,000, of which 6000 were cavalry, the finest troops of Europe. Some conception may be formed of the multitude of visitors to the museums of the Louvre and Versailles alone, from the fact that $20,000 are annually received for the deposit of canes, umbrellas, and parasols, which are not allowed to be taken into the galleries. As the charge on each is but two sous, this would give a million of visitors who carried these articles, and they form but a small proportion of the entire number. Nearly one hundred thousand dollars are received from the sale of catalogues. That Yankee thrift which judges of the utility of an investment solely by its monied dividends, may hence conclude that on the ground of a national speculation the government have not greatly erred in the establishment of these institutions. Their effect on the civilization of the people, and the cultivation of the noble and beautiful in art, it is difficult to over-estimate. It is equally difficult to realize that any population, however brutal, would vent their political hate in the destruction of objects which add so much to the glory and prosperity of their country. Yet we find no learning, however venerable; no art, however beautiful; no association, however sacred, spared by the revolutionary hordes that seek to impose their tyranny alike on kingdom and republic. After the Revolution of 1848, the provisional government was obliged to conceal the beautiful statues of Joan of Arc and the Duke of Orleans to prevent their loss. The mob in their attack on the Tuileries and the Palais National, spared neither literature, paintings, nor furniture. In the latter edifice they destroyed the queen's private library, burned six hundred thousand engravings belonging to Louis Philippe, and broke so much glass and china, that more than sixty thousand pounds of fragments were afterward collected and sold by order of the liquidators of the civil list. Such are the citizens that shout "Vive la République Sociale et Démocratique!"

The French government forbade the passage of Kossuth through their territories for fear of his influence over the Socialists, but I noticed they had of late allowed to be struck at their mint a medal with his bust on the face, and on the reverse, in English, "Set at liberty by the United States, 1851." This is the more strange, as they had arrested and fined all those who sold his effigy about the streets. The mint enjoys the monopoly of casting medals, by the sale of which it derives a considerable income. In it, there is preserved a fine series of French medals from Charlemagne down to Louis Napoleon. Those of the Emperor are exceedingly beautiful, and form a complete history of his remarkable career. A model in bronze of the cast of his head, taken a few hours after his death, is here to be seen. I was disappointed in the apparent volume of the brain and breadth of the forehead. The gigantic bust of Napoleon in marble, done by Canova in 1806 for Fouché, which stood close by, was evidently much flattered. His features by all accounts were classically beautiful, but it is quite apparent from his portraits and medals executed when he was simply *General*, and those afterward done in honor of the *Emperor*, that the artists of the latter had made a sudden discovery of a wonderful increase of personal beauty.

CHAPTER XV.

SECRET POLICE AND SOME THINGS NOT SECRET.

When a newly arrived American is informed that all his movements are known to the police, that there is nothing he can do, and scarcely any thing he can say or think, but what he will find duly chronicled in its records, he looks incredulous. Nevertheless it is in the main true. The first care of the police is to ascertain the nation and occupation of the stranger, his business and general habits. If these are satisfactory, he is subject only to a general surveillance. Should he become an object of suspicion, the Argus eyes of this mysterious power are upon him every where. They report when he goes out and when he returns; where he visits and whom he visits; who visits him; what letters he receives; where from; and his habits of every name and nature, even to the number of glasses of wine he may take in the course of a day, and his very conversation. So thorough is this watch, that when Caussidière, the companion of Louis Blanc, became prefect of the police of Paris, having the curiosity to examine the reports made relative to himself before the Revolution of February, 1848, he exclaimed with astonishment. "Not only my actions but my intimate thoughts!"

How is this effected? In various ways. There are, firstly, the uniformed agents of the police, its external eyes, whose duties and appearance are so well known, that they are easily avoided. But in avoiding Charybdis, the suspected seldom see the more dangerous Scylla, or the secret agents, whose eyes and ears are in every café, restaurant, corner, or place, where men do congregate, and under every disguise. They have as many shapes as Proteus, and as many colors as the chameleon. There is no locality, from the salon in the Faubourg St. Germain to the lowest haunt in the quarter St. Antoine, in which they can not make themselves completely at home.

The employées relieve each other in their watches with the regularity of sentinels. The following note from an ex-préfect of police to his successor, on finding himself incessantly followed by two police agents, got wind immediately after the change of ministry in November last, greatly to the amusement of the people of Paris :

"MONSIEUR LE PRÉFET—I have the honor to announce to you that I leave to-morrow to have a few days' shooting in the country. It is, therefore, perfectly useless to send your agents charged to watch my house and to follow me. I will do myself the honor of informing you of my return.

"Accept, etc., CARLIER."

The finest broadcloth, or the richest satin, the profoundest courtesy, or the most fascinating manner, will not insure one from being in the presence of an informant. The very musician who plays his organ under the windows has his mission; the commissionaire at the corner of the street, his; and if any knowledge is desired of internal movements, there is the porter, generally a woman, who as the Cerberus for every house, knows every person, package, or note that enters, and generally every thing that goes out, and who, for a "consideration," can open a channel of communication, viâ the kitchen, as to what transpires in the parlor. This system of espionage is not confined to public exigencies. It ramifies through all classes of society according to individual wants. I can not better illustrate this, than by Sir Francis Head's entertaining narrative taken in short-hand from the mouth of one of the twelve thousand commissionaires of Paris, who best answer to the literal truth of "Jacks of all work," of any class of human beings. They are to be found all over the city, clad in blue velveteen trowsers and blue corduroy jackets, with brass plates affixed to their breasts, containing their numbers, orders, and names. They are faithful and intelligent men, and can be relied on for any commission, from the conscientious delivery of the Koh-i-noor itself to the most sentimental note that love-stricken swain ever indited; they black boots; carry baggage; wash floors; beat carpets; carry up fuel; in fine, do all the chores of a domestic establishment, even to making the beds. They watch with the sick and dead, pawn and redeem articles at the Monts de Piété, curry horses, travel; in short, it is impossible to find any thing they are not ready to do at a moment's notice, even to giving you the news of the day or the gossip of the neighborhood. But I will let the "commissionaire" speak for himself, on one branch of his accomplishments.

"Sometimes, when a beautiful woman passes by, a gentleman says to me, 'Commissioner, follow that lady, and try to find out her name; you must bring me back her name and address; here is my card and direction where I live; get the name very exact, and bring me back the answer to my house at six o'clock this evening; I will pay you liberally for your commission.' I answer him, 'Sir, Madame lives in —— Street (never mind where!) etc. She is called Mademoiselle ——. Now, Sir, you can write to her, if that is agreeable to you.' This gentleman then says to me, 'Come to-morrow morning at nine o'clock; I will give you a letter to deliver to Mademoiselle.' Now I go and carry the letter; Monsieur sees me return. 'Here is the answer to your letter!' 'Ah! I thank you, Commissioner! Well! how much do I owe you, Commissioner?' 'Sir, this young lady kept me waiting a long time for her answer; so, Sir, it is well worth thirty sous; you know it is a long walk.'

'Well, here are thirty sous, Commissioner; if I want you to-morrow, I shall pass by your station.' Now, this gentleman puts to me some questions. He asks me, 'Has this young lady got handsome furniture?' I answer him, 'Yes, Sir, I saw a good bed, a convenient writing-table, a beautiful clock on the chimney-piece, and the floor was carpeted. In short, Sir, I have told you all I saw. Sir, I am going back to my station.' 'Well! that will do, Commissioner! If I want you I will let you know.' 'I thank you. Good-day, Sir.' Now, when a door-keeper refuses to tell me the name of the person I describe to him—for example, a tall, fair lady who has just come in, who has crossed over to the back of the court-yard, to the stair-case on the right hand—I say to the door-keeper, 'Monsieur door-keeper! would you be so good as to tell me the name of that tall lady who has just gone in there all alone?' The door-keeper says to me, 'But what do you want with her name?' I say to him, 'It is a gentleman who has given me the commission to learn the name of that young lady (correcting himself)—of that person, because I have not known sometimes whether she was a married or an unmarried lady.' The door-keeper says to me, 'If such is the case, to oblige you, I will tell you. She is Mademoiselle, such a one:'—on my part, I show a little civility to the door-keeper, by giving him a glass of wine.

"Now, there is another subject which I will explain to you. When a gentleman has no confidence in his wife, he employs a Commissioner to follow her when she goes out alone. Then the gentleman says to the Commissioner, 'Follow that lady; you must tell me of every place where she stops; I shall come to your station this evening for an answer.' Then I say to the gentleman, 'Sir, Madame stopped in —— Street, Number —. Madame remained for half an hour in that house; during the time I walked up and down opposite to the carriage-gate on the other side of the street, in order to know when she should leave the street, Madame went to the warehouse for novelties —— Street, Number —. From thence Madame got into a hackney coach, which she stopped in the street on coming out of the warehouse. As for me, I ran as fast as my legs could carry me to follow the carriage. Madame got out of it in —— Street, say Number —. Madame sent away the carriage, after having paid for it. Madame went into that house, where she staid an hour and a half. On coming out of that house, Madame went straight home. Madame returned home at half past five. I did not see any description of gentlemen speak to Madame. In short, Sir, these are all the details and information which I can give you, to-day.' The gentleman says to me, 'Well done, Commissioner; how much do I owe you?' I say, 'You are generous enough to comprehend how much the commission is worth.' 'Here, Commissioner, are two francs. Are you satisfied?' 'Yes, Sir, I am satisfied.' 'If I want you to-morrow, I will let you know, or I will go to your station myself.' I say to him, 'Very well, Sir, it is all right. I thank you. Good-day, Sir.' Well, the next morning the gentleman arrives. 'Tell me, Commissioner, can you do me the same commission that you did yesterday? You understand;—come with me; you will keep yourself opposite my carriage-gate; when a lady comes out—a little brunette—she is to come in half an hour; she has a gown of tartan silk, a green bonnet, and a large shawl, with a blue ground and red flowers—you will follow her. Keep yourself at a distance, some way off, so that she may not suspect that you follow her; bring me back a very exact account; you must tell me wherever she has stopped, the name of the street, and the number of the house, and of all the houses, where she may stop. I shall come and get your answer this evening, at seven o'clock.'

"It is now seven o'clock. 'Sir, I have done your commission very exactly. On leaving her house, Madame stopped on the

Boulevard, at a shoemaker's shop. Madame staid there fifteen minutes; from there, Madame went to —— Street, Number —; Madame staid two hours in that house; from thence Madame came out; she went to the Garden of the Tuileries; Madame was talking for about an hour with a gentleman, well dressed, not very tall, of a dark complexion; a gentleman who may be about eight-and-thirty; this gentleman wears mustaches. From thence Madame parted from this gentleman; she returned home to her own house at half past six. This is all the tour that Madame has made to-day.'

"Sometimes a lady in the same way makes me follow her husband, whom I know. In order that this gentleman may not recognize me, I dress myself decently, like a citizen. My comrade, opposite, once followed a gentleman for ten days, at the rate of six francs a day; in the course of all those ten days he was not able to discover or find out any thing!"

Every government of France, whether monarchy, empire, or republic, has preserved the system of secret police. It must therefore arise from the exigencies of French character, or be deep-rooted in the necessities of the public authorities. When its application is solely confined to individuals obnoxious to the civil laws, the result can not but be beneficial. But diverted into a political weapon, it becomes the most insidious as well as dangerous antagonist to liberty. No individual can be safe from the malice of an enemy directed through a spy. Society grows corrupt because dissimulation becomes a necessity. There is no option left the individual other than a passive acquiescence in the will of his rulers, or imprisonment or banishment without appeal to jury.

It is its comparative value as a regulator of society, and as a political machine, that I wish to notice. Of the latter, there can be but one opinion in the United States. In regard to the former, there is much to be said on both sides. The two republics present the extremes of policy in this respect. In the United States the authorities direct their efforts more to punish than to prevent. So jealous are they of civil liberty, that they leave much latitude to rogues and charlatans, rather than intrust any power with the arbitrary control of individual acts, even though the general welfare may seem to warrant its exercise. Hence formal acts of the legislature become necessary to combat every evil. And so subtle is law and so cumbrous its forms, that it is only where a nuisance has become intolerable that society bestirs itself for a remedy. We leave our moral sores to come to a head, and discharge themselves. The result is, that many lives are lost and much injury done by carelessness, quackery, imperfect construction of edifices, bursting of boilers, burning of boats, or collision of cars, before the public become fully sensible that the right of public safety is paramount to the right of private gain. At every great catastrophe, there is a periodical excitement and call for reform. But personal enterprise hurries so rapidly on, that the warning is lost in some new invention or some fancied improvement of private interest, and the public quietly submit to the same risks as before.

This system is not without its advantages. It leaves every thing to individual competition. It develops enterprise and improvement, because success depends upon presenting something to the public better and cheaper than existed before. In the great strife of private interests the public must gain. It leaves the great tidal wave of commerce quietly to seek its own level. Talent, genius, enterprise, and industry, have each a fair start, with the entire public sitting in judgment. The consequence is, that though many quacks may find their way into every profession, yet real worth is sure to rise to the head of its legitimate sphere.

It is also an essential element of our individual independence and self-reliance. With less to lean upon, we become more capable of supporting ourselves. Although we may run more risks in our frame of social life, we are better prepared to meet and overcome them, than if we had been carefully protected from every chance of mishap. The social element, like water, purifies itself; the sediment gradually sinking to the bottom, leaves the top clear and healthy.

We leave to every one the exercise of his own judgment in the supply of his wants; at the same time establishing the government upon the aggregation of individuals. In France this is reversed. The individual rests upon the government, which forms the great base of society. Withdraw this foundation, and the nation is immediately precipitated into anarchy. In the United States, were a plague to destroy at one moment every public officer, the people would soon quietly fill their places by new elections. Order rises from the one, from the other it descends. Hence with the former, it is an exhaustless fertilizing spring; with the latter, an uncertain cloud, from which there may come the tempest as well as the genial shower.

France has eighty-six departments. At the head of each there is a prefect. Every department is divided into forty arrondissements, under the charge of sub-prefects; the arrondissements are subdivided into cantons, and these last into communes, each of which is regulated by a "maire," whose simple order carries with it an authority in matters of the internal welfare of his jurisdiction, equal to that of an act of our legislatures.

Paris alone has a Prefect of Police, with a corps of three hundred clerks. His bureau is subdivided into different departments of active service, each having its particular functions, but affording mutual assistance as occasion may be. Thus there is the chief of the conservers of public safety, who commands a brigade of adroit criminal hunters. The chief, who watches over all persons of doubtful political views, clandestine gaming-houses, etc. There is another who regulates the houses of ill-fame; another, the public vehicles; another, the boats that navigate the Seine, possessing authority to prescribe what they shall bring, and how they shall unlade their cargoes. The "Chef des Halles et Marchés" regulates the price and sale of provisions. The "Chef de Service de la Salubrité" has the important charge of all that relates to the public health, such as the drains, closets, gas establishments, &c. These "chefs" are immediately responsible to the Chief of the Municipal Police.

Paris has four Commissioners of Police to each of its twelve arrondissements, each having in charge one of the forty-eight "quartiers." Without giving farther details of the organization of this half-political and half-sanitary hydra, it is sufficient to add that its arms, ears, and eyes, embrace all France, concentrating its knowledge and direction in one trunk, the newly created Minister of Police, the sum of whose duties is to allow nothing to exist in France unsanctioned by the government.

Thus, the first notice an individual may receive, that his presence can be dispensed with in "La belle France," is a brief notification, that by calling at the proper bureau, he will receive his passport. Last autumn a simple decree of the Prefect compelled all foreigners residing in the department of the Seine, to apply for permission to remain, under penalty of immediate expulsion. The object was to examine into the history of each individual, and if, in the opinion of the police, the public safety required his banishment, he was immediately sent out of the country. Several hundred were in consequence banished. However salutary such a purgative might be in a city like New York, our institutions require that a citizen must be considered innocent until adjudged guilty by a jury of his countrymen. Consequently, we are compelled to await crime before we act. The French seek to prevent it, by placing society as much as possible out of the risk. We punish; they protect. It is not astonishing that each new government of France, in its turn, cherishes an institution, which, in return, can give it such efficient support.

The necessity of this despotism arises from a principle universally acknowledged in France, "that no member of the community has the right to do that which is hurtful to the public at large." It results, therefore, that he must be prevented from so doing. When we compare the general security of their public conveyances, the strength of their buildings, and all those points in which prevention is so much more valuable than remedy, with our own carelessness on these points, the comparison is greatly to the disadvantage of the United States.

No steam-engine is allowed to be put into operation within the city, until it has been thoroughly tested, and then only under prudential regulations in regard to the building. Every manufacture deleterious to health, must be completely isolated from human habitations. No one has even the right to kill a pig in Paris; but the meat for the capital is slaughtered at authorized establishments, with the utmost regard to humanity compatible with the business, and an economy of material that leaves no waste.

There are no expensive suits arising from the prosecution of nuisances. A simple order of the police is all that is required to remove any manufactory, however expensive, should the neighborhood find it "incommode," inconvenient.

The most rigid supervision is exercised over the exterior of buildings, to see that the public be not endangered or incommoded by faulty chimneys, insecure shutters, sign-boards, or incumbered sidewalks. This excess of care at times produces the very evil which it is the intention to obviate. Thus I have been annoyed for several days by an open drain because it was necessary to obtain permission from the police to close it.

The care exercised over poisonous drugs, or whatever may jeopardize individual health, is more rigid still. Each profession is not only protected in its rights, but it is required to be competent to exercise its calling; and it is not allowed to combine with it any other. There are no French Brandreths or Swaims. Quackery has but an indifferent chance in contest with the police. Each chemist or apothecary is required to pass a strict examination. He can not sell any poisonous substance without a license, and then only under the authorized prescription of a physician, who is required to register all the particulars of a dose. Poisons of all sorts must be kept locked up by the chemist, who is liable to be visited at any moment by an agent of the police, accompanied by one of the professors of the school of pharmacy, to ascertain the nature and quality of his drugs.

No patent medicines are allowed to be vended or advertised until they have been examined and approved by the National Academy of Medicine. This is literally putting the faculty on their honor, or it would be in the United States, for the business of doctors would materially decrease if pills and lotions were made contraband. The police of Paris have been obliged to make an exception in favor of the quackery so yearned for by the bowels of John Bull, for fear, if he were not allowed to swallow his favorite nostrum, he would quit Paris in disgust.

The provisions are subject to the same inspection as the medicines. Meats must be wholesome, and the metallic utensils of cook-shops kept bright and clean. Wine and liquors have their regular tasters before they pass into the hands of the retailers. But all this care does not prevent very dubious substances from finding their way into the stomachs of their customers, from both sources. My cook satisfied me on this point, by observing, wherever there was a disposition to cheat there was a way, and proving it also.

The price of meat and bread is regulated by this same all-meddling authority. The latter depends upon the price of grain in the corn-market, and is fixed by the prefect twice a month, averaging about three cents a pound. The weight and quality of the bread is also carefully looked after. The result is, that French bread is uniformly good, and at a price satisfactory to buyer and seller, as it is regulated on the most equitable scale for each. I asked a Frenchman, if it would not be better to leave trade free to fix its own prices. He replied, the result would be, that one baker would undersell another, and thus draw to his shop the population from other parts of the city, who would lose much time in consequence, besides creating confusion; whereas now, the price and quality being uniform, all were content. The degree to which this care of the people is extended, borders sometimes on the ludicrous. For instance, the three classes into which railroad voyagers are divided, are locked up in separate rooms until the moment the train is ready to depart. They are then let out, and passed along with the utmost dispatch into their respective places. The reason given for this is, that if they were left, as with us, to take care of themselves, they would stand talking on the platform, and the train would go off without them.

The following judgment, copied from one of the daily papers, will astonish our race of Ichabod Cranes:

"Two persons, named Bapeaume and Mondière, were yesterday fined five hundred francs by default, by the Tribunal of Correctional Police, for having opened a school without authorization; and the school was ordered to be closed."

How much at a loss would be one of our "free and independent" citizen house-agents, for words to express his indignation at such a violation of his personal rights, were a constable to inform him that, under penalty of being fined, he must hereafter have all his advertisements of unfurnished houses printed on *white*, and those furnished on *yellow* paper. Such is the order of the day here, and very convenient it is too.

Among no class of public servants does this arbitrary power

produce more satisfactory results than the hackney coachmen. There are two thousand six hundred and seventy licensed public carriages, including three hundred and thirty-three omnibuses, producing to the city, from their taxation, a net income of about $70,000 per annum. Their numbers, fares, and regulations, are so plainly exposed on each, that the stranger is subject to none of the annoyances arising from the habits of extortion, so common in the cities of the United States. They are inspected daily, and any attempt at imposition is severely punished.

The statistical knowledge of the police is exact and comprehensive. It tells every article left by accident in the public vehicles ; thus, in 1849, there were restored to their owners one thousand six hundred and forty-two articles, besides eight thousand two hundred and twenty-four francs in money. It gives each month the receipts of the places of amusement, as follows : For December, 1851, the theatres received six hundred and forty-eight thousand four hundred and twenty francs ; the concerts, sixty-five thousand seven hundred and ninety francs ; and minor exhibitions, eight thousand five hundred and ninety-three —a total of seven hundred and twenty-two thousand eight hundred and three francs, which was less by one hundred and fifty-six thousand six hundred and ninety-seven francs than the preceding month, owing to the closing of the doors during the "Coup d'Etat." It reports each day the arrival of strangers; their nation, profession, lodging, and any other particular the curiosity of the chief may desire to be satisfied about. In December, 1851, there arrived at Paris from the provinces, eleven thousand eight hundred and eighty travelers, and from foreign countries two thousand three hundred and seventy-nine—a total of fourteen thousand two hundred and fifty-nine. Of this latter there were nine hundred and ninety-eight English, one hundred and eighty-four Americans, and twenty-six Turks.

A citizen of the United States abroad is greatly puzzled to

nationalize himself. An American means an inhabitant of any portion of the continent; and almost invariably when I have been spoken to as an American, the parties addressing me supposed I was from a tropical climate. Our national vanity constantly suffers from the ignorance so general of all matters relating to our republic. The inhabitants of Europe at large have about as indefinite ideas of the United States, as had the old Romans of the then wild and unexplored regions of northern Europe.

Every workman is required to have a "livret," or species of passport, indorsed by the police, without which he is treated as a vagabond, and any one employing him is subject to a heavy fine. It must always bear the acquittal of his last employer.

This supervision extends to every thing in any way affecting the welfare and interest of society. It is a species of conscience for the body corporate, warning, checking, and punishing, as the case requires. Whatever may be its ultimate effects upon the national character, the stranger is bound to look upon it with gratitude. It protects him in the street; it watches over him by night; it is prompt to redress a wrong; it makes smooth the public places; it gives him useful information; in short, saves him from a goodly proportion of the thousand-and-one ills which are the usual heritage of travelers.

Skillful as the police are in preventing and tracking crime, they are often baffled by a body of men equally skilled in their nefarious profession. Vice has likewise its systematized organization. Paris appears to be a poor field for the ordinary pickpocket. I have not heard of a loss from this source, and no one seems apprehensive of the public places which usually are harvest-fields for this class of depredators. The world of robbers, notwithstanding the incessant surveillance of justice, is a numerous one, and embraces every category of crime. The average number of inmates of the nine prisons of Paris is about ten thousand, of which three thousand are children between twelve and eighteen years of age. In the month of December, 1851, there were arrested three thousand one hundred and fifty-two individuals, of which two thousand three hundred and fifty-two were men, six hundred and thirty children, and but one hundred and fifty women. Two thousand three hundred and fifty-four knew how to read and write; fifty-six only were entirely without instruction. More than one half, or one thousand four hundred and eighty-three men, two hundred and thirteen boys, and three women, were imprisoned for political causes, which, however, must not be understood in the literal sense of the United States, as simply a difference of opinion. A political cause in France may mean an interdicted cry, a malediction upon those in authority, an attempt to assassinate a soldier, or a shot at the President. It comprises every thing, trivial or grave, calculated to disturb the security of the existing government, or bring it into disrepute.

There exist in Paris professors of robbery, who hold regular courses of lectures, in which they not only explain theoretically every species of theft, but give practical illustrations before their pupils upon manikins constructed for this purpose. Their scholars pursue their studies for the usual term of an academic course, acquiring skill, no doubt, at the expense of the public.

Vagabondism and beggary were, until recently, extremely rife. But the late stringent measures of the police have mostly cleared the streets of these nuisances, giving an example which our Atlantic cities would do well to imitate. Individual cases are examined, and the really necessitous are relieved through the legitimate sources of public charity. The "maires," by circulars addressed to the inhabitants of their respective arrondissements, request offerings for the poor to be placed in their hands. In this manner, becoming the systematic dispensators of benevolence, they have the means to relieve the deserving, and to punish imposture, which has as many colors and shapes as a kaleidoscope.

Beggary, like robbery, in the progress of civilization has become an organization. It also has its schools and professors. No people give more generously, and perhaps indiscriminately to distress, than the French. In consequence, benevolence has given birth to the bastard vagabondism, which, true to its parasitical nature, threatens to strangle the very source of its strength. Happily, the government has undertaken so to direct the gifts of charity, as that they shall fulfill their legitimate intent, without becoming a premium to vice. Paris is being freed of these social pests, but it is at the expense, in some degree, of the United States, where they will continue to resort, until salutary stringency convinces them that a land of liberty does not imply a land of vagabondry.

There are some individuals of this class whom the police, thus far, seem to leave in quiet possession of their stands, to which they appear to claim a prescriptive right; possibly that the sight of a certain amount of misery and deformity shall be always before the eyes of the public, to keep active the sentiments of pity and benevolence, and also to afford that species of contrast in social positions, which goes so far toward inculcating individual contentment. None who promenade the Boulevard des Italiens can have failed to remark the woman with wooden legs, seated on the sidewalk, ever plying her inharmonious fiddle to attract the gifts of the charitable. I am told she is one of the worst of the "mauvaises sujettes" of Paris. On the bridges there are always to be found the blind and maimed, generally with some instrument of music. It is gratifying to see with what apparent sympathy and pleasure little children drop into their hats their pennies as they pass.

French benevolence overflows in good works. The natural kindness of heart is greatly stimulated by the exhortations of the clergy. One sees constantly touching and delightful instances of impulsive goodness. One that happened under my windows a few days since occurs to me. A carriage dashing along the street, upset an old woman's stock of apples, and scattered them over the pavement, besides frightening her prodigiously. At that moment a fashionable crowd was pouring out of the Tuileries gardens. Ladies and gentlemen, and even the little children, immediately stopped, re-arranged her cart, picked up her fruit, carefully replacing every apple, condoled with her, gave her money, and sent her in a few minutes on her way rejoicing. The only objectionable feature was, that the apple-woman appeared disposed to exaggerate her misfortune, in order to speculate on the sympathies of the white-kidded gentry around her.

Paris has its foreign vagrants as well as New York. All classes, with an intuitive knowledge of strangers, make them the special objects of their dolorous solicitations. I have been followed for squares by young men, well dressed, plump in flesh, and with every appearance not only of sound health but full stomachs, most pathetically imploring charity on the score of not having had any thing to eat for forty-eight hours, being out of work, having a numerous family, and that it was the first time they had ever begged. If a "sergent de ville" appeared, they disappeared with an alacrity that left no doubt of their agility. One of them told me so often that it was the first time he had begged, that he began evidently to think it a good joke himself, and finally left me unmolested, as one of the initiated.

I was much amused with an incident that befell a friend, who on these occasions, to disembarass himself of their importunities, always buried himself under a feigned ignorance of their desires. A stout vulgar-looking woman, with a bruised eye and other unmistakable evidences of a recent debauch, addressed him in the terms most in vogue, with which, as with a philosopher's stone, they hope to turn into gold all the sympathy that they touch.

Between disgust at her appearance and abstraction of mind, he exclaimed in reply, "Je ne don't speak English pas." "Arrah, is it you yourself that is English then," replied the Amazon in the purest of Hibernian. It is needless to add that it required some silver to arrest her brogue, when she found she had a supposed countryman for an auditor.

The police have also of late cleared the streets of the numerous peddlers, who obstructed the public ways by their awkward carts, which frequently were of dimensions that required as much space to manœuvre in as a Boston truck. They have also made war upon the newspaper boys, who, however, have not been silenced without stoutly battling for their privileges. The places of these noisy, turbulent urchins, making night and day alike hideous with their cries, have been filled by a class of middle-aged men and women, the former of whom may be seen half asleep, and the latter quietly working or nodding, at the corners of most of the principal streets until late at night, either entirely in the open air with a chair to sit upon and a bench in front, filled with the daily journals, sheltered from rain by only an umbrella, or else in a sort of sentry-box, fashioned after those extraordinary habitations of the "toupet" holders in the churches. The regular newspaper carrier is a man of distinction, sports a uniform, and levies contributions at New Year's; but that race which in New York has shown itself able to cope even with the city government, has here been blown out of existence by the mere breath of the prefect of police.

I have nowhere more forcibly realized the truth of the paradox, that the extremes of civilization and barbarism meet. The females at both these degrees of life, supersede the natural affection for children by a depraved attachment for dogs or other animals. Infants in Paris are sent into the country to be reared among strangers, because they would interfere with the fashionable follies of their parents. A Polynesian mother leads her child and carries her dog. I have known a rich carriage, in which were ladies in costly toilets, to be stopped on the boulevards that one of the ladies might alight to pick up, with her own delicately gloved hands, and to place upon the seat beside them, a canine pet, which had gone into convulsions with all the disgusting accompaniments of a dog in a fit. No human sufferer could have received more careful and affectionate treatment. Frequently, more money is lavished on a single worthless animal, to say nothing of the nice attention to its natural wants, than would support a family, while its habits are a never-failing topic for conversation. I love a dog, but it is in its proper place, and not exalted above immortal beings.

If further analogy between these two extremes is required, it is to be found in the labors imposed by the lords of creation, of both races, upon the female sex. We all know what a savage exacts of a woman as a help-meet. Whether the requirement in France is as rigid or not, the effect is the same, and the sex work with an assiduity and severity not at all behind their savage sisters. *They* say French *men* are lazy, and they must work or starve. The fact is a Frenchman's gallantry is of a practical character. His attentions are seldom lavished without an eye to his own pleasure or interest, especially in his intercourse with women. He is not a self-denying animal. If he have a good seat he keeps it. If his feet are on a dry side-walk, it is not so certain but that the weaker vessel must step into the mud to pass him. I am not sure but he is half right when the arrogant incivility of many young American women is considered. Too much deference has a tendency to make them thoughtlessly selfish. I had scarcely landed in the United States before this feature of American society was practically brought home to me. I was sitting in the saloon of one of our Long Island Sound Steamers with a number of spare seats about me, when a young lady, who fancied my position came up to me abruptly, and pointing to my seat, said to her mother, "Here, mother, is a nice place;" and without a look of acknowledgment coolly seated her mother in it, as I rose and offered it, to save myself from more pointed rudeness.

The same indecencies which characterize savage life, are exhibited not only every hour but every minute by the gentlemen of Paris, in the most public promenades, and with a disregard to modesty absolutely painful to the novice in these sights. Habit has undoubtedly reconciled the Parisians to a condition of the streets, and wanton exposure that fills every stranger, not only with disgust, but surprise, that a nation which attaches so high a value to the refinements of art, should tolerate so unnecessary a nuisance. The police that are so effectual in other reforms, could certainly reduce this within the limits of necessity and privacy. Even the beautiful and retired Madeleine is protected solely by notices threatening the penalties of law on those who would defile even a sacred edifice. This nuisance is absolutely forced upon the sight of the public, and engenders a disregard to the proprieties of life, which no home restrictions can fully counterbalance. With many these sentiments may be considered mere prudery. But for their justification I appeal to the standard of female character as exhibited in New England, and I may add in the United States at large, where the sentiment of modesty is carefully guarded as the bulwark of chastity.

But it is not in this respect alone that Barbarism finds its counterpart in Paris. The beautiful Gardens of the Tuileries exhibit daily scenes that are usually confined to the privacy of a nursery. Let any one wander from out of the beaten track of travelers, and he will see sights not to be described, but more common, if possible, among the females than the males, which will convince him that all habits, bad as well as good, converge toward Paris as toward a centre. Paris is indeed the capital of the world; not only of the world of civilization but of barbarism also.

This tendency to extremes has become a national characteristic. Heroic in virtues, demoniacal in crimes, they, with equal facility, glide from the refinements and luxury of civilization into the coarseness and poverty of savage life. I have seen Frenchmen in all conditions, and I have ever found them equally at home amid the saloons of Paris, the wigwams of America, or the more captivating huts of Polynesia. The nature of the Anglo-Saxon is unyielding. The savage must either climb to his elevation or perish. Whereas a Frenchman, whom, to hear speak, you would believe could not exist out of Paris, by his ductility accommodates himself speedily to all races and events. Like hot iron thrust into water he sputters greatly at first, but soon cools into what, at heart, he really is, the true citizen of the world.

If every government which has ruled France for the last half century had not been compelled to devote its energies chiefly to its own preservation, the march of improvement would have been much more rapid. With all their disadvantages, they have made much progress in the work of reform. It is greatly to the credit of Napoleon, that he was inflexible in his exactions of outward decorum at his court, while his police were active in suppressing the more public exhibitions of vice. To judge correctly of what has been done, it is necessary to recur to the public morals bequeathed to his reign by the depravity of the preceding monarchs and the license of the Revolution.

CHAPTER VIII.

SOMETHING CURIOUS FOR MORALISTS.

THE print-shops of Paris swarm with pictures of the most meretricious character, while books and engravings, of the vilest description, are widely though clandestinely circulated. The mind of youth is thus early poisoned through one of the least guarded avenues. In representing the human figure, whether in marble, painting, or engraving, the artist has it in his power to elevate the sentiments of the beholder by giving to his work the expression of what is most noble and pure in human nature. The galleries and museums abound with these elevating triumphs of art. But, unfortunately, interest finds a more profitable market in pandering to depravity.

These pictures are of every class and design, but all more or less illustrative of sensuality. The semi-official organ has of late the following announcement, which if it be carried out to the utter exclusion from public view of every print of an exceptionable character, will be one important step toward guarding youth from contamination: "The authorities are about to take the severest measures to prevent the sale of obscene engravings and books, which are of so much injury to the public morals."

This species of corruption has been doing its work for more than a century almost unheeded. From 1790 to 1793, the demagogues distributed among the people the most filthy and infamous caricatures against Louis XVI. and Marie Antoinette, indifferent to the effect upon the morals, so that they excited hatred toward the unhappy royal family. The public mind thus becoming familiarized with these productions, a morbid taste was created for whatever was most licentious in art. The shops in the Palais Royal and other fashionable quarters began to vie with each other in the production and exhibition of the vilest of compositions. Napoleon caused these abominations to disappear for a while, but in some form or other they have continued from that day to this to do their errand of pollution.

The public sentiment that would support this traffic would not be over-fastidious at any other shape which licentiousness might assume. Consequently, we find that with the same effrontery that the forms of prostitution were exhibited in shop-windows, prostitution itself marched triumphant in the streets. After sunset, no respectable person could enter the Tuileries or other public gardens. Nothing could exceed the indecencies of posture and dress to be seen in the streets; and at the windows of their houses prostitutes exhibited themselves entirely naked. The generation that witnessed these things has not entirely passed away.

The same disposition to shameless exposure among this class is still apparent, but the watchful eye of the police is ever upon them. From the public gardens and the Palais Royal they are entirely excluded. I refer only to those who are registered on the books of the police. Their deportment in the streets is no worse than that of the same class in our Atlantic cities. But I shall show in another place that they are the least dangerous to public morals of the class of females, who are at once the victims of the corruptions and the corrupters of Paris. At the risk of incurring the charge of unnecessarily exposing the vices of society, I shall give some statements from authentic data, believing that, to contend understandingly with an enemy, we should know his resources.

Prostitution in the United States is left alone so long as it does not intrude itself upon the public by the violation of some ordinance. History demonstrates, that wherever there are large collections of men there will be courtesans. The most cruel persecutions, and the severest legislation have been equally futile to eradicate this evil. French legislation assumes the ground that they are an inevitable adjunct to society in masses, and undertakes to regulate what it can not suppress. Much can be said on the relative effects of the two systems upon public morals. One thing is certain, that the French have succeeded, to a great extent, in diminishing the frightful physical suffering which has resulted to humanity from this vice within the last five centuries, and that they have hopes, if not of eradicating it altogether, of making the scourge comparatively innoxious.

They do more than this. Every public woman is required to be registered, that she may be under the immediate surveillance of the police. No improper houses are allowed to exist near a school, public institution, or church. A female who has become "une fille inscrité" (and no one is allowed openly to pursue this "métier" without becoming so), is subjected to most despotic and stringent regulations for the preservation of public health. These are of a nature sufficient to eradicate any lingering traces of modesty, and every subterfuge is practiced to evade their dreaded requirements.

When a girl applies for her license, she is seriously admonished upon the folly of her intentions. Efforts are made to terrify or disgust her with her proposed life. If she be very young, and from the country, her family are written to, that they may be induced to provide for her. In many instances the police actually take them to their paternal homes, only to be, as it generally happens, ejected anew. When there is no other resource, they shut them up in the Hospital St. Lazare, give them work, and make every effort possible to reclaim them. If they finally persist in their design, there is no alternative but to place their names upon the fatal register. It is at their option at any moment to have them erased, by giving evidence of their intention to lead orderly lives. But while they remain registered, they must carry about them tickets, on which are inscribed their domiciles, and the results of the periodical professional visits to which they are subjected.

In my first inquiries, I found that the most exaggerated ideas obtained in regard to the number of known prostitutes in Paris. In two instances they were computed at fifty thousand. This arises from taking the numbers to be seen in their favorite haunts as a standard for all Paris. They are concentrated in comparatively few quarters. I am indebted to A. J. B. Parent Duchatelet's valuable work for the following statistics, not without interest, as they relate to that unfortunate class from whom sprung the repentant Magdalen loved by Christ.

In 1820 there were registered at the bureau of police for that year	2746
1821	2913
1822	2902
1827	2471
1830	3028
1831	3260
1832	3588

This table shows a gradual but not very rapid increase. At the same ratio it would give for 1852, about six thousand, or just five times the number that existed in Boston eight years since.

From 16th March, 1816, to 31st April, 1831, the total number registered was twelve thousand six hundred and seven, of which Paris furnished four thousand seven hundred and forty-four, and the provinces the remainder, except four hundred and eighty-two, who were of foreign origin.

In 1831, there was one prostitute to every two hundred and fifty-five inhabitants; the proportions to the various quarters varied materially.

Rue St. Honoré had one to every fifty-two inhabitants, while the quartier du Mont de Piété had but one to every seven thousand four hundred and forty-two. The Ile St. Louis, with a population of seventy-five thousand, not one.

The causes of prostitution were found, out of five thousand one hundred and eighty-three cases, to be these:

Absolute destitution	1441

Of these cases, one girl who had applied had been three days without food. In the month of November last, a girl of eighteen years of age committed suicide to avoid this life into which her own mother was forcing her.

Loss of parents and expulsion from homes	1255
To sustain old and infirm parents	37
Older sisters to support their younger	29
Widows to support their children	23
Ran away from the provinces	280
Brought to Paris, seduced, and abandoned	404
Domestics seduced by their masters and sent off	289
Mistresses abandoned by their lovers, and having no other resource.	1425

Another examination furnished some unaccountable exceptions to the ordinary reasons assigned for this choice of life. For instance, at the time of registration, there were three midwives, one artist, six instructresses of music, and three women having respectively permanent annual incomes of two hundred, five hundred, and one thousand francs.

The ages of 3250 were as follows:

Of 10	years old	2
11	" "	3
12	" "	3
13	" "	6
14	" "	20
15	" "	51
15 to 20	" "	1250
20 " 30	" "	1909
30 " 40	" "	239
40 " 50	" "	60
50 " 60	" "	4
60 " 65	" "	3

Of 4470 born at Paris, all were of the laboring classes except four.

2332 could not sign their names.
1780 " very badly.
110 " well.
248 ascertained nothing of.

Duchâtelet considers the manufactories as the "centres of corruption, of which we should deplore the pernicious effects while admiring their productions."

By statistics which probably would not be borne out elsewhere, he demonstrates that this class of women enjoy better health than mothers in general. The average of sickness to each is ten days per annum, for all maladies, and less than two and a half for those of a grave character.

Society in the United States recognizes but two grades of female virtue. From the moment a woman becomes unchaste, the irrevocable decree of banishment from her former position goes forth against her, and she sinks at once to the lowest level in the social scale. Reformation becomes almost hopeless. The impassable gulf of public opinion is a far more effectual barrier to vice than the municipal severities which await the "fille inscrite." Virtue has but one language every where, but it is the greater or less degree, which regulates the moral existence of a community. The standard of public opinion in France, on this subject, is widely different from that of the United States. Hence between the legalized prostitute and the pure wife, there exists a variety of social grades, each regulated by its own arbitrary code of opinion, and each distinct in its own sphere.

The influence of this sliding scale of morals is felt throughout the nation. It modifies every character, and penetrates to every fireside. To the student then, who would investigate the causes of national differences, it becomes an indispensable study.

The woman who has sunk her virtue to the purely mercenary character of the public courtesan has become too degraded to have much influence in the ruin of society. She is the sad fruits, and not the cause of its corruption. It is widely different when beauty, talent, wealth, and position combine their efforts to strew the path of vice with flowers. To the moralist there is but the one grand distinction, founded alike on the welfare of mankind and the behests of revelation. Whatever tends to disturb the sanctity of the institution of marriage, is so much weight thrown in the scale of corruption, and no extent of individual happiness that may occasionally arise from ties unsanctioned by God can compensate for the wrong done society.

The term "Lorette" designates that class of women, who, by external decorum or temporary connections, are enabled to evade the dreadful position of "filles inscrites," to which otherwise their mode of livelihood would inevitably doom them. They are subdivided into several ranks, and can scarcely be distinguished, except at their own option, from the more virtuous classes of their sex. Vanity prompts many to make a display in dress and equipage that infallibly betrays their profession. But the newly arrived stranger would be slow to suspect that the young females, whom he meets in the most fashionable quarters, generally in pairs, with miens so modest and tôilets so simple, are but a superior class of prostitutes. If he watches them, he will find that they are on their way to the Valentino or some other ball-room, to which they all have free entrance. Let him enter, and he will perceive that their dress is in general in accordance with their manners, which are quiet, lady-like, and graceful. For an acquaintance, a formal introduction from a friend is necessary, and they exact and receive the same courtesy in public which would be shown to the virtuous.

This is their external character while under the eyes of the police. It is not for me to lift the vail that covers their actual condition. But the licentiousness of this class is the more corrupting, because it is gilded with a refinement of manner and language that strips vulgarity of much of its repulsion, and too effectually conceals the poisonous reptile that lies coiled at its root.

The majority of these style themselves "femmes galantes." In general, they form relations of interest with some one man, from whom it becomes their greatest solicitude to hide their amours with their lovers in general. They often are capable of inspiring the deepest attachments, notwithstanding their known habits.

The powers of captivation possessed by those who combine the graces and charms of a cultivated mind to personal beauty, and that perfection of toilet rarely found out of Paris, is prettily illustrated by the Blue Fairy tale of Stahl.

"One day the Blue Fairy descended to earth with the courteous intention of distributing to all the young girls of the different nations the treasures of beauty which she brought with her.

"Her dwarf Amaranth sounded his horn, and instantly a young girl of every nation presented herself at the foot of the Blue Fairy's throne. All these together made quite a crowd, as you will imagine. This happened a long time before the Revolution of July, 1830.

"The good Blue Fairy said to her friends, 'I desire that you may not have cause to complain of the gifts I am about to present you. It is not in my power to give each of you the same thing, but if I were to make such a uniformity in my favors, would it not make them less valuable?' As time is precious to fairies, she said very little, ended her speech there, and proceeded to the dispensing her gifts. Nobody appeared annoyed at it.

"She gave the young girl who represented all the Castiles, locks so black and long that she could make a mantilla of them.

"To the Italian, she gave eyes as bright and burning as an eruption of Vesuvius in the middle of the night.

"To the Turkish girl, a figure as round as the moon, and as soft as eider-down.

"To the English girl, an aurora borealis to tint her cheeks, her lips, and shoulders.

"To the German, teeth like her own, and that which is no

more valuable than fine teeth, but which has its value—a tender heart all ready to love.

"To the Russian, the dignity of a queen.

"Then going into details, she put gayety on the lips of the Neapolitan—wit in the brain of the Irish girl—good sense in the heart of a Flemish girl; and when nothing remained to be given, she arose to take her flight.

"'And I?' said the Parisian to her—detaining her by the floating border of her blue tunic.

"'I had forgotten you!'

"'Entirely forgotten, madam.'

"'You were too near me, and I did not see you. But what can I do now? My bag of gifts is empty.' The fairy reflected an instant, then calling to her by a sign all these charming beauties, she said to them:

"'You are good, because you are beautiful—it remains for you to repair a great error of mine; in my dispensation I have forgotten your sister of Paris.

"'Let each one of you, I beg, share a part of the present I made her with our Parisian. You will lose little and bestow a great deal.'

"Who could refuse a fairy, and above all, the Blue Fairy? With that graciousness which happiness always confers, these girls approached in turn the forgotten Parisian, and threw her as they passed—one a part of her black hair, another a tint of her rosy complexion; this one a beam of her joyousness, that what she could of her sensibility; and so it happened that the Parisian, so poor, so obscure, so eclipsed by her sisters, found herself in an instant, by this generous division, richer and more attractively endowed than any of her companions."

Foreign youth in Paris, apart from the moral restraints of domestic life, and isolated from those circles which formed at

A MODERN ASPASIA

once its safety and pleasure at home, is thrown into a focus of no ordinary temptations. The rules of the most select of these coteries are as rigid as those of the salons of the Faubourg St. Germain. To be admitted to their reunions, it is necessary to be properly presented. They form societies; they give the most sumptuous of dinners and the most attractive of soirées. Some allow full license of gambling, and a freedom of manners, seductive to libertines who come to lose their money and their health; while others, renowned artists themselves, collect about them the most distinguished names of France. The fact that Mlle. Rachel has several children by different fathers, is no bar to her soirées being the most brilliant of this brilliant capital in point of male intellect, rivaled, perhaps, in this respect, only by those of George Sand.

The race of Ninon d'Enclos is not extinct. The few that rise to the pinnacle of their demoralizing career establish rules as arbitrary and unalterable as those of the Medes and Persians. Some receive their friends only between ten and four o'clock in the day, devoting their evenings to the society of their chosen lovers, whom they frequently support, and in visiting places of amusement.

One of the strangest features of this depravity, and illustrative of a harmony in degradation scarcely conceivable, were it not recorded by Duchâtelet, is the formation by the élite of these courtesans of a clientage, subject to the following conditions: They receive only *married* men, mutually acquainted, to the number even of fifty. The circle once formed, no new member can be admitted, except by the presentation of several of the habitués, and the consent of all; and should any one become a widower he is at once expelled.

Let not the grand ladies of society be deluded into the idea that the rules of conventional morality are solely their property. The audacious complaint of the Parisian mistress, who one day said to her lover, "When will you cease to compromise me? You still continue to appear in public with your wife," will rectify this error.

What has been the book of the season? The history of a Lorette. What has been the play of the season? Her life dramatized by the genius of Dumas. It ran one hundred successive nights, producing more than three hundred thousand francs. Week after week has the Vaudeville been crowded by a fashionable audience, of whom not a few were obliged to engage their seats fifteen days in advance. I have seen gray-headed men and women, as well as the young and sympathetic, weep like children as they gazed upon the fictitious scenes of what was sorrowful reality to this erring girl. Her life was, after all marked by no unusual incident. It was happier than the common lot, because she died before old age brought with it that decay, to them more dreadful than death itself. The toy of Paris while living, now that she is in her grave, she has called forth a sympathy and created an interest, that a Howard or a Dix might in vain labor to excite in the cause of afflicted humanity. True, there is a moral in her life. There is in every life. Of such as hers, the Aspasia of her age, the friend of the Prince of Condé and of Madame de Maintenon, long since said, with a deep sigh of regret, as she recalled her career, "Had any one proposed to me such an existence, I should have died of fright and grief." If such be the deliberate conclusion of her, who, the slave of one passion, preserved to an age seldom attained, wealth, beauty, and an intellect that made her the idol of numerous friends, what must be the reality of those lesser stars who are bought and sold as cattle by the beauty of their limbs and the freshness of their years? The name of this frail one was, singularly enough, Marie Madeleine (Mary Magdalen), though she adopted another while living. Her education that of a peasant girl. Once launched on the sea of Parisian dissipation, her rare beauty and rarer taste made her the butterfly idol of the hour. She dressed magnificently, but with perfect propriety. She expended more than one hundred thousand francs a year, and was ever in debt. Her diamonds, horses, and cashmeres were the envy and admiration of the female world. The luxury of her apartments it would be difficult to describe. They were all that wealth and art could produce even in Paris. The numerous articles of her toilet were of gold or silver, bearing the initials and crests of the titled donors. Furniture of rose-wood, and buhl, Gobelin carpets, vases of Sèvres and China, statuettes of Dresden, and the most exquisite paintings of Saxony, hangings of satin, velvet, and lace, give but a faint idea of the sumptuousness with which she was surrounded. The same clock which had sounded the hours for Madame de Pompadour and Madame du Barri struck for her likewise the passing of time. The most beautiful works of modern art were intermingled with the rarest antiques, with that nice perfection of the coquetry of beauty, that none but the beautiful possess. It is true she ruined those who paid for this luxury, but she astonished the most refined of her sex by the extent to which she carried the costly finish of the minutest details of her wardrobe and toilet. A style of living like this is not uncommon among the Lorettes, though few attain to the magnificence with which she was surrounded.

She was consumptive, and the physicians who attended her, say she desired death to hasten her release from a life which, with its accumulated elegancies, was but a weary burden. Her wish was soon accomplished, for she died at twenty-one. Dumas has made a touching tale of her experience. To what extent he has idealized, it is difficult to ascertain. There are no improbabilities, and the story is in a few words as follows:

Marie was loved by a young man, who finally won her heart by the tender interest he manifested in her health, the only genuine sentiments of affection that she had ever experienced. The new and purer sentiments thus awakened, led her to regard her past life with horror. She persuaded her lover to retire with her to a village near Paris, where the scenes of rustic beauty recalled to her the innocence of her earlier years. In contrast with what she had been, this was virtue, and it brought her peace and a partial restoration to health. Dumas, however, with that spirit which is the bane of the literature of his country, instead of depicting the chaste joys which are the evidence of true affection, debases the passion of love by a picture of delirious sensuality, which, if true, must have inevitably led to satiety and disgust. So thinks the father of Armand, her lover, who has discovered their retreat, and, scandalized at the position of his son, in vain endeavors to withdraw him from his infatuation. As a last resource, he visits Marie, appeals to her love for Armand, and, finally, makes her promise to leave him in a way that any return shall become impossible. Marie fulfills her promise by suddenly returning to her former life, plunging into dissipation with a reckless determination to abridge her miserable existence. Armand, believing her false and perfidious, leaves the country in despair. Before his return she dies, and not till then does he learn the real motive of her inconstancy.

Such is the heroine and such the tale; a type of that class of literature which has in France the same relative influence and success, as do in America the equally dramatic, but far more moral writings of Hawthorne or Longfellow. Bulwer in the Caxtons does justice to the character of the light literature of France. It saps the very foundation of chastity. Another class of writers must arise, before this spring of pollution will give forth cleansing waters. Balzac is the favorite of ladies. Brilliant, witty, and keen, overflowing with that quality so essential to success among those who themselves so thoroughly exemplify it, he becomes the more dangerous from being so "spirituel." His amusing caricature of "The Little Miseries of Married Life," a book elegantly got up, terminates with the moral, that the cure consists in each party, leaving the other in perfect freedom to form such liaisons as fancy suggests, thus creating the anomalous domestic state of "ménages à quatre." I quote the text, "*C'est qu'il n'y a d'heureux que les ménages à quatre.*"

What adds to the interest of "La Dame aux Camelias," is the fact that the accomplished actress who fills the rôle of Marie recalls, in her own life, many striking incidents of her's whose character she represents. Like her she is consumptive, and has shortened her days by dissipation. It is said, also, that the principal friend of Marie has become her's. She displays rich jewels, at all events. Her husband, from whom she has been separated seven years, sits in front as leader of the orchestra. I am told, when Dumas asked her to play the part of Marie, she said to him, "Pray, how do these creatures dress?"

There is yet another class of these females, blending in some degree with that of Lorettes, yet in the main, distinct. I refer to mistresses. Their influence is felt from the Tuileries to the meanest hovel. Louis Napoleon, false at all events in this point to the example of his uncle, sets a pernicious example to the nation of avowed concubinage. The facility with which these relations are formed, and the ease with which they are ruptured, is a serious bar to matrimony, which by French law once entered into, can never be dissolved, whatever causes of misery may arise. The severity of the statute doubtless has its weight in producing the too general state of concubinage. In 1850, the proportion of illegitimate to legitimate births in Paris was one in four; some years it is greater. It has reached one in two; throughout France, it is one to thirteen.

In thirty-three years there have been two million two hundred and eighty-seven thousand nine hundred and forty-four illegitimate births. These figures, however, do not furnish the same guide as to the number of ephemeral unions that they would to those of marriages, from the fact that the proportion of children born to the former is much less than to the latter. Truth, however, constrains the admission that they often give evidence of a sincerity of affection not always to be witnessed in the married state. These connections are more common in cities than in the country, and among the poorer classes spring rather from motives of temporary interest or convenience, than from libertinism. Unfortunately for the sacred ties of family, the government makes itself literally a nursing mother to the fruits of these unions; and by its mistaken generosity not only deprives concubinage of one of its most powerful checks, but undermines the parental sentiment.

The number of foundling hospitals has greatly decreased within twenty years, but the desire to prevent infanticide still keeps in existence more than one hundred and fifty throughout France. The government give encouragement to those who will retain their children, but receive all who are abandoned by their parents. Previous to 1837 no questions were asked, and no one was seen; the infant was received in a "*tour*," a sort of moving box, which, once turned, shut out the child forever from the sight of its mother, unless she formally reclaimed it. These "tours" were abolished, and certificates of abandonment, signed by a commissary of police, required. This compelled the parents to acknowledge their intention. The result of the closing of the "tours" showed so rapidly an increase of infanticide, that the clandestine reception has been lately restored. Mothers, after abandoning their children, frequently present themselves at the hospitals as nurses, with the very dubious chance of being paid for the care of their own infants. Nurses receive from four to eight francs per month, and the children are taken to their homes in the country. At the expiration of two years they are at liberty to give them up, when, if no other nurses can be secured, they are sent to the orphan department. The children are provided for until they are twenty-one years of age. The establishment for them of agricultural colonies has been found beneficial, both in point of health and education. The number received at the "Hospice des Enfants Trouvés," at Paris, during the past ten years, is fifty-one thousand four hundred and fifty-seven—an annual average of five thousand one hundred and forty-five. The total number placed out at nurse in 1850, was twenty-two thousand six hundred and fifteen. The expense of this establishment for the ten years ending in 1851, has been $3,464,732, and the average mortality one in four.

By these institutions the government undoubtedly prevent infanticide to a certain extent. But to what degree of moral abasement or personal destitution must those be reduced who leave to the authorities only the dreadful alternative of preserving life by the destruction of the maternal instinct! An American may well be pardoned for doubting the policy, in every point of view, of so effectually screening the individual from the results of crime or improvidence, at the expense of the State.

In extenuation of the depravity of the lower classes, there are to be pleaded ignorance and misery. Among the higher, a perverted moral education and extraordinary temptation.

That this corruption is, to a great extent, owing to the literature most in vogue, is evident to any one who studies its character. The following extracts, drawing a parallel between wife and mistress, is from the pen of an accomplished writer, Léon Gozlan. It is taken from a work which embodies the first literary talent of France, illustrated by the beautiful and amusing productions of the pencil of Gavarni. It is in every respect a book of "luxe." I mention this simply to show that the sentiments quoted are not, as in America or England, the mercenary productions of unprincipled authors, who seek refuge in obscurity from offended public opinion, but the offspring of accomplished minds, and paraded before the public with the luxury and freedom which are solely the birthright of legitimacy.

"*Mistress.*—This word has no exact equivalent, in the majority of other languages, for the reason, that the object which it indicates with other nations is not, as with the French, a being who loves and is loved. Foreigners have borrowed from the coarse vocabulary of sensuality, terms more or less wounding, to indicate the woman chosen from all others—whom in France we call a mistress. Their unworthy epithets pitilessly dishonor what ours elevates:—they stain with infamy that which we adorn with flowers;—they bespatter with insult the brow which we crown. With them, the mistress is still the ancient slave, standing in the chimney-corner, or crouching in the shadow of the marble steps of the palace; but with us the mistress precedes chivalry and royalty, she followed Rénaud and Tancred to the Crusades, she shared the throne with Charles VII., Francis I., Henry III., Henry IV.—Agnes Sorel, Diana of Poitiers, Gabrielle, Montespan, noble women—loving hearts—charming geniuses! Without them, the princes whom they ruled would have had neither courage, delicacy, loyalty, nor distinction. They would only have been *kings*."

"*Wife.*—I consider the wife in contradistinction to the mistress, as representing the solid, noble, and useful side of life—the architectural side as it were—without which there would be for man neither repose, shelter, nor dignity.

"She is the healthy fruit which contains all the embryos (or buds) of family and society.

"Take away the wife and you almost annihilate the mother, not merely she who produces children, but she whose mission it is to love them tenderly, to bring them up, to make of them men and citizens. Thus a woman, in marriage, is nothing less than society itself, because it is she who makes its force, its greatness, its support, and its continuance.

"This is what I think of the mistress—she is the young and smiling side of life, its month of May, its spirit, its fresh poetry, imagination!—

"Take away the mistress, and you necessarily take away all the grace and beauty which imagination, poetry, and genius give birth to in the sphere of ideality, that is, the arts. Thus it can easily be shown that the finest works (selected by chance) in painting, sculpture, and poetry, were inspired by those independent women whom, in the present day, we call mistresses. I will not quote;—I should have to quote all—to inclose the whole world of art, in quotation marks. This is a truth easily proved, a truth rather wounding to the wife, but why should she be wounded? She is reason, the mistress is only wit; she is order, the mistress only enthusiasm; she is good sense, the mistress only delirium; she is the earth, the mistress only heaven; not—let me hasten to explain—not the heaven to which we aspire for our good deeds, but that where we should desire to go to do no sort of deed, not even a good one."

The same author, after dividing mistresses into two general classes, viz., those who love you, and those who love your money, subdivides the last as follows:

"Those who inhabit the Rue de Grammont at three hundred francs a month, gloves, and flowers.

"Rue du Helder, four hundred francs a month, and a groom.

"Rue Saint Lazare and Mont Blanc, five hundred francs a month, and a one-horse carriage.

"Faubourg du Roule, two thousand francs a month, the pavillion of a hotel, two carriages, a cook, a footman, and two horses.

"To complete the list, it is necessary to cite those who love, for their money, princes and dukes, and who are supported in corresponding style."

These are the females to be seen daily in the Champs Elysées, and at their boxes at the Grand Opera or the Italiens, rivaling in equipage and dress, and excelling in beauty, all others of their sex.

Unfortunately, there is still another shade of immorality, of darker hue, having its source equally in the strongest passions and purest sentiments of the human heart. It is the fearful revenge nature takes for her violatad laws, whenever the principle of religion is not sufficiently strong to bind it in chains. To trace it to its origin, we must begin with the system of education. In France, toward both sexes, it is one of restraint. The girls are either educated by governesses, or placed in boarding-schools, where they are kept in rigid seclusion. The boys are similarly treated. The external world is regarded as one wholly of depravity, from the corruption of which the chief security is in ignorance, or bolts and bars. I know no more pitiable sight in Paris, when contrasted with the free and buoyant spirits of American youth, than the long double files of boys in uniform belonging to the several schools, paraded under the inspection of their teachers, through the public gardens for air and exercise. They remind me, as in long files they drag along their spiritless limbs of the sluggish crawling of caterpillars. There is no liveliness of tongue or manner. Night and day they are guarded as securely as if they were criminals. The same *preventive* system, that obtains in every department of the government, prevents them from acquiring those habits of self-reliance and early development of character, to be seen in the youth of the United States. It is true the temptations are greater. But the result shows that what is gained in present security, is lost in ultimate power of resistance. They are not trusted. Consequently, the firmest basis of virtue is wanting. Curiosity and desire are awakened, and I have the best French authority for ascribing the dissipations into which the youth almost invariably plunge as soon as manhood brings them liberty, to the restraint of their school days. In the United States it has passed almost into a proverb, that ministers' children become the most dissipated men; but it is only in instances where severity supersedes reason.

Confinement being more natural to girls, is less to be deprecated; still, it is the actual application of suspicion in lieu of confidence. They are carefully screened from all outward evils, but in that knowledge, which is in general reserved with us for riper years, they are early adepts. The mind becomes familiarized to a standard of virtue very different from that which regulates the conduct of American mothers. While there are scarcely any theoretical concealments in families of what must sooner or later be known, a conventional platform of morality is erected on a foundation of sand. The reverse of the legal rule, that every one is innocent until proved guilty, sways the minds of the guardians of youth. They are considered guilty, unless known to be innocent. Hence they must ever be in sight. No better germ for intrigue could be devised; for such is the infirmity of human nature, that what is prohibited becomes doubly desirable.

In America, mothers rely upon the principles of virtue implanted by them from infancy in their children for their security The young of both sexes mix freely together. If there can be shown to result from this confidence, and early accustoming them to mingle in the amusements of their years, a condition of things in after-life such as no one disavows to exist in France, then it will be well to practice more restraint. There is, in the United States, a class of young men to whom chastity is as dear as truth. Their characters are due to their early associations with the pure of that sex, which gives them mothers and sisters.

Female virtue is as strong in their honor as in its own innocence. To assert this in France would cause a smile of incredulity. Such differences does education produce in natures essentially the same.

The French girl is fenced in on every side by a rigid conventionality based upon distrust of the male sex. She can not converse with a friend or even a relative, more distant than a brother, except in sight of her parents or appointed guardians. She never appears alone in the streets. In society she is fettered to observances that render her as isolated as the inmate of a harem. The governess of my children, whose family bears one of the most distinguished of the ancient names of France, but who are now so reduced, that the sole choice left her was either a convent or to gain her own subsistence, was a single lady, and not particularly youthful. Wishing one evening to visit a friend who lived in the vicinity, she accepted my escort, but when within a square or so of the house, she requested me to leave her, as it would compromise her were she seen with a gentleman not of her family.

Another single lady of rank, of sufficient years to be entitled to some of the liberties of a Madame, told me that when she first appeared alone in the street, she blushed and felt as if every body was looking at her for doing something wrong.

Marriage becomes their declaration of independence. A young, timid, modest girl, whose heart would palpitate at the thought of an infringement of the slightest of these rules of conventional etiquette, blooms at once into an experienced matron, versed in all the arts of the world. Her first object has been to obtain freedom. In this she is fully successful. The action which in an American girl would be construed only as innocence, would ruin the reputation of her French sister. The reverse becomes true after marriage. No American woman could escape censure were she to follow the example of a French wife.

Affection has no part or lot in a French marriage. Where it exists, it is only as an exception to the rule. The union is based on wealth or position. I am assured by the sex that has the most at stake, that the question invariably in relation to the lady, is, not whether she is beautiful or deformed, good or bad, but what is the amount of her "*dot*," or dowry, to which, in addition, they sometimes inquire if she have any scrofulous taint. Briefly, they are marriages of convenience. The business is one of negotiation between the gentleman and the parents of the intended. She may not even know that there is such an event in contemplation until her fate is decided. The liberty which is in prospect, contrasting so sweetly with present confinement, undoubtedly has much weight in reconciling the minds of the maidens to a custom which, in the United States, would be considered an intolerable tyranny.

Sixty and sixteen are thus often brought together. The first marriage I witnessed was of a couple who had between them well-nigh that difference of years. Strange to say, while the priest was pronouncing their nuptial benediction in one part of the church, a funeral was in progress in another.

French hearts can no more subsist without love than their neighbors. Indeed, impulsive and sympathetic, the necessity of an emotion is a portion of their nature. It is easy to perceive what becomes of a beauty without dower. The plain, God help them! He often does; for hopeless of success in human love, they obtain that consolation in religion that nothing else can bestow.

Those who marry, love their partners if they can. If not, somebody else. Appearances, however, must be preserved. A French woman would die with shame to be supposed to be capable of an elopement. That would be a violation of the proprieties of life. She has no scruples, however, as to receiving her lover under her husband's roof, provided he does not know it. An

English woman will seldom continue to deceive one man, when her heart is another's. She considers it a lesser sin to be true to her affection, than to eat the bread of the man she betrays. Extraordinary as it may appear, you will hear the former abuse, without stint, the latter, not for having a lover, but for proclaiming the fact.

Where there is so much need for it, there is always much mutual discretion. Husbands and wives are blind where all other eyes are open. There is no violation of faith. The one bargained for liberty, the other for money; love would be welcomed were he to make his home with them. Not arriving, each, like Celebs, goes in quest of a companion

The caricaturists show up the condition of domestic affairs in many amusing ways. I have before me an evening paper, containing a print of two ladies of the "haut ton," in conversation. One says, "Yes, my dear, my husband has had the infamy to bring this creature into my house, under my eyes! and that when he knows the only affection I have in the world is two hundred leagues from here!"

The other replies—"Men are cowards!"

Balzac's Philosophy of Conjugal Life in Paris, has an engraving of a tender scene between an enamored couple, the lady exclaiming, "My friend, I sacrifice to you all I owe to the best of husbands. If you ever deceive me, Maurice, O! this would be very bad!"

"Le meilleur des maris," and "Le bon Dieu" of a French intriguante are pronounced in the same tone, and with equal respect, and each is about equally distant from the heart.

I would not be understood as implying there are no happy and true households. Far from it. There are undoubtedly very many. Nevertheless, I describe a reality which no one in France pretends to disguise. Yet I am constrained to believe that, in proportion as a certain class of my own countrywomen imitate the fashionable follies of Paris, they acquire a taste also for its corruptions. A friend, whose experience in his native city led him somewhat harshly to declare he would never marry one of his own country-women, after being initiated into certain circles in New York, to which his title and position made him welcome, declared that city to be less moral than Paris.

Every man is believed to have his mistress. It does not follow that there are no exceptions, only that no amount of argument could induce the belief. It would require as much circumstantial and positive evidence to show the contrary here, as it would with us to prove that a married man kept one. The virtue of mankind, from Adam down, has never been remarkable for its sternness, in sight of the blandishments of Eve and her descendants. My readers, then, need be under no fears of a breach of charity, in believing that a Parisian, after showing his filial respect in making a marriage of convenience, seldom fails to console himself by the more agreeable tie of love.

In a little comedy frequently performed at the French theatre, in which is exposed the condition of domestic life, arising from the substitution of mistress for wife, the plot terminates, after a quarrel, in the marriage of the couple. This is called "The End of the Romance."

Whether there be more romance or not in illegal than in legal unions, moralists have found it expedient to establish societies for the promotion of marriages and the legitimation of children. That of St. François Regis was established in 1826. Up to January 1, 1852, it had taken cognizance of twenty-three thousand two hundred and thirty-four disorderly households, and had sought to recall to religion and good morals forty-six thousand four hundred and sixty-eight individuals. During that period it had succeeded in procuring the legitimation of seventeen thousand children. Of one thousand two hundred and thirty-four marriages which it had induced among couples living in concubinage, eight hundred and sixty-one had been in that state from one to ten years, sixty-eight from ten to fifteen years, twenty-eight from fifteen to twenty years, twenty-one from twenty to thirty years, and ten from thirty to forty years. Several of the parties were from sixty to eighty years of age, and one couple had lived together forty years and three months previous to their legalized union.

I can not close this chapter without relating, on the authority of Madame de Créquy, an historical fact, illustrative of the idiosyncrasy of taste of French ladies. After the first Revolution there was formed a society which imitated the costumes and manners of the ancient Greeks and Romans. It was at a period when much was said about patriotism and the want of children for the Republic. The ladies all aspired to the glory of producing citizens. Those who were "enceinte" made the greatest possible public display of their condition, while those less fortunate invented a style of dress for the street, which should at least give them that reputation. The time and money usually expended in dressing the hair, were devoted in preference to this novel fashion.

CHAPTER IX

AMUSEMENTS.

UNQUESTIONABLY to an American the most "bizarre" of all the sights of Paris is a Carnival Ball at the Grand Opera. The pit being boarded over, and made level with the stage, forms a ball-room of magnificent proportions. The boxes, unless previously hired, are free to the public. The orchestra, two hundred and more in number, led by the famous Musard, is a combination of the best musical talent of France. These balls commence at midnight, and terminate at six o'clock, Sunday mornings. Costumes or dominoes and masks are required of women, but men can enter in plain clothes; the former are free, the latter pay two dollars for admission.

MASKED BALL AT THE GRAND OPERA.

The attempt to give an accurate idea of the mad, bewildering scene, as the visitor first enters the gorgeous hall, would be futile. His eyes are dazzled by the lights, his ears stunned by the united

A CARNIVAL COSTUME.

shouts and merriment of thousands of throats, and his senses bewildered by the variety of costumes, colors, and shapes, which are whirling with frightful activity and extravagant gestures through the mazes of waltz, polka, or quadrille. Collect specimens of all the costumes from Adam and Eve down (of course I exclude the fig-leaves),—of every nation under the sun, and add to them every variety and shade of color; intermingle monsters from the briny deep; sprinkle them thick with shapes hot from Tantalus; invent figures which have no likeness in any created thing; galvanize the whole, so that every tongue, muscle, limb, and lineament, shall assume a convulsive activity that threatens immediate rupture, and make the mass move in harmony with the wild, thrilling, furious notes of a band, that could lend excitement to the very stones themselves, and you would still fail to realize the scene.

The favorite costume among the women is a species of simplified or reformed Bloomerism, consisting of (I proceed upward), satin slippers, silk stockings to the knee, light satin or silk breeches, the legs of different colors, and the whole surmounted by a sort of semi-shirt, or open chemise, beautifully laced, and leaving mostly in "*puris naturalibus*" that portion of the corporeal charms which ladies, in fashionable assemblies, are ever reluctant to hide when there is any thing to display. These costumes vary according to the fancies of the wearers, but their numbers indicate the natural desire of the sex to escape the thralldom of petticoats; a weakness I would by no means counsel them to yield to, as it gives too palpable evidence that in trousers they are greatly inferior in grace to man. Indeed, it is most amusing to witness their attempts at masculine activity or manly dignity, which are sure to terminate in a duck-like pantomime, showing that they are excellent waddlers, but bad walkers. The dress, however, allowed full liberty of motion, in which, I supposed, consisted its charm, for I have seen several avail themselves of it, by springing upon the backs of their partners; and in one instance, one, by no means of ethereal lightness, seated herself upon the shoulders of her gallant, and there, triumphant, made him finish the two-storied quadrille.

Every species of license, not purely beastly, is allowed; loving embraces, jovial slaps, and seductive pinches, meet with no chilling response; kisses explode on all sides like the popping of champagne corks; jokes fly about like swallows in spring-time; "double-entendres" and "jeux d'esprits" fall as thick and fast as hail. Amid all the "giving as good as he sends," perfect good-humor prevails. The lowest apologize for accidents with the grace of drawing-rooms. In a rush by some frolicsome damsels, I was borne back so suddenly, that my heel came down with violence upon the toe of my neighbor in the rear; the pain was so sudden, that nature found instant relief in the common, but unmentionable French exclamation in all such cases known and approved; but the words were not cold on his tongue when he turned to me and apologized, although I was the innocent aggressor.

Hebrews, Greeks, and Romans, were intermining like old and familiar friends, with the courtiers of Louis XIV., and "distingués" of our day. There was a sprinkling of Iroquois, Highlanders, and all the picturesque garbs of Europe. The wardrobes of every theatre must have been in requisition for this "solemnité." It afforded me an opportunity of practically ascertaining that, in respect to them decidedly, "Distance lends enchantment to the view." Amid the variety and oddity displayed, there seemed to be no room for any thing new, when, of a sudden there arose a shout of terror, followed by a recoil among all the masks on the floor. Twelve non-descript devils in shining black suits, fitting tight to their skins, with long green hair falling about their waists, fiery red faces and horns, tails of the same color, barbed, and more than a fathom in length, had burst into the circle of dancers, overturning all in their way, and leaping and shrieking in a manner so vigorous and unexpected, that the throng, for the instant seemed impressed with the idea, that Satan had actually sent them a deputation to see how his work was going on. Men or demons, they soon fraternized with the prettiest girls, and with tails in hand, actively illustrated the vulgar contortions of a dance I shall not attempt to describe. They were numbered from one to twelve on their backs, in huge white letters. Their partners discriminated them as devil number one, and so on through the complement of fiends. Another mask, which kept about it a large circle of admirers, was what Yankees call a "six-footer," clad in a lank cotton night-gown, with a night-cap on of the same material. At every pause of the orchestra there arose a shout of applause, that fell upon the ear like a roll of surf upon the strand.

Fancy costumes are prohibited from entering the saloon. Here assemble the intriguantes in domino and mask, who victimize or perplex the verdant of the other gender. It is impossible in this guise to detect the age, looks, and often the sex of the wearer. As most who sport this disguise, do it to extract suppers or money from strangers, many not very edifying scenes are to be witnessed, if one is curious to observe all the license these balls develope. Sometimes adventures more comical than disreputable are the result. I had a friend whose size admirably qualified him for the feminine garb. He ac-

AN INTRIGUANTE.

cordingly procured one, took lessons from a lady in the use of a fan, and made his way to the ball, where he soon had a circle of admirers. One gentleman well known to him, not only complimented him upon his small feet and hands, but loaded him with bon-bons, and insisted on being his partner in every dance. He prosecuted his suit most perseveringly, and desired an interview. The mask not being able otherwise to disembarrass himself of his admirer, slipped out, jumped into a coach, and started for home. He had not got far before he saw his amorous friend in full chase, and when he arrived at his own door, his late partner was close by. Waiting till he came up, he took off his disguise, and disclosed his well known features, to the infinite chagrin and anger of his partner, who had said to him too many foolish things ever to be able to look upon him complacently again.

A CARNIVAL SUPPER.

Although the female frequenters of these balls are, in general, low characters, yet I am assured, on respectable authority, that parties from the Faubourg St. Germain sometimes go clandestinely, for a frolic. The curiosity of English and American ladies often takes them there; but unless sheltered from the universal license in private boxes, it is indiscreet, if not deserving a worse name. No refined mind can, with pleasure, witness the destruction of all that is modest and lovely in woman, however ludicrous may be the exhibition. To virtuous females these

Saturnalia had better remain among the things unseen. The government require a per centage of the proceeds, for charitable objects; this is not surprising, as they enlist lotteries in aid of religion.

In striking contrast to this scene is one which I can recommend to all ladies. The Jardin d'Hiver forms one of the most charming places of resort, whether as a garden or a ball-room, possessed by any capital. Nowhere does Parisian taste display itself in more fanciful and chaste decorations. A light iron frame supports a front, which opens into a spacious vestibule. The vault is sustained by eight Doric columns. Thence the visitor passes into an extensive garden, protected above and on all sides from the external air by glass, tastefully set in an iron framework. A light and airy gallery, supported on iron columns, runs all along the interior. This is filled with flowers. The advertisements sometimes announce ten thousand camelias in bloom at once. Below is a garden fragrant with orange-trees and rare exotics, which, to quote from Galignani, "with the basins in the form of enormous sea-shells, cascades, statues, and groups, by the bloom and beauty of the scene, reminds the spectator of Tasso's enchanting description of Armida's garden. Indeed, but for the welcome absence of the tiger and cobra capello, it would need no great stretch of imagination to believe one's self transported to the most luxuriant regions of the East. Here the camelia, the yucca, and the cactus will meet the visitor's eye, in juxtaposition with the palm-tree, the araucamia, and the banana. An aviary filled with exotic birds is to the right; in the centre of the garden is a grass-plot, extending to a romantic grotto; while the few walls that connect some portions of the iron frame-work, are completely roofed with mirrors, and lined with passifloras and other creeping plants." The author of this extract had evidently never bewildered himself in the interminable interlacings and dense foliage of an Eastern jungle, or he would never, for a moment, have conceived that glass and iron could cover their endless variety and gigantic proportions. The dwarfish representatives of hot-house culture, bear no better comparison to the originals amid their native forests, than does the cage-born lion to his free-born brother, roaming at large in his native wilderness. However, I saw enough of tropical beauties, to recall many a delightful association with their more genial native climate.

Nothing has been neglected for accommodation or refreshment. There are even places for various games. The price of admission to all this loveliness is but a franc.

I was present at a ball given under the patronage of the Princess Mathilde. The area was illuminated by sixteen thousand six hundred candles, four hundred lamps, and an electric light, so disposed as to give most brilliant perspectives in all directions. From the lofty gallery over the entrance, the effect was singular. The absorption of light by the vegetation was so great, that it gave the scene the appearance of an empyrean, viewed through a hazy atmosphere; the clusters of lights appearing to be so many firmaments, one succeeding the other in the illimitable distance, until the faintest twinkle proclaimed that human sight had reached its limit.

There were present at least four or five thousand representa tives of the middling and higher classes of society at Paris besides the usual complement of strangers. I was struck with the lack of female beauty, when so much is to be met with in the street. There was a brilliant display of diamonds in the balcony of the Lady Patronesses. The ladies generally ranged themselves like so many wall-flowers on the circular seats around the transepts, which though forming somewhat of a barrier to social intercourse with the gentlemen, yet heightened the beauty of the coup-d'œil upon entering. A band of music at the further extremity, concealed among the shrubbery, played alternately with the orchestra for the dancers. The candles unfortunately kept up a constant shower of grease, so that in a little while most of the coats of the gentlemen looked as if their linen was making its way through numerous air-holes.

From this ball I went to that of the Artists at the Opera Comique. Here the crowd was, if possible, greater, and the dancing from want of space much more restricted. The ladies present were the actresses of all the theatres, and it is but justice to say, that I have never seen assembled a more beautiful collection of women. But what particularly attracted my attention was the exquisite beauty of their toilets. There was nothing overdone. Richness of material was beautifully blended with simplicity of design.

To see a Frenchman under his most amiable aspects, he must be visited at his places of amusements. Scattered throughout the city are halls for dancing, graduated in respectability by the fees of entrance. They are all frequented by Lorettes, who are admitted gratis. The best of the class is the Valentino, fitted up somewhat after the Moorish style, with pistol galleries, billiard tables, dynamometers, and tables of games of skill, the prizes being some articles of trifling value. The police are ever on the alert to prevent the dances from degenerating into indecencies. In the few that I have entered, there has been no indecorum. The toilets are those of the street, and hats are not removed. I have nowhere seen more graceful dancing, and if their uses were confined to the innocent gratification of this exercise, there could be little that was objectionable to urge against them.

The most beautiful of the summer gardens devoted to this amusement is the Chateau des Fleurs. When illuminated it has the air of enchantment. But it would be wearisome and unsatisfactory to the reader for me to attempt to convey to him a correct idea of the seductive taste displayed in these places. The numerous class that live in illicit domestic relations, or who pander to the passions of men, find in them those excitements of which their position makes them so covetous. The middle classes, with their families, frequent them to a considerable extent; but what an American parent would view with horror or shame, would amuse a French mother. Under no circumstances can they be considered as favorable to morals; and while the government exercises the most rigid precautions, to prevent the sale of any medicine which could be used as a poison, except under the responsibility of a physician, and fines those who open schools without a license, it permits a thousand sources of corruption to the public morals to exist under its eye, seemingly believing that its highest duty is to amuse the people. Its principle, to regulate what it is forced to tolerate, is right. But there are some evils it is by no means forced to tolerate. Among them I would enumerate what I saw at the "Salle des Délices," which I visited to witness the etiquette of the lowest of these resorts.

The entrance fee was five cents "en consommation;" this last phrase was unintelligible to me. It purported to be a masked ball—but there were no masks or costumes present, and the "en consommation" I soon deciphered to mean something to drink, for the chief business was done at the bar. The dancing was decent, and the place orderly, as they all are, while the "Sergents de Ville" are in sight, and there are always too many of the military on guard to admit of any contravention of public order. The hall was filled with a rowdy looking class of young men, most of whom were smoking pipes. A girl of not more than twelve, with fine features, but whose manners showed that she already was familiar with vice, was persevering in smoking a cigar that made her sick. One table was filled with girls, some as young as eight, and one certainly not over six years of age, who with a party of boys, not one of whom I judged to be over twelve years old, were tossing off tumblers of abominable beer with all the convivial forms of old topers.

The boys were also smoking pipes filled with the vilest tobacco. The girls having drunk enough to make themselves unsteady, joined in the dance. I turned away sickened at the scene, satisfied that the Devil had his infant schools, as well as the Church.

The Salle de Montesquieu affords a school of a different character. It is the rendezvous of the sporting gentry and the arena of amateur and professional combatants. Upon entering I came upon a cloud of tobacco smoke, so dense as to cause me to gasp for breath. There was a numerous and in general well-dressed class of spectators, including several women who appeared to be respectable. The contests this evening were limited to a novel species of wrestling. Those who tried their skill were entirely naked, except to the last point of decency. There were some heavy throws, but there was no disposition to brutality. On the contrary, the spectators frequently called out "enough" to the panting champions. The lions of the evening were Messrs. Arpin and Turc, between whom the struggle was long and doubtful. One was at last handsomely thrown, and although he lost a considerable bet, besides the mortification of defeat, he walked up to his antagonist, shook his hands, and kissed him on each cheek, to signify that he entertained no animosity, and that it was fairly done.

There was a boy of about fourteen present, who performed extraordinary feats of suppleness. He stood firmly on his feet, and bending backward touched the calves of his legs with his lips, and kissed the floor. He put his legs over his shoulders and walked on his hands. In short, he did all that could have been done with an India rubber manikin, frequently extorting involuntary exclamations of sympathy from the spectators, while he smiled at their tenderness.

The drama plays the same relative part in the education of a Frenchman, that religion does in that of an American. The latter loves his meeting-house, and looks askant upon the theatre; the former, indifferent to the church, or merely tolerating it, could not exist without the play-house. It is his school of manners; his forum of education; his teacher of history; the parent of his ideas; a living monument, in which antiquity reappears in the present. He can no more live without it than the American without his newspaper. It plays the most important rôle in his "Art de vivre," a science which in his own estimation exists only at Paris. It is the necessary superfluity. Sainte Beuve gravely says, "The French public, who respect so few things, have preserved the '*religion*' of the French theatre." Churches have been sacked and desecrated; the clergy have been massacred or banished; but the drama has triumphantly held its own, through every revolution, oftener giving law to society than imitating it. The same author, the popularity of whose "Causeries" attests how truly they reflect the public sentiment, speaks thus: "When Paris recommences to amuse itself, it is not only a privileged class that is amused, but all classes profit and prosper. Paris then is in good train to save herself, and France with her. The theatres present the means of action the most direct, the most prompt, the most continuous, upon the masses. To abandon to chance the direction of the theatres, would be to despise the custom and the exigencies of our nature, the energy of the French mind itself." He views it, properly directed, as a means of opposing the increasing national coarseness of manners, in which, he says, in many points we are fast becoming as rude as the English and Americans. Not for a moment contesting the superior polish of French manner, yet as an attentive observer, I must confess, that while he has not exaggerated the importance of the theatre in the estimation of his nation, its influence is not favorable to the moral welfare of society. If amusement be the highest aim of existence, the theatre has attained its correct position. But if useful and solid qualities, the purity of domestic life, and the development of correct principles, be of more importance to the human race, then the "art de vivre," as understood in France, is a moral imposture.

Attracted by an advertisement of Comte's theatre for children in the Passage Choiseuil, which promised all "new cats" in the play of "Puss in Boots," I entered, and found myself in a very indifferent building, though it had been much patronized by the young Count of Paris, during the reign of Louis Philippe. The audience was chiefly composed of "bonnes" or nurses, having on an average about two children each in charge, some of whom had not certainly been long strangers to a draught from nature's fount; and if I mistake not, a few were then employed in drawing nourishment therefrom. The parterre was in fact a very dirty nursery; resounding with every cry compatible with the strength and variety of infantine lungs, except when the curtain was up. Every time it rose, there was a shout of joy, which subsided into occasional ejaculations of wonder and admiration at the efforts of the young actors, who really performed very creditably. There was a slight attempt to point a moral in two of the four plays, but to amuse by jokes, and ludicrous spectacles, or to frighten by hobgoblins and phantoms, was the chief object. In this M. Comte showed his accurate knowledge of the character of his audience, whether children, nurses, or parents. In one piece there was a bear hunt. The animal so frightened his pursuers that one climbed a tree, and the other fainted from fear. The bear turned him over with his nose, then approaching his head, smelt it, and expressed his contempt by imitating the usual performance of dogs at all corners with which their noses are satisfied. This was the "hit" of the evening, and was received with shouts of applause.

The drop-curtain represented children engaged in a variety of frolics, one of which was giving a clyster to a cat. I have some doubts as to the propriety of mentioning these sights, but as those who take their children to this "reward of merit" will find such scenes are prominently displayed, it is but well that they should be forewarned. They are specimens of those anomalous exhibitions, so often met with in France, to the disgust of those whose education has not prepared them to overlook in the ridiculous what is really loathsome. The plays lasted until eleven o'clock, and were succeeded by a distribution, by the young gentleman who played the part of Puss, of numerous bon-bons, toys, and bouquets, among the juvenile audience, who appeared to enjoy the scramble and their prizes more than any thing else. It is hardly necessary to observe that none of these infants get to crib before midnight, though sleep had had for not a few more charms than even the wonderful cat.

The love for spectacles, thus early fostered, begets a patience in riper years which to a "go-ahead" Yankee would be a physical impossibility. Those who purchase their tickets in the morning are required to pay about one fifth more than the evening rates. Consequently, the economical take their chance at the opening of the doors. To secure a place, on the performance of any attractive piece, it is necessary to go early and "faire la queue," literally to make tail, or stand in a line until the ticket-office opens. The arrangements at all public places are perfect in the respect of order. There is no crowding, either in the line or office; only a few are admitted together, and when served, the sentinel passes in as many more. I have known individuals to stand six hours in these "queues" awaiting their turn.

The most amusing theatre is the Montansier at the Palais Royal. None is better known among the bloods of Paris, for it is here some of the most celebrated mistresses make their débuts gratuitously, or even paying a bonus to the director for the privilege of exhibiting their attractions and making their market among the connoisseurs in female charms. Young girls who are carefully educated are not allowed to visit this, or its rival, the Vaudeville.

The pervading character of the pieces enacted upon the French stage is loose and corrupting. There are annually brought out between two and three hundred new plays. They are calculated to increase the prevailing sentiment of ridicule toward a deceived husband, and to enlist the sympathies in the success of the intriguing of either sex. They also pander grossly to the taste for "double entendre" and wanton exposure of the female person. Indeed, in this last respect, the ballet corps use the light costume, in which they exhibit their "poetry of motion," simply as an attractive auxiliary to their next to nude figures. Constantly there are sights and allusions which few American female cheeks could witness untinged, but which fail to produce a corresponding emotion among the ladies of this metropolis. There are exceptions to this censure, and among them I could name three of the most successful pieces of the winter: "La Mariage de Victorine," by George Sand, in which the charming Rose Chéri appears at the Gymnase; "Mdlle. de la Saglière," by Sandeau; and "Diane," a tale of Richelieu, both of which enjoy successful runs at the Française.

In two respects Yankee managers and shop-keepers can receive useful hints from the French stage. The first, is in the excellent arrangement of lights, by the glare of which the eyes of the audience are not blinded as in the United States; the second, is in the use of the drop-curtain for an illustrated advertising sheet, a sort of mammoth directory, from which the play-goers can derive information as to the sources of supply for almost every want human flesh has inherited. The curtain in this manner produces an income to the manager, and is ornamental enough for all scenic purposes.

The poison of the French stage is the more subtle from being united with so much that is captivating to the senses and gratifying to the intellect. That I am not alone in this judgment, the following extract from a late newspaper will show: "The

President of the Republic has approved of a decree by the ex-Minister of the Interior, M. L. Faucher, dated October 12, by which it is decided, in order to attempt to remove the complaints made of the immoral and dangerous political tendency, and the literary imperfection of a great number of theatrical pieces, that the following prizes shall be annually given: A sum of five thousand francs to the author of a successful dramatic work in four or five acts, in prose or verse, represented at the Théâtre Français, and which shall be moral in character and brilliant in execution. A sum of three thousand francs, to a piece of the like character, of less than four acts, represented with success at the same theatre. A sum of five thousand francs to the author of the work in four or five acts, in prose or verse, represented with success at any theatre in Paris, or even if given for the first time in a provincial theatre, 'which shall be of a nature to serve in the instruction of the laboring classes, by the propagation of sound ideas, and the spectacle of good examples.' A sum of three thousand francs to the author of any such piece of less than four acts, represented with success in any Parisian or provincial theatre. A commission, consisting of the Director of the Department of Fine Arts, of four members of the Academy, and of four members of the Commission of the Theatres, is to make a report on the pieces to be recompensed, and the minister is to choose the author from the list it is to present. The funds are to be taken from the subvention of the Théâtre Français, and from the budget of the Fine Arts." It will be noticed that politics, quite as much as morals, are at the bottom of this effort to remedy the evil.

The "Patrie" of April 20th contained the following paragraph. "This morning the directors of the theatres of Paris were convoked by the Minister of the Interior. The minister had assembled them to express the intentions of the government, in respect to the lamentable tendencies of the present dramatic literature."

"In a few and concise words the minister explained how he understood the mission of the theatre and its influence upon manners, and he announced to the directors his resolution, firmly expressed, not to suffer longer upon the stage any work of a nature to excite the passions and corrupt the public mind."

To sustain the unrivaled representations of the Grand Opera, the government gives annually, about $176,000 ; to the Italiens, $10,000 ; to the Opera Comique, about $50,000, and to the Théâtre Français nearly an equal amount—making upward of $280,000 to support these schools of "taste and good language."

In 1600 there was but one theatre at Paris, in 1791 there were fifty-one, in 1807 the number had decreased to thirty-three, which were further reduced by Napoleon to eight, compensation being made to those closed. Now there are four operas and twenty-five theatres, capable of accommodating thirty thousand spectators, beside eight circuses, that hold thirty-one thousand. These last are open only during the warmer months. Add to this list nine musical halls for concerts, sixteen for winter balls, eight gardens for summer balls, and a variety of dioramas, panoramas, and georamas, independent of the legion of ambulatory shows, and it will be conceded that the national taste has ample resources for its gratification.

From 1807 to 1811 the annual receipts of the theatres averaged $920,000. In 1847 they reached, $1,920,000 ; in 1848, $1,120,000 ; in 1849, $1,220,000 ; and in 1850, $1,180,000. These sums are reported to the government, but it is believed they are underrated, as eight per cent. of their receipts is required for charitable purposes. In 1849 the places of amusement contributed to the hospitals and charitable institutions of the city $88,000. The number of actors and singers in Paris is estimated at two thousand and thirty-three, who average but $350 per annum, which, without other resources, must leave the majority in a condition approaching to penury.

The subsidy granted to the Théâtre Français is to counteract any decline of the public taste, and to preserve a school for the classic productions of French dramatic literature. Here are enacted the delightful comedies of Molière and the refined tragedies of Corneille and Racine, in a manner worthy of the genius of those authors. The part is given with such a fidelity of detail in costume and character, that the grave seems literally to give up its dead, who walk and speak among us as they did in life. True to nature and tradition in their minutest points, it may be questioned whether the vivid exposition of the brilliant corruption of the Court of Louis XV., reproducing, as in Adrienne, le Couvreur, scenes of intrigue gilded by the high-toned gallantry of the language of love of that era, is not demoralizing to the youth of the present day. This favorite play of Scribe's is founded upon the unfortunate passion of Adrienne, the first actress of France, for Maurice of Saxony, the most illustrious warrior of his age. It is a scandalous development of intrigue, pride, lust, revenge, and murder, unrelieved by better sentiments, unless the love of Adrienne for Maurice may bear this character. It is her fate, poisoned by her treacherous rival the Duchess of Bouillon, rather than her love, that excites the sympathy of the spectators. Rachel fills her rôle, and in the dying scene is so true to nature, that death itself might mistake the feint for reality.

In one act the Théâtre Française is itself rolled back in history to 1730, and its green-room and side scenes turned toward the spectators. There appears in review, as in life, the theatrical stars of that day, with their train of noble friends, engaged in the scandalous pleasures of that corrupt epoch, and which in any, are better for all concerned with the curtain down than up. Among those who have the freedom of the green room is a reverend abbé, lover and retailer of scandal of the Duchess of Bouillon. He plays a part in his sacred habit by no means edifying to the friends of religion.

The audience at this theatre, as may be supposed, is composed of the élite of the lovers of the dramatic art; for it is here alone that Mlle. Rachel by her genius revives the ancient glories of the great masters of French tragedy. I am told she is preparing herself to appear in the characters of Shakspeare. Her powers, great as they are, must eventually succomb to the life of dissipation and excitement which she leads. On the stage her action flashes like lightning. Her tone and gesture are fierce, quick, and startling. They electrify, but fail to excite sympathy. In one of her stormy passages, she was so carried away by her simulated passion, that she brought her foot down upon the stage-lights, crushing the glass chimneys and scattering them all around. She did not notice the accident, and the audience gave her a unanimous burst of applause.

To my judgment, she appears to refine upon the emotions of the heart, as did Le Nôtre upon nature in gardens. She astonishes, but leaves no permanent impression beyond wonder at her art. Yet it is in the overstrained expression of the sentiments and passions, as in the stiff trimming of trees and prescribing right angles to vegetation, that French taste finds its highest gratification.

The stage in France dates its origin as far back as 1402. Few who witness its present scenes would suppose that it owed its origin, if not directly, to the clergy, at least to the attempt to represent in public the *mysteries* of the life of Christ. Such however, is the fact. The first theatre, was in Trinity Hospital, Rue St. Denis, a street that takes its name from the saint who is said to have walked through it after his execution, with his head under his arm, seeking a spot to his taste for a grave. He chose that which has since become the site of the Abbey of St. Denis. As an unbeliever remarked, the only difficulty would be in the *first* step.

In the same street, says Froissart, upon the entrance of Isabella of Bavaria, there was exhibited at the gate of the Painters, a representation of heaven, with numerous and brilliant stars; the Almighty sitting on his throne in Majesty, with his Son and the Holy Spirit, surrounded by innumerable angels. The queen passed under the gate of paradise, from which descended two angels, who presented to her a costly crown, chanting at the same time this verse—

> "Dame enclose entre fleurs de lys,
> Reine êtes vous de Paradis,
> De France et de tout le pays,
> Nous retournons en Paradis."

Louis XI., on his state entrance, was greeted with a different sight. He was welcomed at the fountain Ponceau by three beautiful girls, entirely naked, in the attitude of sirens.

CHAPTER X.

THE ORNAMENTAL *VS.* THE USEFUL.

Frenchmen claim for the Place de la Concorde the enviable distinction of being the most beautiful public square in the world. The view from the foot of the obelisk of Luxor, justifies their pretensions. On the Eastern side are the attractive gardens of the Tuileries, extending to the palace; on the west, the more rural Champs Elysées, and the noblest of avenues, reaching to the Arch of Triumph, which is shortly to be crowned with a colossal chariot and four steeds in honor of Napoleon. The Madeleine and the beautiful palaces of the ministers, form its northern boundaries, and on the south, separated from it by the Seine, with its magnificent quays and graceful bridges, are the Hotel d'Orsay, the Palais Bourbon, and the new Palace of the Minister of Foreign Affairs; the "tout ensemble" forming an unrivalled "coup d'œil" of architectural beauty. On a clear night, with the stars overhead, and the innumerable lights beneath, extending in long vistas on all sides, the effect is magical.

My object in alluding to this square is not to attempt to describe it, but to call attention to the extraordinary efforts made by the government to render Paris as distinguished for its architecture as for its museums. As the capital of civilization, the aim is to make it worthy of its title in point of embellishment. In this respect all governments concur, and none have made more lavish expenditure than those which have emanated more directly from the people.

I will name some of the more recent expenses to show at what cost this policy is pursued by a government already in debt $1,083,500,000, on which they pay an annual interest of $67,000,000 :

The Hotel de Ville, palace of the city government, has cost	$8,000,000
The Triumphal Arch of the Champs Elysées	2,086,400
" " " Place Carrousel	280,000
The labor on the Column Vendôme—Russia and Austria contributed the bronze at the battle of Austerlitz	300,000
Embellishments of the Place de la Concorde	300,000
" " and Improvements in progress of the Place Carrousel (estimated)	2,000,000
Alterations and Improvements of the Palace of Justice.	2,000,000
Palace d'Orsay	2,270,000
Hotel of Minister of Foreign Affairs (incomplete)	2,500,000
Central Market and Improvements—government estimate to cost	4,000,000
To connect the Tuileries with the Louvre, ordered by Louis Napoleon ; to cost	5,134,000
Repairs of the Abbey St. Denis—unfinished	3,600,000
Spent on the Palace and Museum of Versailles, by Louis Philippe	5,000,000
Decorations of the Louvre—(of this $215,000 were spent in the ornaments of one hall)	400,000
Column of July	240,000
Total	$38,110,400

Napoleon during his reign expended $27,000,000 in embellishing Paris.

The expenditure of sums like the above for objects chiefly decorative, in one city, by a government so largely in debt, clearly demonstrates that the gratification of taste is more considered than either mere utility or economy. This species of disbursement belongs rather to royalty than republicanism. The former has nurtured in the people a love of display, which the latter is compelled to gratify.

Paris expended nearly $100,000 on every republican May fête; or nearly half as much on a day's amusement as on her primary schools for a year; while four theatres actually receive an equal sum.

The annual cost of the Legion of Honor, which gives 50,000 individuals the privilege of wearing publicly red ribbons in their button-holes, is $1,600,000. The yearly cost of the Paris Prefecture of Police is $1,680,000. Upward of $11,000,000 are disbursed every year in pensions. The yearly expenses of the Army and Navy are nearly $100,000,000; for public buildings, &c., $15,000,000, and for public instruction for the 18,000,000 youth of France, $3,400,000. Louis Napoleon, since he has assumed the supreme power, has increased the expenses of the army, public buildings, and his own disbursements as Chief of the State, upward of $7,000,000, while the budget for public instruction has been decreased nearly 2,000,000 of francs. He has appropriated 50,000 francs for the purchase of busts of himself. These sums show the relative importance of the objects in the eyes of the government. No expense is spared in the education of a soldier in the art of war. The present army of France is probably the most efficient in the world. This army is, however, considered more necessary as a protection to the government against its own citizens than against foreign powers. It affords the conclusive evidence, that the people of France who are not the friends of a monarchy, are ranged under the banner of revolution. This will ever be the case where authority relies upon force to control, rather than education to enlighten ignorance.

Another fact speaks volumes. The entire number of the youth of France receiving education in 1850, above that of elementary knowledge, was but a fraction over 92,000, while 394 prisons contained 66,000 prisoners, or one three-hundreth part of the adult population.

No government can be really republican that sanctions expenditures so inconsistent with democratic economy. Where the people control their own expenses, they keep constantly in view, that every disbursement calls for a proportionate contribution from their pockets. Hence utility, and not display, becomes their standard. The people of the United States are lavish in support of education, because it is the basis of their republic. In France, the government are equally lavish for the army, because upon it depends their existence.

Another point in which there is an equal difference between the fundamental principles of the two nations, is the substitution of the ornamental for the useful. The lust of the eye is of paramount consideration to the comfort of the body. This is manifested by all classes of society, from the domestic who spends a third of her earnings in caps and ribbons, to the princely proprietors of hotels, who decorate a single saloon at the expense of $200,000. A Frenchman dines upon two francs that he may spend eight at the theatre. He lives in a garret that he may be a dandy in the street. He gilds his apartments and furniture to such an extent, that he appears literally to occupy a golden palace; yet, in many items of actual convenience, he is content to be far in the rear of ordinary households in America. He is as much inferior in the useful and unpretending mechanical arts of the United States, as he is in advance in all that appertains to ornament. In most French houses one seeks in vain for the conveniences of bathing-rooms, good closets, ample kitchens, economical fire-places, nice fitting doors, or easy and ingenious locks and door handles. In lieu of these we find numberless looking-glasses, clocks, bronzes, candelabras, furniture *doré*, and sumptuous curtains. This species of extravagance has become a general tax upon the community. It enters into the price of all articles consumed. Many of the shops so greatly admired are decorated at an expense of upward of $60,000 each. Nothing can exceed the taste and neatness displayed in the arrangement and packages of all descriptions of merchandise. The shop windows divide with the galleries of the Louvre the public admiration. Even in wood-yards the fuel is piled so as to form a species of mosaic work. A turkey which in the market can be bought for two dollars, by the time it has passed through the epicurean hands of a Palais Royal restaurateur, and attained the honor of a place among the costly delicacies of his window, mounts to the price of twenty-four dollars, and, for American appetite, is actually a much less desirable morsel than in its original state.

Fruits are now 300 to 500 per cent dearer than in 1800. Fish have acquired a three-fold value. Coal the same. Rents have nearly doubled, and general expenses have increased fifty per cent. The present government has given a fresh impetus to this extravagance, by the re-establishment of titles, and the revival of the etiquette of the Imperial court, with its costly decorations and profuse salaries. The attendant expenses undoubtedly contribute to the prosperity of certain branches of trade; $10,000 are sometimes expended in Paris on flowers alone, on the occasion of a fête; but it is the people at large on whom the burden of the governmental prodigality falls.

The average annual expenditure of each inhabitant of Paris some years since, and which probably has not varied much since, was about $204, of which the chief items were—

Rent	$18
Wine and brandy	18
Food	49
Clothing	9
Charities	2 : 25
Amusements	2
Newspapers	50
Taxes	26 : 50

At the present time the cost of the following articles in Paris is as follows. Tea per lb. $1,25. Coffee 48 cents—sugar 17 cents. Milk per quart, 6 cents. Eggs per dozen, 24 cents. Common meat by law 14 cents. Good beef 30 cents per pound and upward. Wood per cord, $10. Bad coal per ton, $8 to 10. The best claret, $17 per dozen. Champagne $6 to $15.

At these prices it is evident that the laboring class, whose average of wages is not sixty cents per day, fare very differently from artisans in the United States, to whom each one of these articles, excepting wines, is considered as an absolute necessary of life.

Salt until recently paid to the State annually from five to ten millions of dollars. The land taxes fall more heavily upon the peasantry than upon the rich proprietors. Sugars are taxed $14,500,000, and the duties levied on articles of necessity consumed in Paris, in addition to the State taxation, amount to $6,500,000 per annum. Doors and windows pay $625,000, city tax.

Paris proper has a population of more than a million souls including sixty-thousand strangers. Of these, 160,000 are either rich or earn more than sufficient for their wants. 800,000 are in an unsatisfactory or wretched condition. 150,000 are constantly in the hospitals or receiving charity from other sources. Each of the above 800,000 is supported by benevolence on an average two years out of thirty-five, their average existence. There is one indigent person to every 12¾ inhabitants. There are 64,816 master workmen, and 342,530 work people, including 240,000 men, 112,000 women, and 26,530 children. The average wages of the men 75 cents a day; of the women 33 cents. There are 80,000 domestics, who average less than 20 cents. The worst paid workmen are the cotton-spinners, who gain only from 20 to 40 cents a day. Women, often not over 15 cents. The daily cost of food to journeymen is from 20 to 30 cents, and of lodging, from $1 to $1 : 25 per month.

The lodgings of the poorest class are of the most wretched description. The proprietor frequently provides nothing but straw or rags for beds, and no other furniture. The chambers are unventilated, uncleaned, and crowded with the miserable and depraved of both sexes, who pay as dearly for these filthy lodgings as for those with some pretensions to comfort. Those who pay from five to eight francs per month are entitled to a dish of soup each evening, and to have a shirt washed once a week.

The figures of the saving's banks show that one workman out of five deposits something each year, and of domestics one in two. Sums as small as a franc are received.

In all France there are 4,500,000 paupers, and four million bordering upon this condition.

For some years past the elements of a statistical account of pauperism and public charitable establishments have been collecting at the offices of the department of the Interior, under the direction of an inspector general. There exist 1133 administrations of hospitals and benevolent institutions established in 1130 communes. The departments which have the greatest number are the Vaucluse, Var, Haut-Rhin, Nord, Seine-et-Oise, and Bouches-du-Rhone; those which have the fewest are the Seine, the Hautes-Alpes, Corsica, the Hautes-Pyrénées, the Haute-Saone, and the Tarn. The department of the Seine has only two hospital administrations, but one of them—that of Paris—is so considerable from the immense revenues at its disposal, by the number of establishments which it directs, and by the number of poor which it assists, that it reckons for a fifth part of the hospital assistance given in the whole of France. From 1800 to 1845 the amount of donations and legacies officially made to the poor was not less than 122 millions, exclusive of sums given direct and authorized by the prefects. The venal value of the productive estates of the hospitals and almshouses is estimated at five hundred millions. They have also large revenues derived from other sources, such as the duty on the receipts of the theatres, grants from the communes, &c. The most considerable revenues of the hospital administrations are those of Paris, which are about 12,690,823f.; of Lyons, 2,279,990f.; of Rouen, 1,136,908f.; and of Marseilles, 1,069,257f. The food of the poor stands for a sum of 22,191,141f., of which the charge for wheat or bread is nearly one half. The number of beds in the hospitals and almshouses in France is 126,142, of which there are 15,353 in the department of the Seine. The number of patients in the hospitals in 1847 was 486,083, and in the almshouses 77,053.

In 1848 the destitution of a portion of the working classes in Paris was so great that having sold all their clothing for bread, they were obliged to lie a-bed during the day, or borrow from some less unfortunate the necessary clothes to go into the streets to seek employment.

There exists all over France, under the direction of the government, to the number of forty-five, five of which lend gratuitously, the useful establishments of Monts de Piété, institutions where the poor and needy can pawn their effects on certain fixed rates of interest, and at fairly apprized values. Their establishment, like that of so many hospitals, is a striking evidence of the necessitous condition of the poorer classes. During periods of great public misery they return, free of interest, all articles pledged not exceeding, say, ten francs value, consisting of indispensable tools, furniture, clothing, &c. In 1847 the Mont de Piété received 3,400,087 articles valued at nearly $10,000,000, Paris alone doing more than half the business. One half the loans are for sums varying from twenty cents to one dollar.

I have collected these data from official reports. I leave to the political economists to solve the connection between the deplorable condition of the lower classes and the profuse expenditure and heavy taxes of the government. My readers will, I am sure, agree with me, that it is not from such materials, and from such a policy of government, that republicanism can germinate. Yet 7,500,000 voters have sanctioned the return to the extravagance of Imperial rule, after having witnessed, in 1850, under a nominal republic, a saving of $35,500,000, when compared with the disbursement of the last year of the reign of Louis Philippe. The people feel their burdens, but are still blind both to the true causes and remedy. On the ground of their pernicious influence, Louis Napoleon has suppressed the chairs of Political Economy in the colleges of France. The only doctrine now allowed to come before the people, is, that the luxury of the rich, and the expenditure of the government, are essential sources of welfare to the nation at large. When it can be shown that fast living benefits the constitution of the individual, or that public extravagance is of more value to a nation than private economy, then, but not till then, will the virtue of the present financial policy of France be discovered. Unhappily, there is an agent far more direct and active in the degradation of the nation than either taxation or extravagance. No one who has made a tour of curiosity around the "octroi" wall of Paris can have failed to make the discovery. Here, for at least three days in the week, he will find from 20,000 to 30,000 of the most dissolute of both sexes occupied in drinking and debauchery of the worst kind in temporary liquor shops.

The increase of licensed retailers of wines and spirits throughout France has been rapid since 1830. Then, there existed but 250,000. Now there are upward of 350,000, an increase of 100,000 in twenty years, and of 20,000 during the last three years, under the Republic. This augmentation has been among the lowest class of cabarets, of which there has been an increase of 70,000 within nineteen years, paying a license of only six francs each. Were Beelzebub permitted to select an agent for the demoralization of humanity, he could not find one better adapted to his purpose than that which is sanctioned by the government of France. That I may not be accused of exaggerating the evil influence of the licensed dram-shops, I quote the following from the work of M. Villermé, upon the physical and moral condition of the working classes. The description he gives refers to the cabarets of the quarter Etaques at Lille:

"I could have wished," says Villermé, "to have entered the places, where I have seen through the doors and windows, across a cloud of tobacco smoke, crowds of people, agitated like the inhabitants of an ant-hill; but it was evident that notwithstanding the precaution I had taken to disguise myself in a manner not to create suspicion, my appearance among them would have created surprise if not violence. A great number stood, from want of room to sit down. All drank the detestable corn brandy or beer. I heard even children utter the vilest obscenities. I can affirm, that I have never seen at once so much pollution, misery, and vice, and nowhere under an aspect more hideous and revolting"

In Paris it is estimated there are 17,000 habitual drunkards, of the most brutal character. The mayor of Paimpol, in his official report, says: "I affirm that the greater part of the paupers of this town owe their misery to the excess of drinks, particularly brandy; that almost all the disorders and crimes which have come before me, have been committed by persons either drunk or given to intoxication."

Such evidences should destroy the common delusion, that, because light wines are cheap in France, intoxication is rare. Brandies of the most deleterious nature are equally cheap, and more generally used.

The government actually encourages the consumption of ardent spirits by public lectures. M. Payen, member of the Academy of Sciences, in his fifth lecture on Public Health, says: "Brandy in itself constitutes a beverage, either very dangerous or very beneficial. Alcohol, taken pure, is a violent poison; mixed, on the contrary, with water, it is an extremely healthful drink." ("Une boisson extrèmement salubre.")

In the department of the North there are nearly 18,000 dram-shops, averaging *one* to every *sixty-four* inhabitants. So says the "Constitutionnel" of the 10th of May ult.

There are some facts relative to French productive industry not without interest. The manufactures of Paris of all kinds produce yearly merchandise to the value of \$268,000,000. Of the minor articles, which find their way to every quarter of the globe, we find the amounts as follow: Infants' toys, \$800,000; buttons, \$1,200,000; canes and whips, \$600,000; fans, \$600,000; artificial flowers, \$2,200,000; gloves, \$2,800,000; umbrellas, \$1,400,000; perfumery, \$2,000,000; pianos, \$2,200,000; memorandum-books, \$1,200,000; corsets (of which 1,200,000 are annually exported), \$3,000,000; baby, table, and toilet linen, to the fineness of which the French ladies attach even more importance than to the quality of their silks and satins, \$5,400,000.

CHAPTER XI.

EDUCATION—SOCIALISM.

I BROUGHT my children with me to Paris under the belief that I should find for them superior advantages of education to what exist in the United States. As I shared this opinion with many others, it may not be amiss to give the results of my experience, for the consideration of those who desire to educate American youth in France.

Having a son and daughter I was prompted to examine into the system pursued toward both sexes. Of the seclusion and restraint, and the effects of sexual isolation I have already spoken.

For a girl, the choice was only between an entirely home education or boarding schools of the most exclusive kind. The former is the course in general pursued by the best families. It renders education much more expensive than in the United States. But by it the evils attending the latter are avoided.

Boys are sent to boarding schools or the seminaries under the supervision of government, where the discipline is rigid and the exclusion of external influences as complete as stone walls and watchful guardians can render it. Teachers sleep with them, watch them at table, are with them during their play hours, and they are never allowed to leave the walls of their seminaries without their presence; in short, they make themselves the pupils' shadows. The rule is never to leave them alone on any occasion, and the strictest watch is held over the servants and porters lest they should connive at procuring forbidden indulgences from outside the walls. If the tutors were of irreproachable morals this system would work better than it does; but when it is considered that frequently in what is called a fashionable school, they receive salaries of not over $100 per annum, no very lofty qualifications of either character or attainments should be expected. They are as likely to be the accomplices as the preventives of the pupils in their attempts at mischief or depravity. It is no uncommon event to find that those youths who have been most zealously watched, even in the least exceptionable of these establishments, have acquired sufficient address to convince their anxious parents that they are as innocent of even the knowledge of evil as babes, while they are in reality adepts not only in theory but practice of what their mothers least wish them to know. The American system undoubtedly allows too much latitude to youth, particularly in not subjecting them to wholesome discipline, but it preserves them from systematic hypocrisy and fixed habits of falsehood.

If education were simply the acquisition of general knowledge, the sciences, classics, or accomplishments, the American parent would find the institutions of France unexcelled by those of any other country. In the solid and ornamental branches they furnish for both sexes every desirable advantage. Intellectual knowledge is, however, but one part of education. Without principle it becomes the worst foe of society; with principle, its best ally. I do not mean to be understood as implying that the morals are neglected. On the contrary, they are rigidly cared for after the French standard. But this in my judgment is one cause of the unfitness of the nation for the republicanism of the school of Washington. After an attentive examination into their system of education for youth, I am decidedly of the opinion that if American parents wish to rear a generation of American children, they by far had better intrust them, both for their morals, and the principles which are to be their guides in civil life, to the public schools of their own country, rather than to the highest seminaries of France. I have seen the results of this nurture in too lamentable shapes to come to any other conclusion than, that, while it rarely is calculated to make an American successful abroad, it is quite sure to destroy his capacity for patriotism at home. Dissatisfied with the genius of his native country as being adverse to his acquired taste, he finds himself, as it were, expatriated, without the solace of being nationalized elsewhere. American citizens can best be reared amid American institutions.

Corporeal punishment being entirely done away with, French teachers are as much at a loss for a substitute to preserve discipline as are our worthy reformists in the navy. They resort to a multitude of penances, the most efficacious of which is perhaps imprisonment; but their general aim is to create shame or mortification. They seek to arouse emulation by a graduated system of rewards, which results in the early development of a passion for prizes and decorations. This is pushed to such an extent that the bauble often becomes the substitute for the principle, and the vanity of display takes the place of love of knowledge. These "rewards of merit" are coveted with an eagerness by all classes that to their graver neighbors savors of childishness. Hence, through every department of society, they are distributed with a profusion that elsewhere would destroy their value.

Boys who are not yet emancipated from frocks are to be seen with decorations attached to their breasts, treading in the footsteps of the legiondaries of Honor, whose ribbons, crosses, and grand crosses are to be met at every step in the street. The acquisition of a ribbon or a medal would be a penance to a Frenchman if he could not display it. If this innocent vanity be a spur to worthy actions, it is undoubtedly to be cherished in default of a better motive. The Legion of Honor already numbers upward of 50,000 members, and scarcely a day passes without additions to its ranks. A recent calculation gives a decoration to one individual in every ten in France.

The history of French Exhibitions of Manufactures and Arts shows to what a ridiculous extent the distribution of prizes is pursued. Indeed, they are so general, that merit becomes equalized, and in the end they will be of no more value as an evidence of truth than the certificate of a seller of pills. The ratio of increase has been rapid. In 1798 of the one hundred and ten exhibitions in the Champ de Mars only twenty-three, or a little more than a fifth, had prizes. In 1801 there was distributed one prize to every three exhibitors. The succeeding year it rose to one to every two. In 1823 the proportions were two prizes to every three persons. Each succeeding exhibition followed the same policy, until the prizes have nearly caught up with the exhibitors, the last on record being 3253 prizes to 3960 exhibitors. Much complaint ensued at the awards of the commissioners of the London Exhibition in 1851, although France received sixty recompenses for every one hundred exhibitors, while England was only in the ratio of twenty-nine to every one hundred, and all other nations but eighteen.

Such is the effect of substituting in infancy the desire of artificial distinctions, for the more solid principle of action from the simple sense of duty. It was with difficulty I could prevent one of the most simple-hearted and conscientious of professors from bribing my children to learn their lessons. The perpetual argument is, "Do this, and you shall have that."

The vanity of display in dress is one of the earliest lessons taught the infant. The Tuileries' garden, of a fair day, resembles a bed of tulips. The children appear as if dressed for fashion plates to a milliner's window. The really good taste displayed by their mothers in themselves, may spring from this early education ; but when it exalts attitudes and frocks above the more important training of the heart, it becomes a bad school for any child.

That vanity becomes the ruling passion of the young girls is readily seen, from the enthusiastic admiration with which they greet any novel or striking toilet of their companions, and the importance which they are taught to attach to the rules of fashion. Their indulgences are all of a nature to foster this evil. They are made up and trained as "show" children, or as toys ; the praises they receive being bestowed upon their looks rather than their conduct; which, however, in the rules of politeness, is in general unexceptionable.

There are public fancy balls every winter for children, attended by all classes. The most select of these is that of the "Jardin d'Hiver," which takes place just before Lent. On this occasion, that beautiful and spacious winter garden is crowded to excess. No expense is spared in making the fête rival the adult balls. The toilets and costumes are as elaborate, varied, and costly, as parental indulgence and means can create. The children mingle in the dance with all the "abandon," and more than half of the coquetry of older heads. I have seen urchins that could just totter about, dressed in full fancy suits of pink trousers and jackets, cap and feathers ; and little girls, mere babies, for they were carried in arms, with their hair powdered, their arms and necks loaded with valuable jewels, and their bodies displaying in miniature the court toilets of the time of Louis XIV. and his unworthy successor. Their elder brothers and sisters exhibited every fashion and costume of Europe, since the Middle Ages, and some that had no likeness to any thing, either in the past or present. It was a pretty and animated scene, but a deplorable stimulus to vanity and assurance. Each child of more than ordinary attractions, was overwhelmed by the public generally with compliments upon its beauty and charming attire, and taught to consider the éclat of its appearance as the most important triumph of its life.

Some one, with more severity than truth, has said that all children are by nature liars. The teacher of one of the best conducted boarding-schools of Paris, who had several American children under his charge, remarked that they were the only boys in his establishment on whose word he could rely. Where appearances are the chief aim of life, there must exist a corresponding amount of deception. The material lie readily becomes the moral lie. Truth is not placed upon its right foundation in the young. How can it be when there is no reliance put in their good faith? The education of the children prepares the way for those lies of convenience or etiquette so prevalent among the adults.

The simple English yes, or no, has no weight in France. To induce belief, adjurations are added, or a sort of sliding scale of expressions, by which you are made to comprehend with what degree of certainty you may rely upon any promise or assertion. I shall never forget the expression of surprise with which a young American girl, to whom falsehood was an unknown tongue, explained to me that her teacher required her to swear to keep a promise; and on another occasion, with mingled indignation and astonishment, exclaiming, "my teacher tells lies." She had detected some of those petty larcenies of truth which here would not be called by so harsh a name.

Children are no casuists. They should be taught, by precept and example, the plain rule, to tell the truth under all circumstances, and leave the consequences to take care of themselves. The French habit arises not so much from evil design, as from a desire either to convey pleasure, or to avoid giving pain. A physician deceives his patient to convey encouragement; the tradesman promises, to secure patronage; gallantry is proverbial for its falsehoods, and vanity must be fed upon lies. The domestic is more ingenious in evasions than a Cretan; and your friend will never be frank at the expense of wounding your "amour-propre." Suspicion is so disguised in the finesse of courtesy, that its sting is scarcely felt; while deception treads so lightly as barely to leave a trail. Wherever manners and morals have their source in the head, and not in the heart, this condition of things will exist. Yet, it is impossible not to admire that exquisite tact, which, in seeking a favor, seemingly confers an obligation. Perhaps the most prolific source of falsehood arises from the wish, as they express it, "pour faire plaisir," to give pleasure. A lady of my acquaintance had an old domestic, in whom she placed great confidence. She gave him an order one day, and, some time after, asked him if he had attended to it. "Certainly, Madame; it is arranged as you wished." She afterward discovered that he had not obeyed her, and asked him why he wished to deceive her, as he well knew she preferred always to know the truth. "Ah, Madame; I told you so to give you pleasure—a little lie does no harm."

In another respect have my opinions undergone a change since my arrival in France. A republican myself, I sympathized with all that bore the name. France, as a republic, was a country to be loved as well as admired. But further acquaintance has convinced me, that neither by genius, habits, nor education, are Frenchmen republicans. Fifteen centuries of absolutism are no preparative for republicanism; and, were they to-morrow to be governed by the constitution of the United States, they would no more be republicans than would ducks be chickens, though hatched under a hen.

Americans justly consider religion and education as the wells whence they draw their republicanism. But it is religion and education carried home to each individual. Not a pompous ceremonial, to dazzle the eyes of the multitude, while it leaves their hearts as cold as the marble altars it rears; nor arts and sciences for the favored few; but a vital principle, warming souls into action, and a system that carries the elements of knowledge to every fire-side. Exile from the United States the clergy, blot out our common schools, and the next generation, ceasing to be republicans, would become anarchists. Give Frenchmen the same education, not only of schools, but of the ballot-box, and the popular forms of government, from village selectmen up to legislative assemblies, and you prepare them for republicanism; but, until a people have learned to govern themselves, they must be governed.

I have no need to recal the past, to prove that free principles have never been firmly rooted in France. There have been continual struggles against oppression, and repeated contests for power. Whichever gained the prize, prince or people, ruled with the authority of a despot or the cruelty of a tyrant. Terrorism has ever been the favorite weapon, because existence was only insured by success. Those who gave no quarter, could expect none; and, thus, though there has been blood enough spilt in France to regenerate a world, it has enriched no soil but that of despotism.

The Fronde gave the Parisians Louis XIV. for a master, who wrote to his loving subjects whenever it was necessary to elect a prévost—" We desire that you give your votes to Monsieur ——;" and the man of the court was elected.

The revolution of 1789, in its general destruction, swept away a multitude of abuses. But the nation exchanged only one despotism for a greater, and gladly welcomed imperial rule to screen them from their own. In 1848, they again essayed republicanism; were well nigh engulfed in anarchy, and now have sought safety and security in a dictator.

When history has given so many proofs of the incapacity of a nation to be free, it is the part of wisdom, if she would remedy the evil, to investigate the causes. One of these I believe to be the Catholic religion; which began by making the people bigots, and ended in leaving them infidels. In requiring implicit faith and obedience, it destroyed individual judgment and action. But the cause which at present prevents republicanism is ignorance: the actual ignorance of the masses, who, unable to read or reason for themselves, are alternately the tools of the demagogue and despot.

Statistics will be found to sustain me in this opinion. The population of France is 36,000,000. In her primary schools she has 2,332,580 pupils, or the ratio of one-sixteenth of her population, supported at an annual expense of $1,800,000, or an average to each pupil of about 75 cents. The State of New York, in 1851, expended on 726,291 pupils in her common schools, $1,432,096, or an average of nearly $2 a-head for one-fourth of her population, while she has a fund of $6,612,850 devoted to purposes of education. The actual difference is, that while New York expends twice and two-thirds as much on each pupil as France, she educates her population also in the ratio of fourfold in point of numbers. France expends more upon the tomb of Napoleon than upon her entire "Ecoles Primaires;" and the city of Paris, from 1800 to 1845, has spent at the Hotel de Ville, in fêtes to the several governments of France, $2,000,000—a sum sufficient to support its common schools, at the present rate of appropriation, for fifteen years. Previous to 1830, the cost of primary instruction in Paris was but $16,000 annually. Since then it has been increased to $250,000, and the number of children frequenting the schools is about 45,000, or one twenty-second part of the population. In the colleges, institutions, and boarding-schools of the city, there are 11,000 pupils, but these embrace the élite of the youth from all parts of the country. The total number of pupils in the lyceums, colleges, and private institutions in France, for 1850, was 92,231; making a total of 2,424,811 children only, out of the 18,000,000 in France, receiving any degree of education.

The military conscription shows, that out of every thousand young men drawn, about 40 know how to read and write, 500 to read only, and more than 400 have no instruction whatever.

Latterly the government has paid more attention to the establishment of primary schools; but I am assured that the people are not forward in educating their children. This arises, partly from suspicion of the motives of the government, and partly from necessity, which requires the incessant labor of all the members of a family to procure the means of subsistence. The great cry of the people is for work that will give them bread, and the energies of the authorities are greatly directed toward providing them with labor. Luxury and extravagance are encouraged among the rich, that the poor may live. Public works are prosecuted, to prevent émeutes. The necessity for present relief is always so urgent, that permanent improvement advances but slowly. The government is ever in the position of a rider to a restless horse; if he relax the rein for a second he is thrown. There can be no radical change in the character of the people until religion and education combine to teach them the duties they owe to God and man. While they remain half-starved, or fed like animals in a cage—their highest aim a full stomach—they will chafe and growl in their confinement. Louis XIV. expended $200,000,000 on one palace. That money devoted to education would have kept Louis XVI. on the throne, and advanced the civilization and freedom of Europe a century. Versailles is the wonder of art; but France pays for it in the socialism of to-day.

In the United States, where the nice adjustment of counterbalancing powers and general intelligence makes the political machine move on quietly in its accustomed track, no adequate conception can be formed of the evils to which France is exposed, from the passions and ignorance of its laboring masses, misled by unprincipled demagogues or conceited theorists. There is no spirit of conciliation in French politics. A difference of views is a war to the knife. Falsehood, force, treachery, and every kindred weapon is employed to attain the desired end. The government strangles liberty, as it alleges, that society may exist. Independence of speech, action, or writing—every thing which gives political importance to the individual—becomes a crime. The press, army, judiciary, and even the church, exist only as the slaves of authority. Spies are every where. The government spreads a thick web over France, ready, like a spider, to dart upon any intruder upon the slightest movement. With this annihilation of political freedom, which in the United States would be the signal of universal dissolution, she prospers—growing mightier and richer as liberty recedes. Call her by what name you will, the freedom of America becomes her curse, and the despotism of Russia her security. This being the case, she has no alternative but to maintain a strong government, until education and tranquillity shall have prepared her citizens for the rational enjoyment of those privileges, which are the birthright alike of all men. It is not so much political as individual reform that France needs.

I will show in few words what is this scourge that, upon every struggle for freedom, drives her back into despotism. It is socialism, directed by faction. Not that vain theory, which, if left to itself, would die from its own want of vitality; but a wide-spread conspiracy to undermine society and overturn authority, that atheism and brutality may renew their orgies of 1793. Like Catiline, it gathers under its banner the discontented and dissipated, of every opinion. It has its honest advocates, who seek only general good. So had the first revolution. They became its earliest victims. Finding its strongest support in ignorance, irritated to madness by social contrasts, it proclaims property and chastity to be crimes against nature. Barricades, assassination, and rapine, are its arguments. Its oracles are Robespierre, St. Just, and Ledru Rollin; its code, the guillotine; and its traditions, the massacres of September and the confiscations of the Assembly.

It is worthy of remark, that it has been whenever there was most political freedom that France has incurred the greatest civil danger. The press and ballot-box, which in the United States are the guardians of freedom, become here the slaves of authority or the emissaries of disorder. The government emphatically perpetuates its own dangers by over-severity. It chains, but does not tame. It exasperates, but does not instruct. It rules by the sword alone, and perishes by the sword. If it were wise for its own good, or patriotic for the nation, instead of muzzling the press to arrest its licentiousness, it would use it to counteract the disorganizing doctrines of its adversaries. It should unfetter it entirely; offset one doctrine by its opposite; encourage discussion; disseminate education; imitate the organization of the socialist, by establishing every where associations for lawful, salutary objects; feed the minds of the people as well as their bodies; leave their tongues free, but direct their energies to useful ends. The government would then rest far more securely than it does at present on its army and police; and the money which is now expended to sustain this terrorism, or to add to the embellishments of Paris, would yield a rich return of patriotism, by being expended in disseminating among its citizens those principles of law and order which are the only sure foundations for the prosperity of a State.

Socialism falls lifeless to the ground in the United States, because it is met by a free press, a zealous clergy, and a matter-of-fact population, who, if they begin by shouting hosannahs for doctrines they do not comprehend, always end by a close investigation into their merits. Some practical good, or some recognized principle of humanity, must be adduced before they subscribe their time or money. If they are misled, a thousand presses proclaim it; and, upon the great ocean of discussion, truth at last quietly floats.

Not so in France. The government refuses to trust the people with the liberty of political organization and discussions. But, as they will speak and think, no other resource remains than secret societies, which being illegal, are so many nurseries of political corruption, by being compelled to a system of fraud and treachery to maintain their existence. Thus organizations, which, if they were open and avowed, might be made serviceable to the cause of patriotism, or at all events, neutralized by those of opposite tendencies, become propagandas of disorganizing doctrines, under the direction of master-spirits of intrigue and ambition.

In 1849, the Constituent Assembly interdicted clubs. They were replaced by the most formidable organization of secret societies with which the civil existence of a government has ever been threatened. An association entitled the "Solidarité republicaine" was formed, with the express design to propagate the doctrines of the democratic and social republic. Its centre was in Paris, with branches throughout the entire territory of France. Repeated judicial condemnations finally broke it up, but only to appear in other shapes; so that, during 1850 and 1851, France became covered with a frame-work of secret associations and their affiliations, to the number of several thousand, extending to the remotest hamlets. Many were disguised under the appearance of philanthropic institutions, literary circles, or musical reunions, with titles appropriate to their nominal functions. Others took the names of masonic lodges; while not a few were christened with alarming or blasphemous appellations, such as the "Malcontents," and the "Robe of Christ."

The "Solidarité republicaine" had for its object to embrace France in one affiliation. After its ruin, two centres of action were established—one at Paris and the other at Lyons—distinct in action, but united by correspondence. That of Paris was directed by a superior committee, constituting "the revolutionary government of socialism." It was in direct correspondence with

Lyons and the chief cities of France; also with London, and all other foreign parts in which there existed kindred societies.

There existed, in addition to the parent association, other centres of action, known as "The Committee of Refugees;" the secret society of "Union of the Communes," and the "Central Committee of Resistance," directed by two national representatives of the Mountain. The last circulated revolutionary bulletins, clandestinely printed.

The Lyonese organization was less extensive than that of Paris, but stronger. The reports were more frequent, correspondence more active, and the unity of action better established.

The means of communication was ordinarily by agents, who bore from one place to another the instructions of their chiefs. They assumed various disguises—generally that of workmen in search of occupation. Their credentials were the impressions of the seals of the leaders upon the papers transmitted, which were seldom signed. These seals represented the emblems of equality or terror, such as the Phrygian cap, the compass, or the lictor's ax.

The societies recruited their ranks by the usual means of corruption and stratagem. Before, however, admitting a novice, he was compelled to answer certain questions, and to undergo a particular ceremony, of which the following was the usual practice:

The candidate, blindfolded, knelt upon two knives crossed, and upon two five-franc pieces. He was then asked—

"Do you wish to join this society?"—"Yes."

"Do you promise never to reveal its secrets?"—"I promise it."

"Swear to obey all orders which may be given you, even if they prescribe to you to kill your brother."—"I swear it."

"What do you feel under your hands?"—"I feel two knives and two pieces of money."

"These objects are placed there to teach you that if the lust of money draws you to betray the society, you will be put to death."

His eyes were then unbandaged, and two of the oldest brethren seized the knives and brandished them over his head, exclaiming, "Yes, the brother who sells our secrets will deserve death, and we will kill him!"

There is another form of initiation still more savage: "I swear upon these arms, symbols of honor, to serve the social and democratic republic, and to die for her, if it be necessary. I swear, besides, the deepest hatred to kings and royalists; and that my bowels shall sooner become the food of wild beasts, than that I shall ever fail to my oath. I swear it three times, in the name of my Saviour, Christ!

"I swear upon my honor, in the name of the sacred cause into which I have been received, to march to any place with my brothers of the Mountain, to give aid and assistance to all democrats. I swear this three times, in the name of Christ, the Redeemer."

He is then baptised "child of the Mountain;" previous to which he must reply satisfactorily to these interrogatories:

"Tell me, citizen, what motives have brought you here?—Tell me, citizen, have you been denounced; is it true?—Now you have your eyes blinded, and your hands bound behind your back, we are your masters; but we wish to examine you. If, by example, your brother or your father are not found on your side, will you avenge yourself; will you assassinate them?—Will not that be painful to do?—If it is necessary to take arms for the republic, will you take them?—You wish then to become a republican?—Your life belongs to us."

Members recognised each other by signs, the mode of salutation, or by watchwords. For instance, on meeting, one asked, "L'heure?" the other replied, "Sonnée;" the first exclaimed, "Nouvelle!" to which the proper answer was "Montagne."

The societies every where prepared arms and munitions of war, and enrolled its members for the general insurrection; the object of which is thus explained in an intercepted letter of one of the chiefs, proven before a judicial tribunal:

"It is in 1852 that the combat should commence. Then we should vote with our constitution in hand; organize for that; not to force the gates of the college and then peaceably retire home, but to march upon the chief place of the department, and proclaim anew the revolution triumphant over its enemies." The rallying cry for this organized insurrection appears to have been "*Marianne,*" and "*De boire à la santé de la Marianne,*" the substitute for "*Republique démocratique et sociale,*" by which the brethren knew each other throughout France.

The confidence inspired either by ignorance or a knowledge of their own strength, and faith in the ultimate success of the bloody drama they were preparing not only for France but for all Europe in 1852, prompted many individual acts of crime in the autumn of 1851. Their assassinations were chiefly confined to the gendarmerie, a number of whom suffered from their assaults. They openly proclaimed their anticipated triumph in the following May, when the election of a new President was to be their signal foı rising. The numbers actually committed to measures of violence it is impossible to ascertain, but one successful movement would have agitated the entire country. The peaceful inhabitants were in a state of continual alarm; they felt that they lived over a mine, ready at any moment to explode, and yet were ignorant of its extent. Often in sallying from their habitations in the morning they would find threatening writings on the walls, calculated to inspire them with terror. Sheltered in the obscurity of the night, unknown voices would cry, "Long live the reds! death to the whites!" with maledictions upon the President and the aristocrats, coupled with praises of the guillotine. After the events of December, one of these instruments of decapitation was found actually prepared in the house of a mechanic, who asserted that he had made it on speculation, believing in a few months there would be a sudden demand for the article. After this there is nothing to be said of the shipment of ready-made coffins to California.

I give one of the many inscriptions with which socialism hastened to signalize its advent. It was taken from a wall in the Rue de Grenelle, and was an attempt at versification, in capital letters:

"Malheureux ouvriers, sans pain et sans travaux,
Vîte, dépêchez vous, brûlez les aristos,
Puisqu'ils sont sans entrailles, montrons nous sans pitié,
Et qu'ils expirent tous sous leurs toits embrasés."

In plain and uncomfortable prose—

"Wretched laborers, without bread and without work, quick, hasten and burn the aristocrats. Since they are without bowels, let us show ourselves without pity, that they may all expire together under their roofs."

The following letter from a refugee at Geneva, addressed to one of his "frères" in France, residing at Montelimart, named Staupany, was found among the papers of the latter, on his being arrested for having taken part in the insurrection of December:

"Dear Brother of the Union, Staupany—The day of vengeance is arrived; I make it known to you in order that you may have arms and abundant ammunition in readiness; fifty of us are about to leave Geneva, and we shall direct our course toward Montelimart. There are some belonging to the Ardèche, the Drôme, the Alps, and elsewhere; we wish to massacre all the aristocrats and the black robes; to burn all the châteaux; no quarter, no pity for those wretches, and that monster Bonaparte—we must assassinate and poison them. Remember us to our brethren; we shall write to you when we are nearer, in order that you may come and meet us, in order to avenge the blood which was shed in Rome, and which is every day shed in France, by those wretches of soldiers, whom we will hunt down. It is now that we are going to enter on the great hunting match against all the kings of the earth; the red flag must float on all sides, and the Phrygian cap before 1852.—Your brother of the Union for life,
Peysson Antoine."

While preachers and practicers of such doctrines are about, society is in the condition of a man groping in the dark amid pitfalls, not knowing but the next step will plunge him to destruction. This was the democracy of Marat faithfully transmitted to their children by the readers of the "Ami du Peuple." The same instruction is made the primary education of the infant race of socialists of 1851. I translate from a journal, which pledges itself for their authenticity, two pertinent illustrations:

"A child of six years, son of one of the insurgents of Surgy, awoke suddenly during the night of the fifth of December. 'Papa,' cried he; and hearing no answer, he called to his mother, and said, 'mamma, where then is my papa? I will wait for him patiently, because he has gone with those others to kill the bourgeoisie (rich citizens).'"

The other is yet more atrocious: "A young woman of Tairnay, mother of a child of but eighteen months, was in the habit of asking him before a circle of Socialists, 'Tin! Tin!' (the child being named Mathurin), 'what is it they will do to the aristocrats?' The infant immediately, to the infinite satisfaction of the spectators and the tender-hearted mother, who covered him with kisses, drew his hand rapidly across his neck, to indicate that it was thus they intended to cut their throats."

The events of December 2d, which placed the supreme authority solely in the hands of Louis Napoleon, disconcerted the plans of the Socialists. Instead of a government weakened by its intestine struggles, and a National Assembly in which they could count upon leaders and co-operators, they found themselves isolated from all extraneous aid, and an army of five hundred thousand men, under the direction of energetic and skillful chiefs, prepared to act against them. Even with these odds, they threw down the gauntlet, and unprepared as they were, took the field in detached parties all over the Republic. They were finally put down, but not until they had given a practical illustration of what would have been the character of their campaign in 1852, had not the President frustrated their intentions by seizing the supreme power himself. Their insignia were red caps and cravats. Their first acts were the pillage of the local treasuries, and whatever their wants dictated, burning of public archives, registers, and title deeds of property, abuse of women, and the murder, and in some instances, torture of soldiers who fell into their hands. At Neury, the venerable curé was shot while in the act of addressing them; and at Nissan, M. Bernard Maury was assassinated, the murderer exclaiming as he fired, "Here is a proprietor." One of their own number met his death from wearing a dress-coat, by which he was mistaken for an aristocrat. Buildings were burned, property destroyed, and many lives lost on the part of the troops as well as the insurgents, in these detached struggles of communism for the mastery of France.

The nobility and the clergy are not now the immediate objects of the hatred of the Socialists. These classes were too effectually prostrated in 1793, ever to attain again a position which shall contrast so invidiously with that of the people, as did theirs previous to that revolution. A new class of society has arisen, possessing the wealth of France, and living in all the luxury and style of the old noblesse. It is thus of the rich "bourgeoisie," and it is against them, the men of property, the practical and striking examples of inequality, that the enmity of the modern revolutionists is directed. The alarm cry of the government is not now as then, "Preserve your privileges"—but, "Preserve your property." And its greatest strength is in the fear of the rich for their possessions.

The intense hatred with which the Socialists and partisans of the government now regard each other, is often manifested in acts of treacherous violence on the one side, and questionable justice on the other. A soldier is attacked, as if he were a wild animal, on every favorable opportunity. On their side they are not slow to avenge the proffered insults and injuries. It is but a few days since, a sentinel on guard in the Rue Richelieu, one of the most fashionable streets, being provoked by a party of Socialists, who threatened his life, fired upon them, and killed an innocent student, who, by a fatal coincidence, had just turned the corner in the direction of the shot.

On the 20th of February, the Court of Assizes of Nevers, acquitted, almost with acclamations, a woman who had killed her husband, because he had joined the secret society, and sworn to forsake his wife and child, and all he held dearest, for the cause of the democratic and social republic. At the moment she gave the fatal blow, the deceased had said to her, in reply to her question, whether he had taken the customary oath: "Yes, I have sworn to abandon you and my child, at the first call. While I go to kill others, perhaps they will come here to kill you."

CHAPTER XII.

THE NATIONAL ASSEMBLY.

BETWEEN the crimes of socialism and the quiet of despotism, there can be but one choice. The nation at large may thrive under one master, but with a thousand it is rent asunder. The doctrines and deeds of the advocates of the social and democratic republic prove that those who have most to gain from political

THE CHAMBER OF DEPUTIES.

reform are those who, in the name of liberty, are most prone to violate its sacred principles. Were, however, the ignorance and evil passions of the masses, the only obstacle to the progress of republicanism in France, much might be hoped for from the gradual dissemination of education and spread of democratic institutions. But when we find that its greatest hindrance is in the legislative body elected by universal suffrage, the cause becomes almost hopeless.

The talent and education of the National Assembly, composed of nearly eight hundred members, were chiefly to be found among the Legitimists or partisans of the house of Orleans. However friendly Berryer, Montalembert, Larochejaquelin, Molé, or Thiers might be to civil liberty, they were pledged to it in no other form than that of royalty. It was for that they labored, and by that tenure they held their seats. They carried with them a large proportion of the intellect and wealth of France. Republicanism in name existed rather by reason of the disagreement of the rival branches of royalty than by its own strength. Still it was respectably represented in the Assembly by about eighty-three members of the conservative order, of whom the most eminent names were Lamartine, the Generals Cavaignac, Lamoricière, and the eloquent divine, M. Coquerel. The reds, or the Mountain, the ultra democrats, among whom every shade of opinion was to be found, from moderate republicanism to the worst errors of socialism, embraced nearly one third of the National Assembly, and numbered in their ranks Victor Hugo, Eugène Sue, the Abbé Lammenais, Emile Girardin, and others, whose literary talents have gained them reputation. A more heterogeneous body of legislators could not have been assembled. Members of the Bonaparte family were to be seen supporting all opinions except that of legitimacy, while there was a party of Imperialists who looked forward to the re-establishment of the empire as the national panacea. The National Assembly in lieu of being a body of republican legislators, was an assemblage of Imperialists, Bourbonists, Orleanists, and Socialists, with a moderate number of members who were sincere in their attachment to a republic. It was a legislature of partisans and not of patriots. Yet they were elected by the broadest principle of suffrage, and may be fairly supposed to represent the actual political condition of the people. If so, on the principle of numbers, it was evident that republicanism had no root in the nation.

Admitting it was a republican assembly, has their conduct shown their sincerity or their fitness for republicanism? They embraced the best minds of the nation, so that ignorance has no apology to offer; and if they failed in their duties as republican legislators, it has been from incapacity or design. That they have failed, and incurred the opprobrium and contempt of the nation is evident from the fact that, while the usurpation of Louis Bonaparte was universally deplored or condemned, not one solitary voice of commiseration was raised for the Assembly. It had become the laughing stock, or object of the indignation of the community; and they saw it fall to the ground, so far as the individual members were concerned, with as little concern as they would have shown for the dropping of rotten fruit in an orchard. Instead of laboring for the republic, in accordance with their oaths and duties, they had presented to the world the unseemly spectacle of fierce contentions, unprincipled intrigues, and a total disregard not only of forensic rules, but the ordinary forms of individual courtesy. In general, they were united in one point—hostility to the executive authority; each party hoping that in its destruction their own might rise. It was a wild scramble for power, with "the devil take the hindmost" for its cry. My own country has a sufficient weight of disgrace, arising from the individual passions of its hot-brained and ignorant legislators, to deplore; but it has been true to the principles of legislative action. The National Assembly of France has to charge itself with doing more in one session to discredit republicanism in the eyes of Europe, than could have the combined efforts of all its enemies in a century.

If it were not for the importance of the results to humanity, I should be disposed to place the proceedings of the National Assembly, during their last ephemeral career, among the amusements of this capital. As a republican, I feel too deep a regret at this last sad solution of the problem of a liberal form of government in France, to speak of its faults and overthrow, otherwise than in sorrow. Making every allowance for the greater vivacity and excitability of Gallic eloquence, and of habits foreign to our own, what a spectacle of tumult and confusion has the Assembly presented up to the period of it forcible dissolution on the 2d of December ! Louis Napoleon saved himself from arrest and imprisonment by forestalling the contemplated violence of the legislative power. I scarcely know what day's proceedings to select, to give my readers a picture of these scandalous scenes, as taken down by their own reporters. Those who have never been in the midst of the hurly-burly of half a thousand French throats, each speaking in its loudest key, and no ears listening, can form but an imperfect idea of this specimen of democratic legislation. It became an established principle with the reds to prevent, by their noise and disorder, any speaker from being heard, that they opposed. This conduct is the more surprising when contrasted with the admirable order sustained by the authority of the police in all public places, and that system of regularity and economy of time and labor introduced into other matters of business.

I shall quote from several days' proceedings. It would be supposed that national dignity, as well as common politeness, would induce a legislative body to receive the reading of the annual report of the Chief Magistrate in respectful silence. The "President's Message" was read November 4th. I give one paragraph only, with the reported interruptions :

"That bill will, therefore, contain nothing calculated to shock the Assembly; for, if I at present ask to have the law of May 31st withdrawn, I do not mean to deny the approbation which I formerly gave to the initiative of that Ministry who asked the majority to support the law which it presented. (Murmurs on the Left, and laughter). I admit even that its effects have been to a certain extent salutary. (Renewed laughter). In calling to mind the circumstance under which it was presented, it must be allowed that it was a political act more than an electoral law—(marks of denial, accompanied with laughter)—that it was a real measure of public safety. (Sneers on the Left). And whenever the Assembly proposes to me vigorous measures to save the country, it may count on my disinterested and firm co-operation. (Ironical laughter). But measures of public safety are only passed for a limited time." (Interruption on the Left).

From the sitting of November 11th:

THE MINISTER OF THE INTERIOR.—I have to state that I have not in any manner endeavored to avoid replying to the interpellations which have been just brought forward. M. Léon Faucher, my predecessor, has a *dossier* of papers on this subject. (Loud interruptions; exclamations on both sides of the Chamber). That honorable gentleman, I say, has in his possession the *dossier* of papers which did not pass from my hands into his. (Renewed interruption).

M. LEON FAUCHER endeavored to speak from his place, but was prevented by the exclamations of the Left. He at last sat down.

THE MINISTER OF THE INTERIOR.—I make that statement because I do not wish it to be imagined that the members of the present Government have need to entrench themselves behind any one; their own acts will speak for them. But you have just heard a report read from the Procureur of the Republic, which shows clearly that all the parties concerned in M. Sartin's affair, had matters to reproach themselves with. (Loud exclamations).

A Voice.—He is seeking votes for the new electoral law! (Great noise on the Right, responded to by ironical laughter on the Left).

The President.—Allow the Minister to proceed. No one ever attempts to prevent a Minister from replying to interpellations; let him then go on whether ill or well. (Tremendous uproar, which continued for some time).

M. de Thorigny turned round, and bowed to the President, speaking to him at the same time with animation.

Voices on the Left.—You are insulting the Minister!

The President.—Do not attach to my words a meaning which they are not intended to convey. I merely desired to impress on you the propriety of allowing the honorable Minister to reply, whether his sentiments were pleasing to you or not. (Laughter; agitation).

From the sitting of November 17th:

General Bedeau (from his place).—Before the vote takes place, I wish to ask the Government one question. Is the decree of May 11, approved of by the ministry of which M. O. Barrot was the head, and posted up in the barracks by General Rulhières, then the Minister of War, still to be found in the barracks, or rather has it not been withdrawn? (Marks of the liveliest curiosity).

The Minister of War (from his place).—The decree which had been posted up in some few barracks, still was to be found in a small number, when I arrived at power. I was applied to, to declare whether I intended to leave it there; and, as doubts and hesitations have been manifested, I gave orders to have it withdrawn. (Extraordinary agitation on every side, and particularly on the Left. We have seldom seen a legislative assembly more moved by the simple statement of a fact.)

M. BAZE, M. CREMIEUX, and some other members, rushed to the tribune, successively entered it, and then abruptly descended.

The agitation on the Left was most remarkable, groups being formed among the members as they stood up in their places, disputing, to all appearance, together most warmly. MM. Latrade, Schœlcher, and Charras, seemed to be addressing their colleagues. The last-named gentleman, as we caught his words amid the noise, asked how the Left could now vote with the Government. M. Schœlcher replied that he could never consent to give such an arm to the majority as the affirmative vote of the proposition. M. V. Hugo was seen standing on his seat, gesticulating most energetically. The scene of confusion was most extraordinary.

M. DE GIRARDIN suddenly rushed up the steps of the tribune, but was received with laughter. He then descended, and after a time, again appeared; but was again badly received. After endeavoring in vain to obtain a hearing, he finally disappeared.

The sitting was again suspended, and with difficulty the President's bell at last procured a comparative state of silence.

GENERAL D'HAUTPOUL.—I by no means, in ascending the tribune, have any intention to deny the rights of the Assembly to provide for its defense by every means which it may deem necessary. But allow me to ask you two questions; the first is this: Is there any imminent danger? No, the most complete calm exists every where except here. (Cries of order, order!)

A VOICE.—But he speaks the truth! (Laughter.)

GENERAL HUSSON.—The exact truth! (Continued laughter.)

ON THE LEFT.—Suppress the state of siege, then! (Noise.)

GENERAL D'HAUTPOUL.—The next question is this: Is this proposition necessary? For my part, I find in the Constitution as many and sufficient guaranties as can be reasonably demanded.

Allow me to consider the question under a military point of view. (Loud marks of impatience.) When the Assembly should desire a battalion, a regiment, a brigade, or a division, it must apply to the questors to demand them. (Loud explosion of impatience, by which the speaker's voice was rendered quite inaudible.)

VOICES ON THE LEFT.—Speak to us of the reviews of Satory.

GENERAL D'HAUTPOUL attempted to continue his remarks, but the noise was so great as to prevent his words from reaching the reporter's gallery. He at last quitted the tribune.

GENERAL LEBRETON ascended the tribune, but could not either obtain a hearing. (Cries of divide, divide !)

M. THIERS.—For the first time the new chief of the public force, General Leroy Saint Arnaud, has made an appeal in novel terms to passive obedience and to discipline. I do not attribute it as a crime to the minister to make this appeal to discipline; but he perverts the spirit of the army when he does not speak to it of respect for the laws—

A VOICE.—Is not the Constitution then a law?

M. THIERS.—And for the Constitution.

A VOICE.—You violated the Constitution by voting the law of May 31.

ON THE RIGHT.—You violated it on the 13th June. (Noise.)

A VOICE.—And you voted against it. (Continued noise.)

ON THE RIGHT.—Allow the Montagnards to speak; they are our future senators. (Laughter.)

M. THIERS.—I will ask my interrupters whether they approve of the omission of any mention of respect for the laws in the circular in question.

M. JOLY.—That question is not fairly put. ("Hear! hear!" on the Left.)

GENERAL DE LAMORICIERE.—Monsieur le President, pray prevent these interruptions.

M. Joly.—We are treated as if we were children. (Noise.)

The President (pointing to the Mountain.)—There are a dozen there who have a mania for interruptions.

M. Thiers.—The circular of the minister, I repeat, is of great gravity. Is it so or not? Do you approve of it? (Cries of "No, no," on the Left, and laughter on the right.)

M. Michel (de Bourges.)—A snare is laid for us.

On the Right.—Citizen Michel has, it appears, the privilege of interrupting.

M. Thiers.—Under no *régime* can such language be held to the army. The army is abroad the defender of the nationality—at home, the defender of the law. That must be well understood by all, and without any reticence. In imposing on the army the absolute principle, without any reserve, of obedience, you should give it for object the maintenance of the law. And you, legislators, who wish that the obedience of the soldier shall have the maintenance of the law for its object, should render the law clear. What is the object of the proposition? I am not the author of it, neither did I suggest it. (Ironical laughter on the Left.)

A Voice on the Left.—And the law of the 31st May!

General Leflo (addressing the Left.)—No one more than you inspired the proposition!

M. Thiers.—Under a constitution which renders the Assembly the temporary holder of the national sovereignty, the necessary principle inspired by the simplest common sense is, that the Assembly shall charge itself with its defense, and shall not delegate it to any one. Now, do you think that that general declaration, without any rule which explains it, is sufficiently clear to put an end to all the anxieties of those who may have to comply with your requisitions? (Interruptions on the Left.)

A Voice on the Right.—Silence, Messieurs les Sénateurs. (A laugh.)

M. Thiers.—Two cases may present themselves. (Renewed interruption.)

A Voice on the Right.—The speakers of the minority have more liberty than those of the majority.

M. Thiers (addressing the Left.)—What! you now deny the privilege of direct requisition, which you admitted under the Constituent Assembly?

On the Left.—Certainly.

A Voice on the Right.—Wait a moment. You are not ministers yet. (Laughter; agitation on the Left.)

The President.—It is impossible to preach passive obedience with greater want of discipline. (Laughter.) M. Valentin, you always interrupt; and yet you will again maintain that you have said nothing.

M. Valentin protested amid the noise.

The President.—I call you to order, since you are anxious to be distinguished.

M. Thiers.—The principle of direct requisition has been affirmed. But it has been denied, and you think that that does not require a new reply from the government.

General Lebreton.—It has been denied by all governments. ("Order!" on the Left.) I will say the same thing in the tribune. ("Order, order!")

The President.—I call you to order.

General Lebreton spoke with great warmth.

The President.—I call you to order, with inscription on the minutes.

M. Thiers.—Will you grant me a few minutes to explain the principle of direct requisition? Do you wish that this immense question, misunderstood now, shall not be unknown to-morrow? The question at stake is the independence of the Assembly—the future of representative government—the last Assembly, perhaps. ("Oh! oh!" on the Left.)

On the Left.—It will be the last for you and for the royalists.

M. Thiers.—Royalist! Call me royalist if you will! But it will be a singular spectacle to see royalists defending the liberty of the Assembly. (Cries of divide! on the Left). I wish to make the question clear in the interest of every body. (Noise on the Left.)

M. Grevy and M. Pelletier (to the Left.)—Let him speak, then!

M. Thiers.—The country will know that when I wished to throw light on this great question, you would not listen to me. (The honorable gentleman left the tribune.)

These scandalous scenes were not always the result of political animosities. That of the 21st of November, both from the subject and the mode of handling it, was one of the most ludicrous that ever took place within legislative halls. It is impossible to render justice to it in English, or to convey the spirit of the "doubles entendres;" still, as it is a subject of interest to the advocates of "female rights," I shall give an imperfect specimen of its spirit:

The President calls M. Leroux to the tribune to explain an amendment which he proposed yesterday. (Shouts of laughter.)

M. Leroux ascends the tribune amid noise and laughter.

The amendment was to add all Frenchwomen, of age, to the list of electors. He proceeded with his speech in support of his amendment, amid boisterous laughter from all parts of the Assembly, who seemed to view his argument as a capital joke. After some remarks of an amusing character, uttered with all the zeal and gravity of the rider of a new hobby, he proceeds:

Well, I ask of you liberty, equality, and fraternity. (Laughter.)

A Voice.—And maternity. (Greater laughter.)

M. Leroux.—I ask you if these great words do not apply to

all human creatures. The authors of the constitution did not wish to exclude women; for they understood very well that the union of the two sexes—(laughter).

A Voice to the Left.—Leave the tribune; you see that you make fun for these gentlemen.

M. Leroux.—The people, gentlemen, the people do not understand the fundamental difference between man and woman. (Roars of laughter). Gentlemen, pursued the orator, let me quote from Condorcet. Are not women, equally with men, part of nature. Do you argue from the physical weakness of woman —then it would be necessary to have the representatives examined by a medical jury. (Boisterous laughter.)

Several Voices.—Enough, enough.

A Voice to the Left of the Speaker.—You see that they are only mocking you.

M. Leroux.—Do you argue upon the inferiority of mind of woman. It seems to me that there are here some representatives who have less. (Renewed laughter; shouts of enough—enough.) I see no motive to prevent females from performing public functions. As to the rest, I quote the sublime words of Olymphe of Gouges: woman has the right to ascend the tribune, since she has the right to mount the scaffold. (Noise.)

General Husson.—Has she also the right to be drawn in the conscription. (Merriment.)

M. Leroux.—Gentlemen, I defend a cause eminently just. Do not condemn a cause because it is badly defended. (Hear, hear.) I examine now the question in view of the actual political situation of France. (General signs of impatience.) For some time, great efforts have been made to destroy centralization, and create a good communal organization. And I also, I wish a good communal organisation; but I believe, that without females, this organisation would be entirely unfruitful. (The most lively laughter.)

NUMEROUS VOICES.—Enough, enough.

M. LEROUX.—To arrive at a good communal organization, it is necessary to call science to your aid; and, if you will permit me—but you will not permit me—(laughter.)

SEVERAL VOICES.—Go on, go on.

M. LEROUX.—If you will permit me, I will show you how to make the organisation of the future. (Hear, hear.) I speak, but you do not listen.

THE PRESIDENT.—Never has an orator been listened to with more patience.

The orator proceeded, in much the same vein, amid indescribable confusion, to defend the propriety of allowing females to vote; at times wandering from his subject, and recalled by shouts of "stick to the women."

M. LEROUX.—If there be a means to make a powerful movement in favor of the public peace; if there be a means to reconcile and conciliate men among themselves, it is to bring between —(laughter, and the noisiest interruption.)

TO THE RIGHT.—Enough, enough. Mr. President, we have no time to lose.

M. LEROUX, making a powerful effort to be heard above the tumult, recalled a conversation that he had had with Saint Simon, who had forewarned him of the contagious success of the socialist ideas.—It is thus, continued he, that when the grippe shows itself in a locality, every body coughs. (Laughter.) Already, you see, my lord the Archbishop of Paris has the "grippe." (Laughter.) Soon you will all have it. (Renewed laughter.) The orator left the tribune; and his amendment, not being supported, was not put to vote.

In this manner women's rights were put to the right-about, among the gallant French legislators.

At the risk of too many plums to my pudding, I give an extract from the report of the memorable sitting of the 22d of November.

THE PRESIDENT OF THE ASSEMBLY.—There remains only one additional proposition, which has been made by General Grammont, in these terms:

During the fortnight which shall follow the elections, the justice of the peace shall pronounce, for the benefit of the communes, a fine of from five to fifteen francs, upon each elector, who, not having voted, cannot furnish legal proof of his inability to do so. The list of names of the electors who have incurred this fine, shall remain posted up, during a month, in each commune.

MANY VOICES.—General Grammont is absent. Take the vote, take the vote.

This proposition is put to vote amid great confusion.

M. DE VATIMESNIL demands to speak before the counter vote is taken.

M. CHARRAS.—You can not speak. The vote is begun—let it be finished.

THE PRESIDENT calls to order.

Loud disputation between M. Charras and several members of the committee.

M. O. BARROT demands the floor, for an appeal to the rule; and mounts the tribune. (Loud protestations from the left.)

A VOICE FROM THE LEFT.—The rule does not permit speaking between the two votes. Mr. President, cause the rule to be observed.

THE PRESIDENT.—It is precisely for an appeal to the rule, that M. Barrot demands the floor.

THE EXTREME LEFT.—Let him wait until after the vote! the rule is strict.

THE PRESIDENT.—Since you invoke the rules of the assembly, let me at least explain what they are! (The clamor recommences on the benches of the first section of the extreme left.)

M. O. Barrot.—It is precisely upon this regulation that I wish to speak.

The extreme Left.—You have not the right.

M. Cholat.—Mr. President, will you preserve order?—The rule is intended for all.

M. O. Barrot.—I demand of M. the President, who alone is charged with maintaining order—(Violent interruption on the extreme left.) I beg, Mr. President, to—(New interruption from the same part.)

The President.—You speak of the rule, and having violated it, you wish to direct according to your own will the deliberation. You do not even allow the President the right of applying or interpreting the very rule you invoke. It is constantly the same thing—always tyranny that you wish to exercise in the name of liberty. (Exclamations become more and more overpowering from the extreme left.)

M. Cholat, who is seated on the left, calls out in a great passion—Mr. President!

The President (turning toward the interrupter.)—I call you to order.

M. Cholat insists with great violence.

The President.—Monsieur, by what right do you speak, when I have not given you the floor? I call you to order a second time, and order it to be inserted in the journal.

The Left.—The vote was begun—nobody can speak between the two votes—respect the rules of the Assembly.

The President.—But, Messieurs, you violate it incessantly by your clamors. Now, as always, you disturb the sitting—you throw continually disorder into the deliberations.

The Left.—Read the rule—read the rule.

THE PRESIDENT reads the rule.

THE LEFT.—Ah!

THE PRESIDENT.—How; you exclaim "Ah!" Without doubt no speaking is allowed between the two votes. But what constitutes a vote? Those who are for, and those who oppose a proposition. It is only after the nays are taken that it is decided. (Ironical applause from the left.)

A VOICE FROM THE LEFT.—Bravo, Escobar, bravo! (Rumors from the right.)

M. O. BARROT leaves the tribune.

The noise and tumult re-commence on the benches of the Mountain.

THE PRESIDENT impatiently throws down on his desk the rule which he held in his hand.

They begin again to laugh on the benches of the Mountain.

THE RIGHT.—It is scandalous—it is the greatest impropriety.

THE PRESIDENT.—I am indignant at the insupportable tyranny of the members who only interfere in the debates to disturb them, and to impose upon their colleagues their will by violence.—(Noisy interruptions from the left.) A certain number of you unite to interrupt simultaneously, and render all deliberation impossible. The President is not free, the majority is not free, the tribune is not free—and thanks to you for it all. You bring nothing but violence and clamor to our deliberations.

M. DE VATIMESNIL rises, and tries to make known the opinion of the committee on the amendment of General Grammont. The noise entirely drowns his words.

THE LEFT.—You can't speak now, the vote is begun!

THE RIGHT.—No, no, there is no vote yet!

M. CHARRAS.—Mr. President, keep order; make them observe the rule—nobody can speak between the two votes.

THE RIGHT.—There is no vote yet: it was to explain the vote that M. Barrot demanded the floor.

The Left.—The Assembly can see how the President maintains order and observes the regulations.

The President.—Oh, be quiet! Yes, the Assembly sees all, and will do me justice. (Numerous cries of adhesion to the President.)

The Left.—The vote had begun—

The President.—There has been no vote. The committee declares there was a misunderstanding. The vote was not explained, and it has not taken place. Be that as it may, the ballot has been called for again on the amendment of General Grammont; it is about to take place.

M. Cholat mounts the tribune.—Citizens (says he), I have been called to order because I appealed to the rule of the House.

The Right.—By-and-by, by-and-by; after the sitting.

M. Cholat.—I have been called to order, because I said that it was forbidden to speak between the two votes. I protest against this call to order.

The Right.—Call him to order, call him to order.

The President.—The member in the tribune, whose name I don't know—

Many Voices.—M. Cholat.

The President.—M. Cholat interprets the regulation as he chooses. I called him to order, because he disturbed the House. He insists that the rule forbids speaking between the two votos; but I repeat again, that what is called a vote and counter-vote, does not make two votes—that it only makes a vote. (Laughing on the extreme left.) No; I repeat it again, there has been no vote. But the ballot has been called for instead of the usual vote. It is going to take place now.

M. de Vatimesnil.—Mr. President, if there has not been a vote, then I demand the floor.

The Left.—No! no! adjourn—adjourn!

The President.—You demand to adjourn—I will consult the Assembly.

A very large majority pronounce against adjournment.

THE PRESIDENT.—The adjournment is not carried. (Exclamations from the left.) The Chairman of the Committee has the floor.

M. DE VATIMESNIL mounts the tribune again.

The cries on the left re-commence with more violence than ever. Many Montagnards add to the noise by knocking on their desks with their paper knives. The orator makes vain efforts to be heard.

THE EXTREME LEFT.—Call the votes! call the votes!

M. DE VATIMESNIL, with impatience.—I will be as obstinate as you! I will not quit the tribune until I have used my right of speaking here.

THE EXTREME LEFT.—You have no right to speak. You violate the rules! The vote! The vote!

M. DE VATIMESNIL.—The Assembly has decided that the discussion is not closed. You revolt against the decision of the Assembly. (The tumult continually increases on the extreme left.)

A VOICE.—This is delightful.

OTHER VOICES.—It is shameful.

M. DE VATIMESNIL makes new efforts to be heard. Most of his words are lost in the confusion.—We do not reject entirely (said he) the amendment of General Grammont; we only request him to withdraw it provisionally, to be brought up again after the third reading.

A VOICE.—M. de Grammont was not there.

M. DE VATIMESNIL.—And the Committee will examine the amendment between now and the third reading.

VOICE AT THE EXTREME LEFT.—Another trick; always sly. (Murmurs on the right.)

THE PRESIDENT—turning toward the extreme left.—You offer, Messieurs, a fine spectacle to the nation!

THE EXTREME LEFT —So do you—so do you!

THE PRESIDENT.—Oh! as for me, I am above board, and do not fear the judgment of the people. (Ironical laughter from the benches of the Mountain.) As the demand for the ballot is not persisted in, I consult the Assembly by requesting them to rise, on the amendment of General Grammont.

The vote is taken. Twenty members only rise *for*—a strong majority *against*. The Montagnards take no part in the vote.

THE PRESIDENT.—The amendment is rejected. (Ironical applause from the left.)

CHAPTER XIII.

THERE were two ingredients of Yankee life that I decidedly missed in Paris. The first was ice, for which "de l'eau frappée" was but a poor substitute. The second, the enlivening bustle of a fire, with the hubbub of bells, the clatter of the engines, and the shouts of the boys. There are fires here, but one rarely hears of them, even through the papers. In the absence of loaded trucks and the din of mercantile business, the noise of Paris becomes monotonous. But once in seven months did I hear the shrill jingle of a dray load of iron ; it was true home music. The excitement of a fire, I frequently thought would be a pleasing relief.

However, I had not lived long in Paris before I found it possessed advantages in the way of excitement peculiar to itself, amply compensating for its disadvantages in the above mentioned respects.

It was the 2d of December, of the past year. I had arisen at my usual hour, breakfasted, read Galignani, and the Constitutionnel, my morning papers, without finding an item of interest, and as the morning was sombre, had prepared myself for a day of more than ordinary quiet. Toward one o'clock, a French lady dropped in. She was somewhat excited, and I inquired the reason. "What," said she, "have you not heard the news? There is a revolution. Paris is in a state of siege. The troops are all in the streets—the National Assembly is dissolved—most of the members are imprisoned—the railroad tracks are torn up to prevent the provinces from marching upon the city—Louis

Napoleon is Emperor;" and thus she rattled off a volley of news, that was genuine news indeed.

I immediately went out. The good citizens of Paris, who had gone to bed under a republic, were just leaving their breakfast tables to read the proclamations which announced to them it had suddenly departed this life, forgetting to add, however, leaving a numerous and afflicted family. Those who had most at stake in this violent change, knew nothing of it until it had been old news by some hours in London.

I passed along the boulevards and the usual resorts of business. All the shops were closed. Groups read in silence the notices, and quietly dispersed. This part of the city, usually so rife with life, appeared as if stunned by a violent blow. Men held their breaths. It was not the settled composure with which the seaman looks upon the coming storm, but the anxiety and terror with which is awaited an expected earthquake.

The public gardens and Palais Royal were closed. There was no thought of amusement. The Champs Elysées, Place Madeleine, and every avenue leading to the Palais Bourbon and residence of Louis Napoleon, were filled with dense masses of troops in fighting order. More than fifty thousand were under arms. They, too, were awaiting, they knew not what—but ready at the order of their chiefs to rise and slay. Certain streets were closed; those who had homes therein, found no little difficulty in reaching them.

That evening the celebrated Jesuist, Le Ventura, was to preach at Nôtre Dame. I started early to obtain admission, as he always draws a multitude. By this time, six o'clock, the troops had returned to their barracks, and Paris looked as gay and busy as on the preceding evening. The church was closed; nothing was permitted at this juncture that would attract the crowd to one spot. News boys were crying at every corner the dissolution of the National Assembly, and the other stringent measures of the President. The people had begun to discuss them; the first sentiments were admiration at the cleverness with which it had been done. The President had conversed even till midnight in the most friendly manner at the Elysée with his opponents. No agitation announced the desperate throw he had then resolved to make of his political dice. Yet his head was upon the cast, and if successful he foresaw that blood was to be shed. In four hours the deed was done. Every printing press, not his own, seized. The Assembly dissolved. The legislative halls closed. Those in whose hands the grasp of his own was scarcely cold, arrested and in prison. Thiers wept, and was alternately fool and coward—Cavaignac, dignified—Changarnier haughty, and Lamoricière, pugnacious. None whom Napoleon feared were spared. His selection was admirable. Not a leader of any party except his own was exempted from the call to exchange a warm bed at four o'clock of a winter's morning for a stone cell at Vincennes, or the prison Mazas. Each had the honor of a special attendance—no questions were answered as to the object of their imprisonment or their probable fate. In twelve hours the bourgeoisie exclaimed, "c'est bien fait!" and were ready to go on with their amusements.

On the 3d there was more excitement. The secret societies were at work. The reds were recovering from their astonishment; ex-members of the National Assembly harangued the multitude, and circulated addresses to arouse the people to resistance. The result was several barricades, which were speedily carried by the troops, with some loss on both sides. On the part of the government, the proclamations became more stringent. Carriages were forbidden to circulate, or the inhabitants to appear in the streets. Those taken near any barricade with arms about them were to be put to death.

In the evening there was shouting; inflammatory speeches; the rallying cries of parties. Immense human masses on the boulevards and the quays heaved to and fro in sullen anger, like the swell of the ocean before an approaching storm. Individuals ran from group to group muttering curses upon the usurper. Some said the excitement would spend itself in words; others, that Louis Napoleon would be killed within forty-eight hours. The police charged repeatedly on the crowds, which, in return, mocked at them. I looked quietly on, and became convinced that the back of the Parisian tiger was up, and was preparing for a leap.

The next morning was the fourth. There was not much stirring; the shops were generally closed. I went to the Rue de Jeuneurs, where I had business. This was before mid-day. As I approached this street, I saw crowds running through it, panic struck, while the residents were barring their windows and closing their doors. I asked the cause. All were too much frightened to speak intelligently. Some thought the faubourgs were rising, and others that the troops were approaching; each added to the alarm of his neighbor. At last I learned that barricades were being erected at the Porte St. Denis on the boulevard of that name.

Being curious to see a barricade, I pushed directly for the spot. On arrival, I found the work going bravely on. Four were already commenced at different intervals in the boulevard. Stagings had been torn from unfinished houses; iron railings from the magnificent gate-way; trees were cut down; all those nameless buildings, at once so convenient and so disgraceful, to this fashionable avenue, were demolished, and their materials added to the fortifications. Carts, carriages, and omnibuses were triumphantly dragged from hiding places, amid shouts of exultation, to add to the monster piles. The stout iron railing and massive stone wall which protects the side walk from the street, long resisted the efforts of destruction. Crow-bars, and the united strength of several hundred men at last brought it down. Pavements were torn up, and shaped into breast-works. The barricades soon began to assume a formidable appearance, and to any force but artillery were well nigh impregnable. They were further strengthened by ropes, which bound firmly together the disjointed parts. There were not very many at work, but those who were, labored like beavers, and evidently knew their trade. Blouses and broadcloth were about equally mixed. Neither were there many spectators. All sorts of rumors were in circulation. The army, it was said, had left Paris, to defend the city against the troops coming in from the neighboring cities—such a regiment had revolted ; the National Guards were arming ; in short, every species of tale to encourage and exasperate the enemies of the President, was circulated by agents of the political parties of the late Assembly.

Having completed the barricades, the mob burst into the nearest guard-house, with wild shouts, sacked it, placed its flag on their most formidable fortification, and used the materials to further strengthen their quarters. The small force usually there had been withdrawn or it would have been massacred.

Sinister individuals in blouses armed with cutlasses, muskets, and pistols, began to appear. These acted as leaders. They broke into all the neighboring shops and searched the houses for arms. When any were found, they marked in chalk on the building, "arms given; death to robbers." From one of the theatres they procured a few muskets and a drum. These were hailed with shouts of joy, and a party began beating the rappel through the adjacent streets.

I was surprised to see how many boys there were in their ranks. They went to work in all these violences as if on a frolic, light-hearted, and even jovial. From their manner, I should rather have supposed that they were gathering materials for a rustic fair, than for a struggle in which no quarters would be given. I saddened to think how many that I saw so busy around me, would be shot or bayonetted before night. The comments of the spectators varied; some said, let the rascals go ahead—they wish to plunder and kill—they will soon be taught a good lesson; others encouraged. One man asked me if I were German or English; on my replying that I was an American, "Ah!" said he, with a sigh, "you live in a true republic."

I asked a fine looking boy of about fourteen, in a school uniform, with a stick in his hand, at the end of which was a bayonet, what he intended doing; "you are too young to fight." He laughed, brandished his weapon, and ran off to join a crowd, listening to the reading of a proclamation announcing the deposition of Louis Napoleon, and calling upon the Parisians to give their allegiance to the provisional government formed by such of the members of the late Assembly as had escaped arrest.

A rough looking fellow, armed with a musket, who seemed to have authority, came up to me, and said, "If you are one of the curious, you had better be off." I thought so too, as appearances began to wear a serious aspect. The houses overlooking the barricades were taken possession of, and garrisoned; sentinels were placed at the principal points; the non-combatants were mostly gone, and few but fighters left. I had been there less than two hours; yet, so rapidly had the mob worked, that all the streets opening upon this vicinity, were already fortified. I was forced to climb three barricades, politely assisted over one by an armed lad in a blouse, before getting clear of their line of operations. It was most injudiciously chosen, for it could be attacked to equal advantage in front and rear; and their flanks were also exposed.

I found the boulevards below almost deserted. A brigade of infantry and artillery were just turning the corner of the street, marching without music, slowly, toward the first barricade. Before reaching it, they halted. One half the artillery passed in front, and was pointed toward the breastworks; the other was loaded with grape, and pointed in the other direction. The few persons about saluted the troops with "Vive la République." The commanding officer ordered the boulevard to be cleared. The troops charged upon us, and we slipped out of the way by the side streets.

I then walked down the Rue Montmartre, where I saw similar scenes. Coming out again upon the Boulevard des Italiens, I found the entire length of the boulevard, from the spot I first left, filled with troops, in order of battle. The line extended into the Rue de la Paix. It was a stirring spectacle to witness regiment after regiment of artillery, cavalry, and infantry, pass up this noble avenue, to take their stations. In the novelty and beauty of their array, I quite lost sight of the fact that they were ordered out to slaughter these misguided people I had so recently left. At one time they cleared the sidewalks, and allowed no one to approach their lines. The sentinels, however, for some inexplicable cause, were shortly removed ; and those of the populace who had more curiosity than fear, allowed to pass along as far as the Boulevard Bonne Nouvelle. This led to the melancholy slaughter of thirty-five individuals, and the wounding of a large number, soon after on the Boulevard Montmartre, just above where I was. Opposite me was the 7th Lancers ; a fine corps, recently arrived in Paris.

I stood talking with a friend, when, from the upper end of the line, the discharge of cannon was heard, followed by a blaze of musketry and a general charge. The stragglers on the boulevards took to flight in all directions. They pitched headlong into open doors, or loudly demanded entrance at the closed. I was fortunate enough to get into a neighboring carriage way, through the grated "porte cochère" of which I could see what was going on. The firing was tremendous. Volley followed volley so fast, that it seemed like one continued peal of thunder. Suddenly there was a louder and nearer crash ; the cavalry in front of me wavered; and then, as if struck with panic, turned, and rushed in disorder down the street, making the ground tremble under their tread. What could have occurred! The first supposition was, that the different regiments had turned their arms upon each other. Another that the reds had proved too strong for the troops. In a few minutes the horsemen came charging back, firing their pistols on all sides. Then came in quick succession the orders "To shut all windows; to keep out of sight; to open the blinds, &c." It seemed an unexpected fire had been opened upon the soldiers, from some of the houses above, by which they at first suffered so severely as to cause a recoil. The roar of firearms was now tremendous. Mortars and cannon were directed point blank at the suspicious houses, within a few rods distance, and fired. They were then carried by assault.

The rattle of small shot against windows and walls was incessant. This was too in the finest part of the boulevards Costly houses were completely riddled; their fronts were knocked in; balls passed through the various floors, and lodged finally whereever their spent force destined them. The windows were destroyed by the concussion of the cannon; and, as for the outer walls, they looked as if a thunder-storm of bullets had passed over them. They were literally peppered with lead from cellar to roof. Some balls had passed through panes of glass, leaving holes as true and clear of their exact size, as if they had been cut out by a diamond. Of the hair-breadth escapes of the inmates, and the general destruction of property, I need not speak. The government afterward footed all the bills for the last. The firing continued for nearly an hour, and then receded to more distant parts of the city; for the field of combat embraced an area of several miles, and there were some 40,000 troops engaged.

As soon as I could with safety, I left my covert; and, by back streets, endeavoured to get near enough to the barricades, to see what work had been done there. It was now quite dark. The troops guarded every possible avenue, and fired upon all who approached the interdicted spots. The streets in this vicinity were almost wholly deserted. The few that were to be seen, cautiously peered round the corners, but did not venture to show themselves. Not knowing the danger, I attempted to go upon the boulevards by the Rue Montmartre. As I walked up the street I noticed the marks of the balls that had glanced along the houses. There was a large pool of blood, but the corpses had been removed. I had nearly reached the corner, when an officer rushed out, and ordered me back in a tone which I thought most prudent to obey. As I was alone, and he had probably seen enough blood-shed that afternoon, he did nothing worse. I turned into the first cross street, and there saw a well dressed man, gasping on a rude bier. Those who had picked him up said he had six balls in him. In the Rue Richelieu, there was the corpse of a young girl. Some one had placed lighted candles at her head and feet.

Emerging from the line of soldiers as I reached the parts of the city removed from their surveillance, I noticed a bitter feeling among the better classes for the day's work. The slaughter was, as it always is, in the heat of a battle, greatly exaggerated. Still it was with no gratifying emotions that one could reduce it, even to a few hundred. It was civil war—fratricide. I reached home indignant and mournful.

The soldiers have been justly blamed for firing upon the unarmed. Those who fought at the barricades knew the penalty of defeat. The inhabitants had been ordered not to appear in the streets. Those who suffered, forgot the danger in their curiosity. One gentleman met his death by standing at a distant corner and looking at the troops with a spy-glass. It was mistaken for a musket. and he fell, pierced with several balls

Those who were killed on the Boulevard Montmatre were non-combatants, but suffered from their rashness. The public feeling in such cases is ever severe on the soldier. But in extenuation it should be remembered, that his exposed position in a street, fired upon from houses on both sides, is by no means calculated to insure coolness and judgment. His enemies are unseen, and he knows, from fatal experience, that a socialist gives no quarter. Several of his comrades had been basely assassinated in the public ways. Numbers had already fallen from the fire of his ambushed foes. In the heat of revenge he believes every citizen's coat to cover an assassin, and kills without pity.

In the evening I again attempted to go up the boulevards. Squadrons of lancers were on guard, and brigades of infantry bivouacked on the side-walks. The public were permitted to go as far as the Rue Lafitte, but obliged to walk quickly, and not allowed to stop for an instant. Horsemen with loaded pistols stood at each corner, and if there was the slightest hesitation, or if two individuals spoke to each other, they pointed them directly upon the delinquents, and ordered them to pass on. The cavalry, with their lances in rest, charged repeatedly upon groups accidentally formed. In passing the length only of a square I was obliged to run twice; and once had just time to dodge under the projecting angle of a house as the troops swept by. These charges were intended simply to intimidate and prevent collections of people. The French rule is to run at the sight of a soldier. There is more danger from the panic of the crowd than from the military. I concluded an accident was as liable to occur to me as any one else, and returned home, fully satisfied by what I had seen during the day, that street fighting in Paris is a serious matter.

Louis Napoleon proclaimed himself master of France, December 2d. The 4th of December made him master. It was a terrible lesson deliberately planned, and intended as such by him.

I say planned, for the Minister of War, in his official report, says, "The troops were withdrawn, and the insurgents allowed to build their barricades unmolested, that the insurrection might come to a head and be extinguished at one blow." It left me nothing to covet in the political institutions of France, but more to love in those of my own country. The poor wretches who suffered most were mere hirelings. A French gentleman of my acquaintance, whose house was near one of the barricades, said a few days afterward to the sentinel in front of his door, "The soldiers have behaved well." "Ah!" replied the man, "it pleases you to say so, but my heart is heavy this morning." "Why so?" "I was drawn with a number of my comrades to shoot thirty prisoners condemned to death. As they marched to the place of execution, they said to one another, it was hard to die for ten francs."

CHAPTER XIV.

"LOUIS NAPOLEON."

France still bears the name of a Republic. Her only claim to the title is universal suffrage. It is evident, however, that the government, by its secret machinery, is able to make even this nominal liberty subservient to its own objects. If it do not, it will be because Louis Napoleon possesses more public virtue than is in general attributed to him.

The inhabitants of the United States naturally take a lively interest in the cause of political freedom and democratic institutions. The events of 1848 were hailed by them with joy, as indicating the progress of republican ideas. What has been the result? In three years republicanism has become extinct in Europe, while monarchy has not only regained its lost ground, but almost annihilated every vestige of freedom.

Why is this? In the United States every movement of the people is an onward one. Religion, education, and liberal institutions march together. In Europe, liberty burns for a while with a fierce, destructive flame—and then expires. It has no store of fuel. Take France, for example, which has oftenest tried her fortune under the republican banner. Her citizens are second in courage to none; light, chivalric, and impetuous, their patriotism flashes brilliantly in wonderful efforts, but sinks under protracted and unostentatious labor. They are easily led by honor, but restless under restraint. The Duc de Richelieu happily illustrates this trait, in relating the effect of a speech of his to his troops, at the attack on Minorca. Great drunkenness and demoralization prevailed in his camp, and the officers counseled severe measures to put an end to the scandal. He understood French nature better. Passing the army in review before him, he thus addressed them: "Soldiers! grenadiers! I declare to you, that those who hereafter get drunk shall not have the honor to join in the assault I am about to make on the Fort St. Philippe." This put an end to the vice, and the fort, which was considered almost impregnable, was carried by their reckless bravery. Richelieu adds, that if his troops had been English, he should have flogged them. With this discipline and plenty of roast beef, he says, they fight well enough. An Anglo-American meets his warmest friend, gives a careless nod, and passes on. A Frenchman, on the contrary, rushes into his arms, and kisses both cheeks. Yet the coldness of the former covers more sincerity than the ardor of the latter.

The discarded Bourbon cock is the most fitting type of the French character, in more respects than one. Like that bird, it can bear no rival. It is brave, quick, gallant, and showy: more fond of war than peace, and impatient of that beaver-like industry, by which alone a republic can flourish.

Thus the elements of Gallic character are, in themselves, adverse to sober, calculating, persevering republicanism. To these are to be added the education and associations of fifteen centuries of monarchy or feudalism. Some of the most important of civil rights have been acquired by the people, but they continue as unrepublican as ever. While the present system of education remains unchanged, this must be the fact. I have already given my reasons why I consider the Roman Catholic religion to be adverse to republicanism. Also, the centralism and emasculating policy of the government in its system of police and forcible constraint of individual enterprise; still more in its preference of ornament to utility; amusements to education; but, above all, in the principles inculcated in the youth by the discipline to which they are subjected, which of themselves undermines the very base of individual reliance and integrity. I mean suspicion and deception.

Republicanism being unsuited to the condition and genius of France, she has the alternative between a constitutional monarchy, like that of England, or an absolutism, allied to that of Russia. She is as incapable of imitating England as she is the United States. Nor are the social and civil institutions of England adapted to her wants. The loyalty that characterizes an Englishman, has no corresponding feature in a Frenchman. Neither has he that idolatry for rank which renders the former almost servile in his homage to his superiors. Thrones, titles, and castes have experienced too many fluctuations in France to be viewed with veneration. It is one of the most promising points of the national character, that the individual in France is gauged solely on his own merits. Nowhere is talent more honored and appreciated, or society more free from petty conventionalities.

Legitimacy in France is an obsolete idea. The Bourbons have no leader to offer suited to the nation. The noblesse, who still cling to the fortunes of the Count of Chambord, worship a chimera. Theirs is like the age of gold; it grows brighter in their imaginations as it recedes. It is the selfish ambition of a titled few, and can never again have weight with the nation. Louis Philippe was more wedded to his money-bags and family aggrandizement, than to the welfare of France. He attained the throne by meanness, and lost it by weakness. His ancestors were the curse of the country, and his children are no objects of its attachment. Their influence was solely through their wealth and those who, like Thiers, sought to elevate their own fortunes by the Orleans' name.

There did exist, however, a man of the people—the roughest master they ever had. Him, they loved as they have loved no other sovereign. He stamped his name on their hearts by the deeds they esteem, by the works they admire; and, deeper than all, by that Code which is his greenest laurel. The name of

Napoleon is the most popular one of France. It was his name alone that elected his nephew.

Of the character of Louis Napoleon, the six millions of Frenchmen who voted him the President of the Republic, knew nothing. They cast the souvenirs of his uncle into the electoral urns. Three years have passed, and they have learned only that he is an unreadable man. Suddenly and without warning, he broke his solemn oath of office—overturned the constitution —drove the legislators of the people from their Hall of Assembly by the bayonet—imprisoned and exiled the best blood and talent of France—muzzled the press by a law severer than the ordinance which cost Charles X. his throne—shot his fellow-citizens by hundreds in the streets—rode rough-shod over all classes—grasping the entire liberties of his country—and yet the people confirmed his power, and his acts, by the largest vote ever bestowed upon a ruler.

It was during the last election, that an aged Frenchman of the provinces came to deposit his vote. "For whom do you vote?" asked the officer at the polls. "For the Emperor Napoleon." "But he has long been dead." "Then I vote for his son." "But he is dead also." "Very well; the Holy Spirit must be left; I vote for him." And he cast it for Louis Bonaparte.

The mass sustain Louis Napoleon on account of his name. The men of property, because his popularity is the only counterpoise to the socialists. The legitimists and noblesse, that they may exist in peace. As one said to me, they must eat and drink. To all, he is the man of destiny. They have submitted to a greater tyranny than even the Emperor dared exercise; not that they accept this policy as their permanent rule—but that France, like the maniac in the straight-jacket, may gradually recover her senses, and learn to appreciate the blessings of rational freedom.

No ruler ever outraged constitutional liberty in a more summary way than Louis Napoleon. Paradoxical as it may appear, perhaps no one has at this moment greater strength in the country at large. They trust him because they believe he has a mission to perform—that he will save France. He has it in his power to ruin or redeem her. If the selfish and vain glorious policy of his uncle is to be his guide, he has every thing to fear. If, on the contrary, he preserves a firm hand, relaxing, as time and discipline prepare the way for popular forms of government, devoting the resources entrusted to him to the moral improvement and education of the people, France may be at this moment nearer republicanism than she has ever yet been.

However severely his government may press upon the citizens of France, the neutral stranger has no cause of complaint. Nowhere is he better protected or more hospitably received. He is required simply to abstain from intermeddling with public affairs. Nor is he allowed, as in the United States, to abuse his asylum by insulting the agents of friendly powers, or plotting against the stability of the government that protects him. He must, however, behave himself with the same propriety that is expected of a visitor in a family—that is, to let alone its domestic concerns.

The hospitality of the United States is, as it should be, limitless. It receives all who come into the privileges of its institutions, without question of birth, character, opinion, or fortune. To do this with impunity, there must be, however, a large store of domestic virtue. With the great, good, or unfortunate of Europe, come also her evil spirits, disorganizers, whose highest aim is revolution, that they may themselves be conspicuous. Availing themselves of the attachment of the citizens of the United States to those principles of freedom which are their political birth-right, they would enlist them in a crusade against all powers whose forms of government differ, whether those nations desire or are prepared or not to receive them. England intervened in the affairs of France. It cost her $2,300,000,000 to send Napoleon to St. Helena. Republican France endeavored to revolutionize Europe. Her lesson was learned when the Cossacks encamped in the Champs Elysées. If the foreign demagogues who are now preaching hostility toward powers with which the United States are on terms of amity, should succeed in embroiling our country with foreign nations, we should buy our experience as dearly. No one class of institutions are adapted to all nations, any more than one suit of clothes will fit all men.

The citizens of the United States owe their unexampled prosperity to peace and the policy of Washington. The same doctrine which forbids European powers from intermeddling in our affairs is of equal weight to prevent us from intervening in theirs. Our sympathies should be limited to our hospitality. If we pledge ourselves to more than this, we run the risk, not so much from external assault as from internal demoralization, of destroying all freedom. There is higher authority for this doctrine in the divine parable of the beam and mote. Assuredly there is still scope enough within the United States for the employment of the entire moral energies of the nation in self-reform. We have our own abuses, weaknesses, and, greater than all, the tide of European emigration, to correct and purify. While we seek to proselyte abroad, we are in danger of losing our own faith at home. There is but one safe and honorable course for Americans. To cherish their own institutions, and leave to their neighbors the task of reforming their own. Example will be of more weight than armed men. The one has a moral force ; the other is mere muscle ; the greatest tenacity wins the day. I came to Europe in all the flush of republican enthusiasm. I write from it with deeper and wiser attachment to its principles. If I have succeeded in making a single one of my fellow citizens at once more patriotic and more charitable, with a juster appreciation of the causes which make nations to differ, I shall feel that my experience has not been without its reward.

THE END.

www.ingramcontent.com/pod-product-compliance
Lightning Source LLC
LaVergne TN
LVHW010245110826
845151LV00004B/1399

* 9 7 8 1 4 2 5 5 2 3 6 2 6 *